"He masterfully uses his own life experiences to force us to take an uncomfortable look at how we've been conditioned to adopt, accept, and extend the unfortunate American traditions of hate and violence."

—Jemele Hill, author of *Uphill: A Memoir*

"Kevin Powell's writing never fails to be both profoundly insightful and brilliantly inciting. His words are unassuming daggers, piercing the skin of racism in America, gender inequality, misogyny, and the sociopolitical impact of our greatest icons while expertly avoiding clichés and pretension. His work provides a compassionate examination of our contemporary ethos and inspires us to move beyond apathy into full social accountability."

—Dominique Morisseau, Obie Award–winning playwright

for *The Education of Kevin Powell: A Boy's Journey into Manhood*

"Intelligent and ambitious . . . Powell's confessional packs a powerful punch, full of urban realness and raw emotions." —*Publishers Weekly*

"[Kevin Powell's] story is powerful and unsparing. By the end, his narrative bears witness not only to the life of one Black man, but to an American society still bound to a tragic history of racism. Raw-edged honesty at its most revealing and intense." —*Kirkus Reviews*

"Explores poverty, pain, and the redemptive power of the written word . . . you feel his hunger, whether for food, knowledge, or the sweet squeeze from his mother that would not be coming." —*Nation*

"A book that you will want to keep close to you as a reminder of the depth of human pain and inhumanity, and the possibility of transcendence and redemption." —*Daily Kos*

"As a charismatic speaker, leader, and a very good writer, Kevin Powell has the courage . . . to be fully human, and this will bring the deepest revolution of all." —Gloria Steinem

"[A] raw, deeply painful accounting of a life . . . as much about a mother as it is about her son, a memoir born out of stunning writing and surprising vulnerability. Powerful, brave, and unforgettable."

—V (formerly Eve Ensler), author of *The Vagina Monologues*

"Poignant and transformative. This story of a Black male's life in our patriarchal culture, from boyhood to manhood, is raw and passionate. It offers a true and honest portrait of all that Black males endure to survive and, more importantly, to cope with trauma, and to heal and thrive. It should be read by everyone who claims to care about the fate of Black males in America."　　　　　—bell hooks, author of *All about Love*

"In telling his own truth, Powell's story is illuminating. His memoir highlights how beneath an angry façade, there often lurks a wellspring of alienation and pain . . . For those reasons, the education of Kevin Powell turns out to be an education for us all."　　　　　—*USA Today*

"*The Education of Kevin Powell* . . . feels necessary in this moment, both for its unflinching look at abuse and its consequences, and for showing the value of working to overcome all obstacles, including those of our own making."　　　　　—*BookPage*

"Powell's 'education' is one with lessons for all of us, a riveting story of conflicted manhood, the ups (and definitely the downs) of the class structure, and the ongoing racial drama that has characterized America from the jump. To understand Powell's triumphs, defeats, and refusal to give up, even when all the odds were against him, is to understand America writ large. His personal commitment to justice and equality for all, made clear here as the outgrowth of a life often marked by in-justice and hardship, is one we should all hope to mimic."
　　　　　—Tim Wise, author of *White Like Me*

"This dynamic memoir takes us through a personal journey of pain, growth, triumph, defeat, and finally reclamations of his gifts and im-portance in US letters. Using his journalist's keen eye, he also recalls key events and people over the past forty years in American culture, music, and politics: the birth of hip-hop, poetry slams, the life and death of Tupac Shakur, Los Angeles's rebellion after the acquittal of police in Rodney King's beating, the rise of Barack Obama, and more. The inter-sections make his story our story, his voice that of a generation."
—Luis J. Rodriguez, Los Angeles poet laureate, author of *Always Running*

THE
KEVIN
POWELL
READER

THE
KEVIN
POWELL
READER

THE KEVIN POWELL READER

ESSENTIAL WRITINGS AND CONVERSATIONS

Akashic Books
Brooklyn, NY

Published by Akashic Books
©2023 Kevin Powell

ISBN: 978-1-63614-101-5
Library of Congress Control Number: 2022947066
All rights reserved
First printing

Grateful acknowledgment is made for permission to reprint the essays, poems, interviews, and speech in this collection. See page 437 for details.

Akashic Books
Brooklyn, New York
Instagram, Twitter, Facebook: AkashicBooks
info@akashicbooks.com
www.akashicbooks.com

For the people of Jersey City, New Jersey,
where it all began . . .

Author's Note: I am very proud of this collection of my writings, which stretches from the 1980s to the present day. Over that time my value system and my thinking have matured greatly, and I sincerely believe that all people, no matter their identity or identities, are equal, and deserve to be fully safe, and fully free, and fully empowered. My life work as both a writer and a civil and human rights activist is reflective of that. This collection is an evolution of my writing, my thinking, and my being—and also highlights how America and the world have evolved since I began writing as a youth—so there may be some language and ideas, particularly in several of the older pieces, where I was not the person I am now. I believe in honesty always, in being transparent always, in taking ownership always, in growing always, which is why I am especially humbled and grateful to present this collection for you, the reader, and for the future generations.

Lovely, dark, and lonely one,
Bare your bosom to the sun,
Do not be afraid of light
You who are a child of night.

Open wide your arms to life,
Whirl in the wind of pain and strife,
Face the wall with the dark closed gate,
Beat with bare, brown fists
And wait.

—"Song" by Langston Hughes

Table of Contents

Introduction
Why I Write

I write because I want to be free. I write because I want to heal from the toxic and dysfunctional behaviors that were passed on to me as a child, that have haunted me throughout my adult life. I write because writing is as important to me as breathing, because writing has, seriously, saved my life, time and again. I write because I believe in telling the truth, the whole truth, about myself, about where I come from and what shaped me, about America, about this world. I write because my grandmother Lottie Burrison Powell—my mother's mother—could not read or write. I write because my mother can read and write a bit, but due to the segregated America into which she was born, my ma only made it to the eighth grade, and to this day I help her to spell and pronounce words she does not understand. As for my father, who was never married to my mother, I only saw him three times in my life, the last at the age of eight, the same year my mother first took me to the library and I fell madly in love with storytelling, with books, with the word. It would not be until after my father was dead—I did not know he had died for over a decade after the fact—that I would learn from close relatives of his that he could not read or write either.

So, I consider myself a miracle. And you can imagine how I am humbled and grateful to be a writer, one with more than fifteen books, hundreds upon hundreds of essays, blogs, articles, poems, pieces of cultural criticism, and screenplay and play ideas at different stages of development. Because, given where I come

from—the poverty, the violence, the abuse, the abandonment, the many years battling despair and sadness, and generations of trauma rooted in American racism going back to the enslavement of my ancestors—I realize it is some divine order that I am a writer, that I figured out a way to use my voice, for myself, for others. And a miracle, too, that I have been able to survive so much, because, as the Pulitzer Prize–winning hip-hop artist Kendrick Lamar has rapped, I done been through a whole lot—

In the beginning, my mother was the first storyteller I ever met. She is a daughter of the American South, the Low Country of South Carolina, and I am the product of the Northeast, of urban America. But inside our home my mother shared tales from as early as I can recall of her life as a girl residing in a two-room shack: her, her three sisters, her brother, her mother, and her father. There were stories of the vicious hatred of them because they were Black. There were stories of their endless financial hardships, of making a way out of no way. There were stories of God and ghosts that visited them in that backwoods area where they had no electricity, no outdoor lights, no toilet save an outhouse. There were stories of my mother and two of her sisters migrating from the South to the North, of them being the help for White folks, of demeaning factory jobs, of men like my father who saw women as nothing more than mattresses or punching bags. These stories and more stuck with me, shaped my vision of myself, of the world, of what life possibilities and equality and freedom ought to be.

And so did my youthful imagination, as the only child of my mother. I wanted to be many things—a baseball player for my beloved New York Yankees, a weatherman, a magician. I marveled at the art of Salvador Dalí as a boy, drew long before I ever wrote anything, and my mother drilled into me that I should be a lawyer or doctor, since one of those careers would be my ticket to a life better than hers. But when I got to the twelfth grade

at Henry Snyder High School in Jersey City, New Jersey, my hometown, my life changed forever. Mrs. Lillian Williams was my English teacher that fateful year, and this middle-aged Black woman with the perfect diction and immaculate dress saw a future for me I could not see for myself. Mrs. Williams encouraged me to enter a citywide essay contest for high schoolers, and, to my downright shock, I won. The theme I had to write to was "A Strong Nation Needs Strong Schools," and I found myself, at age seventeen, with a $100 savings bond and my photo in the local newspaper, the *Jersey Journal*. And, as it turned out, it was the first published piece of my life.

But I still did not know I could be a writer until I entered Rutgers University, one of Jersey's massive state institutions. It was there, amid the madness of the Reagan-Bush years, the AIDS and crack pandemics, and the anti-apartheid movement gripping college campuses nationwide, that I was transformed to spiritual and mental spaces beyond my wildest dreams. Over the course of four years, I went from a terribly awkward boy with a debilitatingly low self-esteem and a grave fear of speaking aloud in any way, to a professional writer at age twenty, while still at Rutgers, and a student leader yelling unapologetically, and often, about justice for all. I had been liberated by my college years, but also because of what I read while at Rutgers. I did not know, honestly, that Black writers existed until I began to hear names like Langston Hughes and Zora Neale Hurston in classes such as Dr. Cheryl Wall's Harlem Renaissance course. I did not know that I could make a go of a writing life until I began to encounter authors like Amiri Baraka and Richard Wright and Greg Tate. I did not know there was an entire tradition of Black literature, dating back to pre–Revolutionary War America, of which I was a part. Reading—words—had saved my life as a child, allowed me to escape the misery and isolation of my youth, and now as a young adult, reading was saving my life once more, teaching and telling me that I mattered, that my life

and history mattered, that my people, Black people, actually had a history—that I needed to figure out, as a writer, as an activist, how to love myself after I had been told my entire life up until then that I was ugly and doomed because I was Black, because I was a Black boy—

Given the above, it is no small feat to slow down and review one's life, one's writing life, because I have been in a hurry since I was a youth. But slowing down allows one to see the past and present in a different light, allows one to have conversations with the different chapters of oneself in a way that is, frankly, both jarring and healing. I have experienced the great highs of major magazine cover stories and endless accolades, and I have returned, more times than I care to admit, to the horrific poverty of my youth. No matter, I am supremely proud of the fact that as a poet, I was one of the young wordsmiths who came through New York City's Nuyorican Poets Café, and Atlanta's National Black Arts Festival. Likewise, I cherish my initial writings in the 1980s and early 1990s, including the very bad pieces, of which there were plenty, because I was learning, painstakingly, how to be a writer, how to edit my work, how to be edited. I still pinch myself that it was me on MTV's *The Real World* as the very first poet to perform their work on that national platform. I still pinch myself to think that I was a star writer for *Vibe*, the groundbreaking publication of the legendary entertainment mogul Quincy Jones, that my cover stories on iconic figures like Tupac Shakur are now considered classics of what became known as "hip-hop journalism."

During this long journey, I have been everything from a news reporter to a poet to a music journalist to a screenwriter to a cultural critic to a playwright to a public speaker to an editor to a filmmaker, whatever it has taken to be a writer, to earn a living, to not be homeless or destitute, to do what I love, to be free, to be fulfilled, to fight the good fight with my words. I think about

how my very first professional piece was on the racist murder of Michael Griffith, a young Black man, by young White males in the Howard Beach section of Queens, New York. Little did I know, back in the day, that a huge chunk of my writings to come would deal with what it is to be Black in America, or, too, to be a Black male in this nation. Little did I know, back in the day, that the same anguish and terror I felt during the Reagan-Bush era, I would feel nearly forty years later, in these times similarly freeze-framed by right-wing fanaticism and brutal racial assaults. Little did I know, back in the day, that what began as a fight against racism would turn into my becoming, through many missteps and trials and errors and much rethinking, anti–all forms of oppression, all forms of hate, all forms of violence, and that this very thought would appear in my writings: if all of us are not free, then none of us are free.

Finally, and as a matter of fact, I feel free and alive in these times, despite all, in a way I have never felt before. I feel born, again, as the Black church folks like to say, and that all I have endured makes me as hungry as I was as a kid writer, back in the day, to never stop putting forth my words, my thoughts, in the service to others. To help the invisible, the neglected, the forgotten, the disempowered. And I overstand, as we say, that even what I have experienced in just the last few years—be it COVID, or a painful divorce, or severe depression, or a second bankruptcy, or a close friend's suicide, or my nagging worries that I myself might not live into my elder years because of the writing life that has called me since I was a child—are bottomless blessings, are love lessons well-earned, are the unshakable fruits of what it is to be a human, to be a writer, to be a keeper of memories—

Part I

Part I

A Strong Nation Needs Strong Public Schools

Originally published as a first-place essay contest winner by the Jersey City Education Association

Fall 1983

Author's Note: This is my very first published piece, at age seventeen.

In today's society there is a constant economical and political struggle between the so-called powers of the world. It is not unconventional for one nation to try to stay one step ahead of its adversaries. As a matter of fact, this attitude is now commonplace. Thus, our nation, the United States of America, must maintain her high status by thoroughly educating the youth of today for the leadership of tomorrow.

The public school system in America is on the decline, however. Many students drop out each year due to boredom and high anxieties. Some teachers have lost all intensity and compassion for their work. Coupled together, these factors do not lead to the making of a solid educational program. Instead, the United States is left with bits and pieces of material, so to speak, that just will not fit in place. A pessimistic future looms large if nothing is done to curtail this ever-growing dilemma.

The present administration on Capitol Hill has done little if anything to boost public school standards across the country. There has been talk about the complicated situation, but

nothing positive has been done about it. State-level governments have been more productive thus far. Many have given incentive pays to teachers and designed various programs to keep students tuned into school. Both ideas have been and should continue to be beneficial. The United States government, however, seems to refuse to even "wet its feet" when it comes to the education of the young people of America. This is a disgrace to the ideals of this great nation. We just cannot relax and allow superpowers, such as Japan and Russia, to continue to advance forward as we steadily step backward.

Something must be done, within this decade, to help the ailing public school system. If little or nothing is done now, the United States can expect to have little or no influence whatsoever in future world problems.

A Letter to My Mother
January 3, 1989

Dear Mother:

I am writing this letter because I have a lot on my mind. As you know, I have made a lot of mistakes in my life and I have gone through a lot of changes. 1988 was a hard year for me because I was not smart with my money, because Lottie died, and because I was suspended from school. Even though I am now twenty-two years of age, I feel younger because <u>now</u> for the first time I am really finding out what being a man is all about.

You see, college is not the real world. All it really is is a place where you go for four or five years so that you can get a better job once you finish. From what I've seen, you can't even be sure if you will get a good job because you went to college. I know a lot of people—especially Black people—who went to Rutgers and still ended up working as waiters or bus drivers or something else you don't even need to go to college for.

But what happens when you go to college for a while is that you get used to people feeding you and cleaning up after you and just basically treating you like a kid. College is just one big playground. It is not different from high school except that you live at college.

So when I got kicked out of school, I did not know what to do. I was scared and I am still scared. For the first time I am starting to realize that I have to do for myself if I am ever to make anything of myself. You are probably saying that I should have known that all the time. But I didn't and I do not think I am totally to blame for not knowing. Look at the way you

raised me. You never let me learn how to cook or taught me how to clean a house or even how to wash clothes. I became used to someone else doing all those things for me. Even though we were real poor, I grew up thinking that someone or everyone was supposed to do for me and that I didn't have to do anything. Yes! Now I see that that was wrong and I am trying to better myself—with the help of God, of course.

It is true that me and you have not gotten along all the time and had a lot of problems in 1988. And I take a lot of the blame for this fact. But Mother, I just cannot understand why you would just completely reject me, your son, when it is so possible that I could become <u>homeless</u>. You tell me to ask those "other Black people" for help but they are not my family and I don't like having a lot of people in my business.

I have a pretty good job now with some nice people but that does not mean I am back on my feet yet. And it is not like I want to live with you forever—because I do not. But where I live is bad. The heat comes and goes when it pleases. I've been sick off and on for the past few weeks. On top of that, I have a very sore foot from these new shoes I bought but it is too late to change them. I have to wear them because they are all I have. And because I had to pay rent every week, sometimes I have had to forget about eating. This is crazy. I feel like I have nowhere or no one to turn to. I am trying my hardest but this is not easy. And now you make me feel like I don't even have a mother. I mean I grew up not having a father, now I don't even have a mother to turn to for comfort. This is too much for me to handle. I cannot even sleep well at night because all I can think about is how lonely I am and how unfair life is. And lately when I have called you, you sometimes do not know it is me—your son. Are you trying to forget me? Do you hate me? Have I hurt you so much that you want me far away from you?

I do not know what else to say. I just know that I find myself crying all the time—wherever I go—even now as I sit at my desk

at work. It hurts, Mother, it really does. I do not think I am a bad person, just a person who has made many mistakes and must learn from them. I cannot understand how you could seriously call yourself a Christian or God-fearing and not feel what I feel or feel for me. Friday is around the corner and I have to get out of that room. I need time to look for a nice apartment—not just anything. And I need time to save money. Can't you understand that? I could see if you were down south and I up north by myself but that is not the case. I only need until February 1 and I would be right back out. All I would bring are some clothes. I would not use the phone and watch the TV if you don't want me to—I would respect you and your apartment. Is this so much to ask?

Is your heart made out of stone? Do you think Judgment Day will come and you won't be asked about this if you just turn your back on me like I am not your son? Do you care that you may see me one day begging for money at the PATH station in Jersey City or at Penn Station in Newark? Do you realize that if I have no place to go on Friday I also will not have a job for too long because I will not have a place to wash up or to change clothes? Do you care? Do you care? Do you care?

Your son,
Kevin Powell

for aunt cathy
1990

life ain't never been promised to nobody
that's what grandma lottie used to say
and you
her youngest daughter
and youngest of six children
snuck into the city
on a greyhound bus
with my mother
and scraped the side of a boardinghouse for good luck
as your life stretched beyond
the wooden shacks
and cotton fields
and the sandy schoolroom floors of south carolina

and you were alive
at last
free
in a city
away from the
comforting stench of down south
and in the big city
with its
musty underarm
and gasoline breath

and you took all ten years of your schoolin'

and applied for a job as a factory worker
on the assembly line
and you assembled parts
and the parts assembled you into
the permanence of minimum wages
and time clocks
and bosses who thought a black woman
was supposed to like work
hell, y'all had been conditioned to be oxes
they figured

and when you wasn't producing like an ox
their tucked-in potbellies would ask:
why you moving so slow, cathy?
and on the inside you licked your tongue
at them the way you used to do
when my mother and my aunt birdie yelled at you
and your heart tightened around your waist
and you ate what your feet could produce
for 8 hours a day
40 hours a week
with
one 15-minute break a day
if you was doing your job

and you needed something else
to keep your tears from spitting out
thoughts and words that would send you
back down south
in a fit of fear
and you met him
and he was fine
that man
and you liked him

and he liked you
and like became love
to you
and like became lust
for him
and he and you
exploded into anthony
my cousin anthony
one april day in 1966
and now you had a shield
to hold against the world
you had a world to shield you against
the heartaches of him
the foot aches of work
and the headaches
of city life

and you raised anthony
the best way you knew how
just like my mother raised me
and anthony grew and i grew
with our frustrated imaginations
to resent each other
to hate you, our mothers
to despise our very existences
in that tiny
cramped three-room apartment
two mothers and two sons
in a three-room apartment
held together
by welfare
food stamps
and the roaches
that always found their way

into our food
no matter how thick
the layers of aluminum foil

and that thirsty, tingling sensation
would often reappear
crawling between your toes
up your legs
across your thighs
teasing your crotch
but it couldn't get any farther
that's nasty,
you thought,
some man between my legs
again
so you stuffed your womb
with the world of anthony
because your spirit
was tired of being probed
by social workers, mailmen, and would-be husbands
for having an illegitimate son

and in spite of reality
burning down every hope we had
we managed to spread out
to a better part of the ghetto
and we even had separate apartments now
but you and my mother
always was in the same building because
my mother was the mean one
who scoffed at the world
with her angry eyes
and you was the nice one
who wanted to be like my mother

but you couldn't
so you followed my mother
everywhere
because at least you'd be safe
from yourself

and when we finally moved out of the ghetto
around white folks
you felt good
we was movin' up
and flying like birds released from their mother's grip for the
first time
and we was happy to be around
white folks
and didn't mind being called niggas
because at least we was good niggas

and me and anthony
knocked off the weight of
that restless city
that dirty city
and we left
me to college
anthony to the navy
leaving you and my mother
grazing in the pastures of midlife

and my mother was happy to be free of a man-child
but you was sad
because anthony had been your reason to live
your reason to work
your reason to exist
and now his departure meant your death
and you were dying

a slow death
dancing with midlife and dying a muted death
the years of working were gone
the years of sharing were gone
the years of being were gone
and the woman inside of your crouching body
died one may day in 1988 when grandma lottie was buried
and as we wiped the tears from our eyes
no one noticed you sinking through the church pew
through the floor
into the earth to join grandma lottie

and even though anthony was there at the funeral
he left again
back to the navy
back to japan
to some strange place
that was not him
because he hated himself
and he hated you
for being him
and he nailed shut
the door
on your life

and no one noticed you drowning in your pain
until you began having conversations with yourself
and tellin' everyone how you was hearing things
and seeing movies on your living room wall
how you was the star in those movies

and even my mother
with her superstitious ways
could not believe
that you were a victim of roots and magic spells

and my mother and aunt birdie did it
they tricked you with a meal and had you straightjacketed
and they didn't tell me
but i found out and i found you
and i leaped inside your body
and begged you to wake up
i swam inside your dried-up tears
and turned back the currents
to your childhood
to your adolescence
to your early adulthood
to anthony
to anthony's father
to my mother and aunt birdie and grandma lottie
and i cried between the lines of your history

and you told me you were not crazy
and i said i know
and you told me you could not understand
why my mother and aunt birdie had put you there
and i said i know
and you told me how they drugged you
how they called you by a number
how they monitored your phone calls
and i knew that you had become a prisoner of your worst fears
 of your own death

and i looked at you and i didn't see you
instead i saw an old black woman
inside your 45-year-old body
and i wanted to rush to you and shake your youth
out of that impostor

but it was you . . .

and now i understand those sounds you heard
and those movies you saw on your walls
you are not crazy
it took me a long time
but i understand
anthony knows what you've been through
but he doesn't know you
i know you
my mother and aunt birdie know what you've been through
but they don't know you
i know you

i carry you with me every day
i see you when i see that black woman
lying on the ground with a mcdonald's cup in her hand
at 34th street
i see you and i say
"here, cathy,
this is all i got"
and i drop a tear into your cup
and curse myself and my mother and aunt birdie
and anthony and anthony's father
and i kiss you with a prayer
because now i understand
why black bodies sag the way they do
and why black hearts don't birth emotions anymore

The Sexist in Me

Originally published in *Essence*
September 1992

My girlfriend and I had been arguing most of the day. As we were returning from the laundromat, she ran ahead of me to our apartment building. I caught up with her at the front door, dropped the clothes at her feet, went inside, and slammed the door behind me. She carried the bundle in, set it down, and started back outside. Enraged, I grabbed her by the seat of her shorts and pulled her back into the apartment. We struggled in the kitchen, the dining area, and the bathroom. As we were moving toward the living room, I shoved her into the bathroom door. Her face bruised, she began to cry uncontrollably, and I tried to calm her down as we wrestled on the living room floor. When she let out a high-pitched yell for help, I jumped to my feet, suddenly aware of what I was doing. Shaking with fear and exhaustion, I watched my girlfriend run barefoot out of our apartment into the street.

I still shudder when I think of that scene one year later. It was my first serious relationship and, notwithstanding my proclamations of "I'm one Black man who's gonna do the right thing," I managed to join the swelling ranks of abusive men with relative ease. Soon after "the incident," accusations of sexism flooded my guilty conscience. Like a lot of men, I tried to pin much of the blame on my now ex-girlfriend. *She must have done something to provoke my outburst*, I rationalized to myself.

But I couldn't delude myself for too long. I kept thinking of all the women I had ill-treated in some way. Without fully realiz-

ing it, I had always taken women for granted, but it wasn't until I committed a violent act that it hit me how deeply I believed women to be inferior to men.

Ashamed of what I had done, I knew that if I didn't deal with my deeply rooted sexism—that desire of man to dominate woman—I could not seriously enter into another emotionally intimate relationship with a woman. Psychologically drained, I consulted young female friends my own age, older Black women and men, and any book that dealt with the issue at hand. Everywhere I turned I found someone who was pointing out the dangers of exhibiting sexism.

For example, one woman friend drew an analogy to racism. If a child is taught from an early age to dislike another child because of his or her race, she said, the former is likely to become a hardened racist by adulthood. The same logic, she offered, applies to sexism.

Keeping in mind my friend's analogy, I recalled my childhood. I evolved as many boys do in this society: machismo gripped my psyche, and by the time I reached my teen years we "boys" did whatever we felt like doing—which ran the gamut from squeezing girls' buttocks in gym class to "gangbanging" girls in abandoned buildings.

My chauvinistic demeanor merely ripened with age, and even after my political consciousness blossomed in college, I self-righteously continued to rationalize that the real battle was against racism, and if the "sistas" on campus couldn't fall into line, well then, those women weren't really down with the program anyway.

In retrospect, what happened in my relationship was inevitable. Left unchecked my entire life, my sexist inclinations were building up to a breaking point. Unable to handle the pressures of a serious relationship, I first sought to "control" my girlfriend through verbal tirades and then finally through violence—the highest form of sexism.

The entire experience has been incredibly stressful—including writing about it now. I will never be able to remove the pain I inflicted on my ex-girlfriend, but at least I've taken measures to ensure it will not happen again.

Acknowledging my inherent sexism was the first step. I then had to recognize that women are not footstools or servants or punching bags, but my equals on every level. And as I've struggled against my own sexism, I've also had to struggle against it when it manifests in my male friends. I can no longer tolerate the use of words like *bitch* or *skeezer* to describe women. Silence is acquiescence and acceptance. Moreover, true manhood does not rest on the subjugation of women—verbal or physical—and meaningful relationships between men and women won't exist until we men understand that.

Native Sons

Originally published in *Vibe*
September 1992

*This is the only real concern of the artist, to recreate out
of the disorder of life that order which is art.*
—James Baldwin

*And now you want me to rap and give? Say something
positive? Well, positive ain't where I live.*
—Treach

Naughty by Nature are the last act on the Apollo bill, and the throng of swaggering, foul-mouthed B-boys and gum-popping B-girls is restless. It has been a typically disappointing evening of hip-hop in Harlem. But when corapper Vinnie steps out and demands, "Throw your hands in the air!" homies jump from their seats in a frenzy, thrusting knuckles upward like mesmerized Holy Rollers. Vinnie introduces DJ Kay Gee as a phalanx of boys from Naughty's East Orange, NJ, neighborhood lines the stage, suited in NBN hoodies, baseball caps, and T-shirts. Kay Gee cuts and scratches Treach's name on the turntables and the audience erupts again. (My own adrenaline is pumping: in the heart of Uptown I'm yellin', "Yeah, y'all, Jersey's in da motherfuckin' house!"—proud, for once to be from *that* state.)

Treach glides across the stage like a panther: Black, lean, his narrowed eyes riveted on his prey; he grips the mic tightly in one hand while the other slashes air with his ever-present

machete. Draped in a baggy blue prison-like outfit, a black Malcolm X tee, and the latest B-boy headgear—a striped knit cap more appropriate for sleepin' than sportin' outdoors (though B-boy logic says otherwise)—Treach savors the moment and looks genuinely inspired by the chorus of screaming voices.

When Kay Gee launches "Guard Your Grill," Treach high-steps across the stage as rapid-fire lyrics eject from his mouth. With his impish charm, long braids, and dark brown baby face, Treach explodes the notion that hip-hop doesn't produce sex symbols. Throughout the evening women fawn over his pelvic gyrations and tongue acrobatics ("How many of y'all ladies like a nice long wet tongue?" he asks seductively), and even the homeboys in the house readily give Treach his props.

Instantly my mind replays the incredible rap shows of yester-year: Doug E. Fresh and Slick Rick at the Funhouse, Public Enemy at Studio 54, Big Daddy Kane at an outdoor rally/concert in Harlem. But nothing compares to Treach's funky coup d'état. There are no gimmicks, no fancy stage design except for Kay Gee's high-rise boulder with an electronic Naughty sign, and no dancers. Treach is just a regular brother from around the way, rippin' the mic and doin' it because he loves his craft. Tonight Treach *is* hip-hop: in dress, in talk, in spirit.

East Orange, New Jersey, to use one resident's term, is "an extension of Newark." Many of the city's Black inhabitants moved here from that larger, crime-ridden metropolis after the riot of 1967. East Orange's population is an eclectic bunch: the spacious homes of upwardly mobile Black professionals butt up against the rat-infested tenements of single-parent families. Paradoxically, East Orange's hill roads, tree-lined side streets, and beautiful row houses give the illusion of a suburb. But packed tightly on many of these blocks are legions of young Black men drifting somewhere between poverty and death. Each year some of these boy-men graduate from the city's two public high schools—East

Orange and Clifford Scott—into a shapeless, unpredictable future. Like inner-city youth elsewhere, some will escape to the military or, if they're lucky, to college. The rest linger at home, forced either to take near-minimum-wage jobs or seek refuge in the streets.

> *If you ain't never been to the ghetto*
> *Don't ever come to the ghetto*
> *'Cause you wouldn't understand the ghetto*
> *So stay away the fuck out of the ghetto!*

Ghetto dwelling breeds distrust and hypersensitivity. I grew up in Jersey City and later in Newark, watching B-boys walk down my block, only to be jumped because they were strangers. As far as we were concerned, the hood was all we had and we would defend it at any cost. I recalled that world, my world, as I rode the 21 bus through Newark—past garbage-filled lots, smoked-out buildings, and nodding junkies—into East Orange for my interview with Naughty by Nature.

"We don't let nobody come around here if we ain't never seen them before," Treach would tell me later. "We live on North 18th Street but we call it 118th Street 'cause there's a hundred real niggas we roll with, and we don't take no shorts. Ain't no female or no nigga from the outside gonna step up and cause any friction between us."

When I get off the bus at Williams Street and 18th, I realize I don't know where I'm going, and even if I did, I'd still be simply an intruder on someone else's turf. I stop at a pay phone and call Kay Gee's house.

"They ain't here," a woman with a sweet, maternal voice says. "They went to the store. They ain't say nothin' about no interview. But I'll tell them you called."

Click.

On the PATH train back to Manhattan, Naughty's Apollo

show floods my brain. Treach's world infuses his lyrics, and his aura makes it impossible for his audience—Black and White, poor as shit and squeaky-clean—to ignore what he's saying. But the music itself is the music of every Black male I know who's hustling on the street or rotting in jail or taking a dirt nap somewhere. After all, as has been the case with me, Treach, Vinnie, and Kay Gee have learned most of their values and guidelines for survival from the streets. There's nothing complex about B-boy culture: we fight, we drink, we bond. The hood is often all we know; it cannot thrive without us, and we cannot live without it.

On the set of *YO! MTV Raps*—a colorful, oversized playground complete with a basketball hoop and dangling *YO!* signs—Treach, Vinnie, and Kay Gee are subdued, watching Ed Lover and Doctor Dre kill time before a taping by dissin' everyone within reach.

"Hey Dre, you know who Kenny looks like?" Ed Lover, the tall, lanky cohost shouts to his shorter, overweight partner.

Kenny Buford, *YO!*'s thin, light-complexioned production assistant, braces himself for the inevitable.

"Sade with a receding hairline!"

The camera crew and other production assistants crack up, but the trio remains mute. Bored by the delay—one camera isn't working properly—Vinnie breaks into a beat-box routine (his skills are amazing) and, like any old-school rapper, Treach jumps in with a crotch-grabbing rhyme. The set quiets down momentarily, and Treach ends the impromptu show with a when-the-fuck-is-this-shit-gonna-start? look. I wonder if he realizes how large he is. How many self-proclaimed ghetto bastards have their first single go double platinum, their debut album do nearly as well, and earn an American Music Award and a Grammy nomination all in the space of ten months? Not Public Enemy, not Boogie Down Productions, not N.W.A or Ice Cube, and not even that other homebred B-boy, LL Cool J.

"Treach is the first authentic hip-hopper I've seen in a long time," Ed Lover tells me after "Uptown Anthem" is taped. "Yeah, he wants to get his, like everybody else, but there's a sincerity there too. Look at him; you can see that he's had a hard life, and it comes out in his music. His hard core ain't made up; it's real. And he wants everybody to know that."

B-boy culture, in order to sustain itself, often exaggerates and creates unrealistic images. These hyperboles are at best coping methods and at worst ludicrously false senses of security. Treach is real precisely because he is not out to startle or please anyone; his life is his music and his music is his life. "Naughty by Nature has this total pop sensibility," says Benny Medina, senior vice president of A&R at Warner Bros., "yet their big concern is about staying true to the street, true to life. Most people in rap go pop at the expense of their street credentials, and don't seem to care." But Treach insists you either accept him for who he is or don't accept him at all.

Midtown's Unique Recording Studios is located in a high, undistinguished building just off the corner of Seventh Avenue and 47th Street. In a dimly lit tenth-floor lounge nestled between two studios, Treach, Vinnie, and Kay Gee's cousin Gene (Naughty's road manager) are playing pool. Across the hall in studio C, Kay Gee (born Kier Gist) is laying down tracks for NBN's second album, tentatively titled *19NaughtyII*. Hidden behind dark glasses, a gray hoodie, and black bandanna, Kay Gee gives the definite impression that he doesn't want to be bothered.

"So why do you always wear the hood and glasses?" I half-heartedly ask him.

Kay Gee looks up from his stack of 45s and, for a second, grins. A gold cap beams from the left side of his mouth. "I'm always in the chill mood," he responds coolly, before turning back to his work.

Kay Gee cues the engineer and she clicks on the anthemic "Hip-

Hop Hooray," a smoothed-out R&B track with a chanting chorus.

> *I live and die for hip-hop*
> *This is hip-hop for today*
> *I will give props to hip-hop*
> *So hip-hop hooray*
> *Hey! Ho! Hey! Ho!*

Besides "Hip-Hop Hooray," Kay Gee lets me listen to a hard-core jam called "The Hood Comes First" and the funk-filled "Lyte Taste of Nature." Although *19NaughtyII* has the band's characteristic hooks and live samples, I can also hear and feel their maturation. Animated for once, Kay Gee insists this album is going to be different from their Tommy Boy debut. "Our music is like classical hip-hop, you know it has that hard-core street sound, but we also like to use live instruments and whatnot," he says. "*19NaughtyII* is gonna let people know how serious we are. Hip-hop is all we think about."

Treach, in a better mood than he was on the set of *YO!*, greets me with a big "Whaddup?" and a bear hug, while Vinnie and Gene argue shots at the pool table. We sit down at a cafeteria-style booth at the front of the room. Bigger up close, Treach's biceps are thick, and save a few old nicks and bruises, his skin has a smooth chocolate glow. Wearing a black T-shirt, sagging black denim jeans, and black Timberland boots, he looks every inch the wickedest man alive.

Born Anthony Criss twenty-one years ago in Newark, Treach moved to East Orange at age two. He has two brothers and two sisters, but only he and his younger brother lived with his mother. The product of a single-parent home, Treach only saw his father sporadically. As in the autobiographical "Ghetto Bastard," anger fills Treach's voice when he speaks of his father. "I met him, yeah, I met him," he mutters, then pauses. "I saw him a few times, but I never knew him."

I think of my father, who disowned me when I was eight, who I didn't really know either and haven't seen since, and I remember, the first time I heard "Ghetto Bastard," how I rewound the tape over and over again to those jarring words: *"Never knew my dad / Motherfuck the fag!"*

"'Ghetto Bastard' is my world too," I say to Treach, and his face relaxes a bit, a serious, solitary "Word" falling from his mouth.

"It's all of us," he says, his eyes moistening. "Me and Vinnie come from broken homes. Most of our friends is like us—ghetto bastards. Kay Gee is the only one that got a pops in the house." He pauses, catching his breath. "The last time I saw my father was when I was thirteen. He was in town for a while, and I would see him every now and then. Around Christmastime I scraped up some money and bought him something—cologne or a tie or something. It was snowing, and I walked to his house, and they told me he had moved again. That was the last time I ever heard anything about him. I don't even remember walking home, that's how hurt I was. I just know I was there."

Throughout his teens, Treach became even more alienated from everything and everyone around him. With his mother struggling to feed two children and school being little more than a hangout, Treach ran the streets of East Orange, immersing himself in the rites of B-boy passage: cutting school, having sex, drinking, and smoking. Though at seventeen he worked for a few months at a Grand Union warehouse packing and unloading boxes, after he was laid off, his mother, fed up, finally threw him out.

"I wasn't comin' home and wasn't making no money to help her out either," he says, resigned as if he'd expected it all along. "I really wanted to work, but I couldn't find nothin'. The streets was the only place I could turn."

Treach slept in parks, friends' homes, and anywhere else he could, selling drugs at night and sporadically attending East Or-

ange High during the day. "A week after my mother threw me out, I got locked up for selling . . . It wasn't for too long, though, and I was right back out there doin' it again. I didn't know what else to do."

Ask most ghetto children what they want to be, and their faces go blank, unsure why the question has any meaning for them. We live, as Ralph Ellison put it, literally on the run, from a world that views us as a threat to be either subdued, intimidated, or even eliminated. As a kid I knew I wanted to be a writer, but I didn't dare tell anyone because I didn't believe it could happen. Treach, too, knew he wanted to be a weaver of words—a rapper—since he was in the seventh grade. From the time he heard the Sugarhill Gang and Kurtis Blow, he knew that *that* was what he wanted to do. Treach is one of those rare brothers who knew he could when everyone and everything around him told him he couldn't.

Vinnie, also twenty-one, joins Treach and me at the table. A short, stocky individual with close-cropped hair, Vinnie is the most gregarious of the three and outrageously funny. The history of Naughty by Nature, he says, dates back to an eleventh-grade health class he shared with Treach. Whenever the teacher was less than inspiring—which was often—Vinnie would do the human beat box as Treach dropped freestyle lyrics. DJ Kay Gee lived on the same block as Vinnie, and the two would team up after school to practice the beat box and turntable scratches.

A year ahead of Treach and Vinnie at East Orange High, Kay Gee decided to participate in his senior class talent show and asked Vinnie to join him. Since they didn't have an MC, Kay Gee invited Treach over to his house and they quickly formed the New Style (a phrase borrowed from a Beastie Boys song). "We wrecked the show," Vinnie boasts. "We kept the name and did shows all over the area. We knew from there that we wanted to be in the music business."

After Vinnie and Treach graduated from high school in 1988, the New Style signed with Sylvia Robinson's Bon Ami label and, like hundreds of aspiring rap stars before them, received a harsh lesson in the music business. They locked themselves into a production deal and wound up making an album, *Independent Leaders*, an unsuccessful effort which led them nowhere. (Naughty by Nature ultimately settled with Bon Ami for an undisclosed amount in 1990.) All three turned back to selling drugs to support their musical ambitions.

"We was dirty niggas clockin'," Treach says reflectively. "We put our money somewhere that would help us in the future. We always knew we'd make another record."

In 1989 Queen Latifah, who the trio knew from neighboring Irvington, released her first album on Tommy Boy. "Latifah was managed by the Flavor Unit, and we figured if they helped her, they could help us," Vinnie says. "Kay Gee called Latifah's producer, DJ Mark the 45 King, and he camcordered us performing in his basement. That tape started all the buzz."

When the New Style gave themselves a fundraiser at East Orange's Upsala College, Flavor Unit members Lakim Shabazz, Apache, and Queen Latifah attended. Impressed with the group's potential, Latifah and Shakim Compare immediately signed the New Style to Flavor Unit Management and then took their demo tape to Benny Medina at Warner Bros., who gave them a contract in 1990. After their album was completed, Medina approached Warner's new subsidiary, Tommy Boy—the label of De La Soul and Digital Underground—about distributing the album. "I liked Tommy Boy's marketing techniques for street audiences," Medina explains. "Sometimes an act, a really significant act, can get lost at a major label because of its stupidity or weakness. Tommy Boy started building street knowledge two months before the release of 'O.P.P.'"

"We actually turned them down in 1989 when they were still the New Style," says Tommy Boy president Monica Lynch. "We

felt they hadn't clarified their style yet." But after that initial contact with Tommy Boy, the New Style became Naughty by Nature (the title of a song on that first album, which, Treach says, neatly sums up the group's persona) and polished their sound, moving away from freewheeling braggadocio to anecdotes about Illtown. Hearing Naughty by Nature the second time around, Tommy Boy jumped on "O.P.P."

"I just thought it was the coolest," says Medina. "I'd never heard anyone use a Jackson sample before, and with the grooves, the smooth bass lines, and melodic structure, it was a totally new sound. I thought we'd have a fairly successful record, but no way did I know it was going to be *the* phrase, *the* rap song of the year."

But Tommy Boy worked the single from the ground with a major promotion including stickers, T-shirts, and a national tour long before the single dropped. "We wanted something everybody could get wit: the kids to the older folks, the girls and the guys," says Treach. "We figured even the hardest of the hard would be like, *Yeah*."

Treach still insists, somewhat disingenuously, that Naughty by Nature "just wanted to be a nice underground group like Brand Nubian." But B-boy culture is about being large—being known in your world as the best, be it a local drug dealer or a hip-hop artist. Indeed, Naughty by Nature has spawned a number of Treach imitators, most recently Das EFX and Kris Kross. Monica Lynch's assessment is blunt: "The effect Treach has had on hip-hop has been enormous. I call it 'Treach-isms': the way he delivers lines, his stage presence, and his charisma. Treach has that star power that is unbelievable. Guys admire him for his rhyme skills, but women want to sleep with him."

Inside the poolroom, Treach's lean body pushes against a window as he peers down on Times Square and the rush-hour crowd. Glassy-eyed and mellow after a long day in the studio,

he's sipping on a forty-ounce of Olde English. Alone with him, I wonder aloud how it feels to be a star.

"Everything is still the same," Treach says, his voice low and raspy. "The only difference is that financially we ain't gotta struggle and hustle on the streets. We still live on the same block, hang with the same people. A lot of people are lookin' up to us, where it wasn't like that before."

The role-model tag will probably stick to Treach for a long time. He's employed many of his homies already, and plans to hire his friends who are in jail when they get out. In addition, Treach, Vinnie, and Kay Gee sell Naughty by Nature paraphernalia—hoodies, baseball caps, pajamas, and condoms—at a profit and expect to build the business at home in East Orange.

Judging by the number of women who have passed through the studio today, it seems the only thing missing from Treach's life right now is one steady love interest. "I don't have time for that right now," he says. "Our music comes first. I have companions, but it's not like I'm home long enough to get serious with someone. And I tell them that. It's an understanding from jump."

If Treach is avoiding relationships—ones that might lead to a family of his own—it may be because he's recently been trying to repair the one with his mother. It is perfect, in a way, that Treach would rise above the resentment he must harbor for her and do what is probably the right thing. That, it seems, is where his success comes from: the ability to control the rage and cultivate the creativity, a powerful combination that will allow him to move up.

Where his mother is concerned, perhaps he's backing up, in a sort of retroactive attempt to make the past right—playing the part that his father so pitifully neglected. He's buying her a house. Sending her to school.

He says resolutely: "I'm not bitter or nothin' about what happened. She had to do what she had to do."

But someday Treach wants to be able to do things differently:

"I wanna have a family with some type of structure, you know what I'm sayin'? That's why I haven't had any kids yet." He looks down at his large hands and ponders them for a minute. "I wanna have it so my kids will know me." He pauses again. And then lifts his head and looks straight at me. "*My* family would come first."

A Dialogue
with Audre Lorde

Originally published in *Emerge*
November 1992

I n the late '60s Audre Lorde, poet, activist, and theorist, was an integral part of the Black Arts Movement. In the '70s and '80s hers was a potent voice in the feminist and gay/lesbian literary movements. Given two years to live in the first of three bouts with cancer in eight years, Lorde continues to endure and write in the '90s. "I feel it's really important," she says matter-of-factly, "that I use what I have, that my whole life is not just focused on preserving my life."

Born in New York City of Caribbean parentage on February 18, 1934, Lorde moved to St. Croix, Virgin Islands, in the late '80s, when the grit and grind of the big city became too much for her ailing health. She was professor of English at Hunter College until her retirement in 1987 and was named New York State poet laureate in 1992. She has published ten volumes of poetry, including the recent *Undersongs: Chosen Poems Old and New Revised* (Norton), and five books of prose. She has lectured widely and has worked intensively with women of color in various nations. She also has two grown children, a daughter and a son. Always upbeat, Lorde described her latest illness as a "very hard time. But here I am, fifty-eight and still making trouble."

KEVIN POWELL: What were some of the things you were doing in St. Croix before this latest bout with cancer?

AUDRE LORDE: I was involved with the Sisterhood in Support of Sisters in South Africa. We were fundraising. Other than my writing, I've been involved in community activities there, like work in the schools. And I've been active in community issues. For people who visit, St. Croix seems like a paradise—and in some respects it is—but we have all the problems of a colonial existence. Basically, we exist in a colonial relationship to the US. There are problems having to do with education, with rebuilding, even though it's three years after Hurricane Hugo. A lot of the effects of Hugo are still evident in the social fabric of St. Croix.

POWELL: What are some of the similarities of being a writer in the US and being one in the Caribbean?

LORDE: I occupy an interesting position. I have made myself a part of the St. Croix community. I believe we have a right to choose the community we wish to be a part of. You have to offer the people in the community something that will make them want you to be a part of it. I am a writer, and I give readings in St. Croix. I had a wonderful reading in February for Black History Month. It was at a Black bookstore. I gave the reading on Black love—you know, Black history, Valentine's Day. And what I used it for was to bring up the issue of domestic violence, which is a real problem there, as it is in many island cultures. I wanted to bring it up in such a way that we could really discuss it. First of all, when you live on an island that's twenty-six miles long and seven miles wide, emotions can get really intense. I think that's because of the social issues endemic to a colonial relationship: rage, inadequate opportunities, unemployment. When you consider that alcohol here is tax-free—in some areas rum is cheaper than milk—you see the availability of alcohol and the lack of opportunities, and together, in many respects, those two factors

create certain social problems that very frequently find their expression in domestic violence.

POWELL: What are some issues on the mainland that concern you?

LORDE: I feel that domestic violence is a problem in the US also. I am most concerned that our younger sisters should not believe that the battles are either lost or won. This is a very, very hard time to keep fighting, to keep goals in mind and continue to pursue them. We look around us at the political situation, at the economic situation, and we say, "Why bother?" Now, more than ever, it is important to keep alive the ideals and visions of the kind of life we want for ourselves and for our children, and follow them. The situation of young Black people is appalling right now in terms of drugs, in terms of narrowed expectations. We've got to be able to keep the fire alive, to keep the vision of a future alive and continue to work for it, even in the face of the most overwhelming odds. As bad as things are—and they are bad now, and I believe they're going to get worse for us—I have to tell you I am very optimistic. They'll get better if we can keep that fire alive and alter and change and fuse our young people, wherever we meet them, with some sense of the kinds of changes we need to work toward.

POWELL: What does poetry mean to you?

LORDE: I believe that poetry is the skeleton architecture of our lives. Poetry gives us a chance to express visions of things that have not been but can be. It's the farthest reaches of our imagination about what we need to construct before we can make those visions real. I think poetry is the most subversive use of language there is, because it's in the business of altering feeling.

POWELL: You write and talk a great deal about sexuality. Do you see a relationship between one's sexuality and/or sexual preference and one's art?

LORDE: I believe that if you cannot be open and aboveboard about your sexuality, that is a restraint. And I think any kind of restraint upon us constricts our creative forces. I think our sexuality is part and parcel of who we are and becomes metabolized in terms of our creativity.

POWELL: You've been critical of the Black and gay/lesbian literary movements in the US from the late '60s to the present. Why?

LORDE: It's so difficult for me to talk about movements. I'm not sure why. Of course, I just live them and wait for other people to talk about them. The Black literary movement was very important in the '60s. It was, in many aspects, incomplete. There were certain efforts of vision that we are now probably reaping the results of. I think it was, in many aspects, restrictive. There were those of us who were not allowed to express ourselves and, you know, became outsiders.

POWELL: Can you be more specific?

LORDE: For example, if we talk about Black poetry in the '60s, there was no room for Black lesbian and gay poets. The very people who were running around raving about James Baldwin were calling him a "skinny faggot." And they didn't want to hear things he had to say. Who is it now that we're not listening to? That's the question. But I think very, very important things happened during the Black literary movement of the '60s, and we built upon it. No one is ever perfect. It's a question of being brave enough to get it out there so that someone can use it to go somewhere else. I think that's true now in the Black gay/lesbian

literary movement. One of the things that just makes my heart sing, for example, is the great surge of young, Black, gay male writers and poets.

POWELL: How were you able to distribute your work given the limitations of both the Black and gay/lesbian literary movements?

LORDE: A lot of it wasn't. A lot of the things that were published in the '70s and '80s were things I had written ten years before. The women's movement was very instrumental in having my work presented. That's also true in terms of the Black literary movement. When Gwendolyn Brooks really encouraged Dudley Randall of Broadside Press to print two of my books [*From a Land Where Other People Live*, 1973, and *The New York Head Shop and Museum*, 1975], she was taking a chance. Broadside Press was very instrumental in presenting a lot of young poets who would not otherwise have had a voice.

POWELL: What does the future hold?

LORDE: I pretty much live from day to day. I would like to do more writing concerning living with cancer and the processes of dying. I'd like to continue work on my novel about a young Black lesbian mother living in the late 1960s. I want to live—which means writing and making trouble.

Reality Check
1994
for Kurt Cobain (1967–1994)

i hate myself and want to die
i can hear you saying that now
the words like gunshots blasted into
the skin silencing the nightmares of a
generation we are not an x or twenty-
something
there is more to our teen spirit
it smells like distorted childhoods
and diapered friendships and parents
who fed us watergate and vietnam
and ronald reagan and saturday-morning
cartoons without giving us a love we could
grip and suck on when the earth
was burning in our direction
and now you are gone
nah! i refuse to believe that
a whole bunch of us were gonna go and listen to you
regurgitate our blues (yours too) and make anxiety-filled
guitar licks into a futuristic rock opera (our opera)
your hair would fly like a stringy flag saluting the knuckleheads of
the world, yes! us! the post–civil rights post-vietnam post-reagan
babies would somehow feel validated when your hoarse, garbled
tongue slapped the world with an indictment that said "you have
neglected us for too long and look, just look at what you have
created"

and we would mosh and slam dance, our bodies contaminated with
this thing called youth, into a fitful overdose (isn't that what
 they expect of
us anyhow?) of icon-worshipping you: but you are
alive!
tongue-kissing your feminine side on *saturday night live*
alive!
eating environmentally sound fruit next to river phoenix
and you whisper in james dean's ear
as janis, jimi, jim, and john, the post–
happy days mount rushmore,
fall stone in love with the grunge thing
and someone will fanzine you
and call you a tragic genius
and bury you in mtv heaven
because no one no one no one
will ever understand why your flannel shirts
and ripped jeans and busted guitars mean
you have loved and lived much longer
than most of us . . .

Hero Today: O.J. Simpson

Originally published in *Vibe*
October 1994

Back in the day, we used to say, "A hero ain't nothin' but a sandwich," because our heroes—at least the ones we saw on television or in the movies—were so intangible. But we allowed their mystique to touch us, to represent us, to be us. One hero we loved was O.J. Simpson. I remember playing football at playgrounds and *everyone* wanted to be O.J.—our bodies shaking and spinning away from defenders; our smiles, like O.J.'s, as broad as a ghetto dream.

That was then, this is now: O.J. is charged with the double murder of his ex-wife Nicole Brown Simpson and a friend of hers, Ronald Goldman. Whether he did it or not we may never know, but speculations and opinions run in mad directions. We do know that most Black folks have a far different take on the O.J. saga than White folks. A month after the murders, a *USA Today*/Gallup/CNN poll revealed that 68 percent of White Americans were convinced of O.J.'s guilt, compared with 24 percent of Black Americans.

Many of us cringed as O.J., driven by childhood buddy Al Cowlings, was pursued for sixty miles by the California Highway Patrol. It was unfair, many of us felt, for one of our own to be ridiculed on national television like that. Many of us have also insisted that the hypercharged wheels of media are working overtime to sensationalize the case because O.J. is a Black man accused of murdering—gasp!—a White woman. Given Ameri-

ca's racial quagmire and media coverage of people of color, that thinking may not be so far-fetched.

But community reaction doesn't stop there. Somewhere in our collective mind, Black folks have managed to turn O.J. into a hero—again. We brandish *FREE THE JUICE* bumper stickers and hawk O.J. watches on the streets. On a single July afternoon, Tupac Shakur said, "I think that White people are evil, what they're doing to O.J.," and Flavor Flav was arrested wearing a *FREE O.J. SIMPSON* T-shirt.

Because of our history in this country, we immediately connect with any Black person whom we perceive to be a victim of "the man." Never mind the fact that O.J. Simpson was a "race-neutral" athlete in his heyday, rarely going out of his way to help Black causes. Never mind that O.J. repeatedly beat Nicole Brown Simpson. And never mind the fact that for every minute of O.J. coverage, there are many thousands of silent tragedies in Black America.

When all else fails, we find a hero to make our sandwich until the next meal comes along. For sure, O.J. will be glorified in rap songs, pimped by political leaders, his image mass-marketed in a Black community near you. Then, once O.J. and his trial are outta here, we will, as the Last Poets put it, party and bullshit until there's another fallen hero to rally around.

 # Ready to Live: Tupac Shakur

Originally published in *Vibe*
April 1995

Make me wanna holler
The way they do my life
—Marvin Gaye

I t was a chilly January morning when I made my way to Rikers Island for a conversation with Tupac Shakur, what would be his first words to any journalist since being shot last November 30. After passing through a series of checkpoints and metal detectors, I reached a dingy white conference room in the same building where Tupac was being held on $3 million bail. Within weeks, he'd receive a one-and-a-half- to four-and-a-half-year sentence for a sexual abuse conviction in his New York rape case.

Tupac strutted into the room without a limp, in spite of having been recently wounded in the leg—among other places. Dressed in a white Adidas sweatshirt and oversized blue jeans, he seemed more alert than he had been in all our interviews and encounters. He looked me in the eyes as we spoke and smoked one Newport after another. "I'm kinda nervous," he admitted at one point. After a brush with death and the barrage of rumor and innuendo that followed, Tupac said he'd summoned me because "this is my last interview. If I get killed, I want people to get every drop. I want them to have the real story."

KEVIN POWELL: How do you feel after everything you've been through these past few weeks?

TUPAC SHAKUR: Well, the first two days in prison, I had to go through what life is like when you've been smoking weed for as long as I have and then you stop. Emotionally, it was like I didn't know myself. I was sitting in a room, like there was two people in the room, evil and good. That was the hardest part. After that, the weed was out of me. Then every day I started doing, like, a thousand push-ups for myself. I was reading whole books in one day, and writing, and that was putting me in a peace of mind. Then I started seeing my situation and what got me here. Even though I'm innocent of the charge they gave me, I'm not innocent in terms of the way I was acting.

POWELL: Could you tell me specifically what you mean?

SHAKUR: I'm just as guilty for not doing nothing as I am for doing things. Not with this case, but just in my life. I had a job to do and I never showed up. I was so scared of this responsibility that I was running away from it. But I see now that whether I show up for work or not, the evil forces are going to be at me. They're going to come 100 percent, so if I don't be 100 percent pure-hearted, I'm going to lose. And that's why I'm losing.

When I got in here, all the prisoners was, like, "Fuck that gangsta rapper." I'm not a gangsta rapper. I rap about things that happen to me. I got shot five times, you know what I'm saying? People was trying to kill me. It was really real like that. I don't see myself being special; I just see myself having more responsibilities than the next man. People look to me to do things for them, to have answers. I wasn't having them because my brain was half-dead from smoking so much weed. I'd be in my hotel room smoking too much, drinking, going to clubs, just being

numb. That was being in jail to me. I wasn't happy at all on the streets. Nobody could say they saw me happy.

POWELL: When I spoke to you a year ago, you said that if you ended up in jail, your spirit would die. You sound like you're saying the opposite now.

SHAKUR: That was the addict speaking. The addict knew if I went to jail, then it couldn't live. The addict in Tupac is dead. The excuse-maker in Tupac is dead. The vengeful Tupac is dead. The Tupac that would stand by and let dishonorable things happen is dead. God let me live for me to do something extremely extraordinary, and that's what I have to do. Even if they give me the maximum sentence, that's still my job.

POWELL: Can you take us back to that night at Quad Recording Studios in Times Square?

SHAKUR: The night of the shooting? Sure. Ron G. is a DJ out here in New York. He's like, "Pac, I want you to come to my house and lay this rap down for my tapes." I said, "All right, I'll come for free." So I went to his house—me, Stretch, and a couple other homeboys. After I laid the song, I got a page from this guy Booker, telling me he wanted me to rap on Little Shawn's record. Now, this guy I was going to charge, because I could see that they was just using me, so I said, "All right, you give me seven G's and I'll do the song." He said, "I've got the money. Come." I stopped off to get some weed, and he paged me again. "Where you at? Why you ain't coming?" I'm like, "I'm coming, man, hold on."

POWELL: Did you know this guy?

SHAKUR: I met him through some rough characters I knew.

He was trying to get legitimate and all that, so I thought I was doing him a favor. But when I called him back for directions, he was like, "I don't have the money." I said, "If you don't have the money, I'm not coming." He hung up the phone, then called me back: "I'm going to call [Uptown Entertainment CEO] Andre Harrell and make sure you get the money, but I'm going to give you the money out of my pocket." So I said, "All right, I'm on my way." As we're walking up to the building, somebody screamed from up the top of the studio. It was Little Caesar, Biggie's side-man. That's my homeboy. As soon as I saw him, all my concerns about the situation were relaxed.

POWELL: So you're saying that going into it—

SHAKUR: I felt nervous because this guy knew somebody I had major beef with. I didn't want to tell the police, but I can tell the world. Nigel had introduced me to Booker. Everybody knew I was short on money. All my shows were getting canceled. All my money from my records was going to lawyers; all the movie money was going to my family. So I was doing this type of stuff, rapping for guys and getting paid.

POWELL: Who's this guy Nigel?

SHAKUR: I was kicking it with him the whole time I was in New York doing *Above the Rim*. He came to me. He said, "I'm going to look after you. You don't need to get in no more trouble."

POWELL: Doesn't Nigel also go by the name of Trevor?

SHAKUR: Right. There's a real Trevor, but Nigel took on both aliases, you understand? So that's who I was kicking with—I got close to them. I used to dress in baggies and sneakers. They took me shopping; that's when I bought my Rolex and all my jewels.

They made me mature. They introduced me to all these gang-sters in Brooklyn. I met Nigel's family, went to his kid's birthday party—I trusted him, you know what I'm saying? I even tried to get Nigel in the movie, but he didn't want to be on film. That bothered me. I don't know any nigga that didn't want to be in the movies.

POWELL: Can we come back to the shooting? Who was with you that night?

SHAKUR: I was with my homeboy Stretch, his man Fred, and my sister's boyfriend Zayd. Not my bodyguard; I don't have a bodyguard. We get to the studio, and there's a dude outside in army fatigues with his hat low on his face. When we walked to the door, he didn't look up. I've never seen a Black man not acknowledge me one way or the other, either with jealousy or respect. But this guy just looked to see who I was and turned his face down. It didn't click because I had just finished smoking chronic. I'm not thinking something will happen to me in the lobby. While we're waiting to get buzzed in, I saw a dude sitting at a table reading a newspaper. He didn't look up either.

POWELL: These are both Black men?

SHAKUR: Black men in their thirties. So first I'm like, *These dudes must be security for Biggie,* because I could tell they were from Brooklyn from their army fatigues. But then I said, *Wait a minute. Even Biggie's homeboys love me, why don't they look up?* I pressed the elevator button, turned around, and that's when the dudes came out with the guns—two identical 9mms. "Don't nobody move. Everybody on the floor. You know what time it is. Run your shit." I was like, *What should I do?*

I'm thinking Stretch is going to fight; he was towering over those niggas. From what I know about the criminal element, if

niggas come to rob you, they always hit the big nigga first. But they didn't touch Stretch; they came straight to me. Everybody dropped to the floor like potatoes, but I just froze up. It wasn't like I was being brave or nothing; I just could not get on the floor. They started grabbing at me to see if I was strapped. They said, "Take off your jewels," and I wouldn't take them off. The light-skinned dude, the one that was standing outside, was on me. Stretch was on the floor, and the dude with the newspaper was holding the gun on him. He was telling the light-skin dude, "Shoot that motherfucker! Fuck it!" Then I got scared, because the dude had the gun to my stomach. All I could think about was piss bags and shit bags. I drew my arm around him to move the gun to my side. He shot and the gun twisted and that's when I got hit the first time. I felt it in my leg; I didn't know I got shot in my balls.

I dropped to the floor. Everything in my mind said, *Pac, pretend you're dead*. It didn't matter. They started kicking me, hitting me. I never said, "Don't shoot!" I was quiet as hell. They were snatching my shit off me while I was laying on the floor. I had my eyes closed, but I was shaking, because the situation had me shaking. And then I felt something on the back of my head, something real strong. I thought they stomped me or pistol-whipped me and they were stomping my head against the concrete. I saw white, just white. I didn't hear nothing, I didn't feel nothing, and I said, *I'm unconscious*. But I was conscious. And then I felt it again, and I could hear things now and I could see things and they were bringing me back to consciousness. Then they did it again, and I couldn't hear nothing. And I couldn't see nothing; it was just all white. And then they hit me again, and I could hear things and I could see things and I knew I was conscious again.

POWELL: Did you ever hear them say their names?

SHAKUR: No. No. But they knew me, or else they would never check for my gun. It was like they were mad at me. I felt them kicking me and stomping me; they didn't hit nobody else. It was like, "Ooh, motherfucker, ooh, aah"—they were kicking hard. So I'm going unconscious, and I'm not feeling no blood on my head or nothing. The only thing I felt was my stomach hurting real bad. My sister's boyfriend turned me over and said, "Yo, are you all right?" I was like, "Yes, I'm hit, I'm hit." And Fred is saying, "He's hit," but that was the bullet that went through my leg. So I stood up and I went to the door and—the shit that fucked me up—as soon as I got to the door, I saw a police car sitting there. I was like, "Uh-oh, the police are coming, and I didn't even go upstairs yet." So we jumped in the elevator and went upstairs. I'm limping and everything, but I don't feel nothing. It's numb. When we got upstairs, I looked around, and it scared the shit out of me.

POWELL: Why?

SHAKUR: Because Andre Harrell was there, Puffy was there, Biggie . . . there was about forty niggas there. All of them had jewels on. More jewels than me. I saw Booker, and he had this look on his face like he was surprised to see me. Why? I had just beeped the buzzer and said I was coming upstairs.

Little Shawn bust out crying. I went, *Why is Little Shawn crying, and I got shot?* He was crying uncontrollably, like, "Oh my God, Pac, you've got to sit down!" I was feeling weird, like, *Why do they want to make me sit down?*

POWELL: Because five bullets had passed through your body.

SHAKUR: I didn't know I was shot in the head yet. I didn't feel nothing. I opened my pants, and I could see the gunpowder and the hole in my Karl Kani drawers. I didn't want to pull them

down to see if my dick was still there. I just saw a hole and went, "Oh shit. Roll me some weed." I called my girlfriend and I was like, "Yo, I just got shot. Call my mother and tell her."

Nobody approached me. I noticed that nobody would look at me. Andre Harrell wouldn't look at me. I had been going to dinner with him the last few days. He had invited me to the set of *New York Undercover*, telling me he was going to get me a job. Puffy was standing back too. I knew Puffy. He knew how much stuff I had done for Biggie before he came out.

POWELL: So people *did* see blood on you?

SHAKUR: They started telling me, "Your head! Your head is bleeding." But I thought it was just a pistol-whip. Then the ambulance came, and the police. First cop I looked up to see was the cop that took the stand against me in the rape charge. He had a half smile on his face, and he could see them looking at my balls. He said, "What's up, Tupac? How's it hanging?"

When I got to Bellevue Hospital, the doctor was going, "Oh my God!" I was like, "What? What?" And I was hearing him tell other doctors, "Look at this. This is gunpowder right here." He was talking about my head: "This is the entry wound. This is the exit wound." And when he did that, I could actually feel the holes. I said, "Oh my God. I could feel that." It was the spots that I was blacking out on. And that's when I said, "Oh shit. They shot me in my head." They said, "You don't know how lucky you are. You got shot five times." It was, like, weird. I did not want to believe it. I could only remember that first shot, then everything went blank.

POWELL: At any point did you think you were going to die?

SHAKUR: No. I swear to God. Not to sound creepy or nothing—I felt God cared for me from the first time the niggas pulled the

gun out. The only thing that hurt me was that Stretch and them all fell to the floor. The bullets didn't hurt. Nothing hurt until I was recovering. I couldn't walk, I couldn't get up, and my hand was fucked up. I was looking on the news and it was lying about me.

POWELL: Tell me about some of the coverage that bothered you.

SHAKUR: The number one thing that bothered me was that dude that wrote that shit that said I pretended to do it. That I had set it up, it was an act. When I read that, I just started crying like a baby, like a bitch. I could not believe it. It just tore me apart. And then the news was trying to say I had a gun and I had weed on me. Instead of saying I was a victim, they were making it like I did it.

POWELL: What about all the jokes saying you had lost one of your testicles?

SHAKUR: That didn't really bother me, because I was like, *Shit, I'm going to get the last laugh.* Because I've got bigger nuts than all these niggas. My doctors are like, "You can have babies." They told me that the first night, after I got exploratory surgery: "Nothing's wrong. It went through the skin and out the skin." Same thing with my head. Through my skin and out the skin.

POWELL: Have you had a lot of pain since then?

SHAKUR: Yes, I have headaches. I wake up screaming. I've been having nightmares, thinking they're still shooting me. All I see is niggas pulling guns, and I hear the dude saying, "Shoot that motherfucker!" Then I'll wake up sweaty as hell and I'll be like, *Damn, I have a headache.* The psychiatrist at Bellevue said that's post-traumatic stress.

POWELL: Why did you leave Bellevue Hospital?

SHAKUR: I left Bellevue the next night. They were helping me, but I felt like a science project. They kept coming in, looking at my dick and shit, and this was not a cool position to be in. I knew my life was in danger. The Fruit of Islam was there, but they didn't have guns. I knew what type of niggas I was dealing with.

So I left Bellevue and went to Metropolitan. They gave me a phone and said, "You're safe here. Nobody knows you're here." But the phone would ring and someone would say, "You ain't dead yet?" I was like, *Damn! Those motherfuckers don't have no mercy.* So I checked myself out, and my family took me to a safe spot, somebody who really cared about me in New York City.

POWELL: Why did you go to court the morning after you were shot?

SHAKUR: They came to the bed and said, "Pac, you don't need to go to court." I was like, *No.* I felt like if the jury didn't see me, they would think I'm doing a show or some shit. Because they were sequestered and didn't know I got shot. So I knew I had to show up no matter what. I swear to God, the furthest thing from my mind was sympathy. All I could think of was, *Stand up and fight for your life like you fight for your life in this hospital.*

I sat there in a wheelchair, and the judge was not looking me in my eyes. He never looked me in my eyes the whole trial. So the jury came in, and the way everybody was acting, it was like a regular everyday thing. And I was feeling so miracle-ish that I'm living. And then I start feeling they're going to do what they're going to do. Then I felt numb; I said, *I've got to get out of here.*

When I left, the cameras were all rushing me and bumping

into my leg and shit. I was like, "You motherfuckers are like vultures." That made me see just the nastiest in the hearts of men. That's why I was looking like that in the chair when they were wheeling me away. I was trying to promise myself to keep my head up for all my people there. But when I saw all that, it made me put my head down; it just took my spirit.

POWELL: Can we talk about the rape case at all?

SHAKUR: Okay. Nigel and Trevor took me to Nell's. When we got there, I was immediately impressed, because it was different than any club I'd been in. It wasn't crowded, there was lots of space, there were beautiful women there. I was meeting Ronnie Lott from the New York Jets and Derrick Coleman from the Nets. They were coming up to me like, "Pac, we're proud of you." I felt so tall that night, because they were people's heroes and they saying I was their hero. I felt above and beyond, like I was glowing.

Somebody introduced me to this girl. And the only thing I noticed about her: she had a big chest. But she was not attractive; she looked dumpy, like. Money came to me and said, "This girl wants to do more than meet you." I already knew what that meant: She wanted to fuck. I just left them and went to the dance floor by myself. They were playing some Jamaican music, and I'm just grooving.

Then this girl came out and started dancing—and the shit that was weird, she didn't even come to me face-first, she came ass-first. So I'm dancing to this reggae music; you know how sensuous that is. She's touching my dick, she's touching my balls, she opened my zipper, she put her hands on me. There's a little dark part in Nell's, and I see people over there making out already, so she starts pushing me this way. I know what time it is.

We go over in the corner. She's touching me. I lift up my shirt while I'm dancing, showing off my tattoos and everything. She

starts kissing my stomach, kissing my chest, licking me and shit. She's going down, and I'm like, *Oh shit*. She pulled my dick out; she started sucking my dick on the dance floor. That shit turned me on. I wasn't thinking like, *This is going to be a rape case*. I'm thinking like, *This is going to be a good night*. You know what I'm saying?

Soon as she finished that—just enough to get me solid, rock-hard—we got off the dance floor. I told Nigel, "I've got to get out of here. I'm about to take her to the hotel. I'll see you all later." Nigel was like, "No, no, no. I'm going to take you back." We drive to the hotel. We go upstairs and have sex, real quick. As soon as I came, that was it. I was tired, I was drunk, I knew I had to get up early in the morning, so I was like, "What are you going to do? You can spend the night or you can leave." She left me her number, and everything was cool.

Nigel was spending the night in my room all these nights. When he found out she sucked my dick on the floor and we had sex, he and Trevor were livid! Trevor is a big freak; he was going crazy. All he kept asking me was, "D-d-did you fuck in the ass?" He was listening to every single detail. I thought, *This is just some guy shit, it's all good*.

POWELL: What happened on the night of the alleged rape?

SHAKUR: We had a show to do in New Jersey at Club 88. This dude said, "I'll be there with a limo to pick you up at midnight." We went shopping, we got dressed up, we were all ready. Nigel was saying, "Why don't you give her a call?" So we were all sitting in the hotel, drinking. I'm waiting for the show, and Nigel's like, "I called her. I mean she called me, and she's on her way." But I wasn't thinking about her no second time. We were watching TV when the phone rings, and she's downstairs. Nigel gave Man-man, my manager, some money to pay for the cab, and I was like, "Let that bitch pay for her own cab." She came upstairs

looking all nice, dressed all provocative and shit, like she was ready for a prom date.

So we're all sitting there talking, and she's making me uncomfortable, because instead of sitting with Nigel and them, she's sitting on the arm of my chair. And Nigel and Trevor are looking at her like a chicken, like she's, like, food. It's a real uncomfortable situation. So I'm thinking, *Okay, I'm going to take her to the room and get a massage.* I'm thinking about being with her that night at Nell's. So we get in the room, I'm laying on my stomach, she's massaging my back. I turn around. She starts massaging my front. This lasted for about a half an hour. In between, we would stop and kiss each other. I'm thinking she's about to give me another blow job. But before she could do that, some niggas came in, and I froze up more than she froze up. If she would have said anything, I would have said, "Hold on, let me finish." But I can't say nothing, because she's not saying nothing. How do I look saying, "Hold on"? That would be like I'm making her my girl.

So they came and they started touching her ass. They going, "Oooh, she's got a nice ass." Nigel isn't touching her, but I can hear his voice leading it, like, "Put her panties down, put her pantyhose down." I just got up and walked out the room.

When I went to the other suite, Man-man told me that Talibah, my publicist at the time, had been there for a while and was waiting in the bedroom of that suite. I went to see Talibah and we talked about what she had been doing during the day, then I went and laid down on the couch and went to sleep.

When I woke up, Nigel was standing over me going, "Pac, Pac," and all the lights was on in both rooms. The whole mood had changed, you know what I'm saying? I felt like I was drugged. I didn't know how much time had passed. So when I woke up, it was like, "You're going to the police, you're going to the police." Nigel walks out the room, comes back with the girl. Her clothes is on; ain't nothing tore. She just upset, crying hysterically. "Why

you let them do this to me?" She's not making sense. "I came to see you. You let them do this to me." I'm like, "I don't got time for this shit right here. You got to chill out with that shit. Stop yelling at me and looking at me all crazy." She said, "This not the last time you're going to hear from me," and slammed the door.

And Nigel goes, "Don't worry about it, Pac, don't worry. I'll handle it. She just tripping." I asked him what happened, and he was like, "Too many niggas." You know, I ain't even tripping no more, you know? Niggas start going downstairs, but nobody was coming back upstairs. I'm sitting upstairs smoking weed, like, Where the fuck is everybody at? Then I get a call from Talibah from the lobby saying, "The police is down here."

POWELL: And that's what landed you in jail. But you're saying that you never did anything?

SHAKUR: Never did nothing. Only thing I saw was all three of them in there and that nigga talking about how fat her ass was. I got up, because the nigga sounded sick. I don't know if she's with these niggas, or if she's mad at me for not protecting her. But I know I feel ashamed—because I wanted to be accepted and because I didn't want no harm done to me—I didn't say nothing.

POWELL: How did you feel about women during the trial, and how do you feel about women now?

SHAKUR: When the charge first came up, I hated Black women. I felt like I put my life on the line. At the time I made "Keep Ya Head Up," nobody had no songs about Black women. I put out "Keep Ya Head Up" from the bottom of my heart. It was real, and they didn't defend it. I felt like it should have been women all over the country talking about, "Tupac couldn't have did that." And people was actually asking me, "Did you do it?"

Then, going to trial, I started seeing the Black women that

was helping me. Now I've got a brand-new vision of them, be-
cause in here, it's mostly Black female guards. They don't give me
no extra favors, but they treat me with human respect. They're
telling me, "When you get out of here, you gotta change." They
be putting me on the phone with they kids. You know what I'm
saying? They just give me love.

POWELL: What's going to happen if you have to serve time?

SHAKUR: If it happens, I got to serve it like a trouper. Of course,
my heart will be broke. I be torn apart, but I have to serve it like
a trouper.

POWELL: I understand you recently completed a new album.

SHAKUR: Rapping . . . I don't even got the thrill to rap no more.
I mean, in here I don't even remember my lyrics.

POWELL: But you're putting out the album, right?

SHAKUR: Yeah. It's called *Me Against the World*. So that is my
truth. That's my best album yet. And because I already laid it
down, I can be free. When you do rap albums, you got to train
yourself. You got to constantly be in character. You used to see
rappers talking all that hard shit, and then you see them in suits
and shit at the American Music Awards. I didn't want to be that
type of nigga. I wanted to keep it real, and that's what I thought
I was doing. But now that shit is dead. That thug life shit . . . I
did it, I put in my work, I laid it down. But now that shit is dead.

POWELL: What are your plans after prison?

SHAKUR: I'm going to team up with Mike Tyson when we
get out. Team up with Monster Kody [now known as Sanyika

Shakur] from California. I'm going to start an organization called Us First. I'm going to save these young niggas, because nobody else want to save them. Nobody ever came to save me. They just watch what happen to you. That's why thug life to me is dead. If it's real, then let somebody else represent it, because I'm tired of it. I represented it too much. I was thug life. I was the only nigga out there putting my life on the line.

POWELL: Has anybody else been there for you?

SHAKUR: Since I've been in here I got about forty letters. I got little girls sending me money. Everybody telling me that God is with me. People telling me they hate the dudes that shot me, they're going to pray for me. I did get one letter, this dude telling me he wished I was dead. But then I got people looking out for me, like Jada Pinkett, Jasmine Guy, Treach, Mickey Rourke. My label, Interscope Records, has been extremely supportive. Even Madonna.

POWELL: Can you talk about your relationship with Madonna and Mickey Rourke?

SHAKUR: I was letting people dictate who should be my friends. I felt like because I was this big Black Panther type of nigga, I couldn't be friends with Madonna. And so I dissed her, even though she showed me nothing but love. I felt bad, because when I went to jail, I called her and she was the only person that was willing to help me. Of that stature. Same thing with Mickey Rourke—he just befriended me. Not like Black and White, just like friend to friend. And from now on, it's not going to be a strictly Black thing with me. I even apologized to Quincy Jones for all the stuff I said about him and his wives. I'm apologizing to the Hughes brothers . . . but not John Singleton. He's inspiring me to write screenplays, because I want to be his competition.

He fired me from *Higher Learning* and gave my idea to the next actor.

POWELL: Do you worry about your safety now?

SHAKUR: I don't have no fear of death. My only fear is coming back reincarnated. I'm not trying to make people think I'm in here faking it, but my whole life is going to be about saving somebody. I got to represent life. If you saying you going to be real, that's how you be real—be physically fit, be mentally fit. And I want niggas to be educated. You know, I was steering people away from school. You gotta be in school, because through school you can get a job. And if you got a job, then that's how they can't do us like this.

POWELL: Do you think rap music is going to come under more attack, given what's happened to you?

SHAKUR: Oh, definitely. That's why they're doing me like this. Because if they can stop me, they can stop thirty more rappers before they even born. But there's something else I understand now: If we really are saying rap is an art form, then we got to be true to it and be more responsible for our lyrics. If you see everybody dying because of what you saying, it don't matter that you didn't make them die, it just matters that you didn't save them.

POWELL: You mentioned Marvin Gaye in "Keep Ya Head Up." A lot of people have compared you to him, in terms of your personal conflicts.

SHAKUR: That's how I feel. I feel close to Marvin Gaye, Vincent van Gogh.

POWELL: Why van Gogh?

SHAKUR: Because nobody appreciated his work until he was dead. Now it's worth millions. I feel close to him, how tormented he was. Him and Marvin too. That's how I was out there. I'm in jail now, but I'm free. My mind is free. The only time I have problems is when I sleep.

POWELL: So you're grateful to be where you are now?

SHAKUR: It's a gift—straight up. This is God's will. And everybody that said I wasn't nothing . . . my whole goal is to just make them ashamed that they wrote me off like that. Because I'm twenty-three years old. And I might just be my mother's child, but in all reality, I'm *everybody's* child. You know what I'm saying? Nobody raised me; I was raised in this society. But I'm not going to use that as an excuse no more. I'm going to pull myself up by my bootstraps, and I'm going to make a change. And my change is going to make a change through the community. And through that, they gonna see what type of person I truly was. Where my heart was.

This thug life stuff, it was just ignorance. My intentions was always in the right place. I never killed anybody, I never raped anybody, I never committed no crimes that weren't honorable— that weren't to defend myself. So that's what I'm going to show them. I'm going to show people my true intentions, and my true heart. I'm going to show them the man that my mother raised. I'm going to make them all proud.

Uncut Funk: bell hooks

Originally published in *Vibe*
May 1995

At first glance, the soft-spoken Dr. bell hooks (née Gloria Watkins) doesn't strike a hard-core pose. Even the way she writes her name seems almost timid. But hard-core bell hooks is. She has written fourteen books in seventeen years (including two new titles this year: *Art on My Mind: Visual Politics* and *Killing Rage: Ending Racism*). Her work is uniformly fearless. No subject is glossed over, and no one is immune from Dr. hooks's brain-shaking ballistics.

Inside her meticulously organized New York apartment, bell hooks offers me some apple juice and answers the phone every time it rings, which is quite often. After all, the City College English professor is in demand these days. Her essays and books have become staples in academia and reading circles nationwide. Unimpressed with sales stats, Dr. hooks points out that "people can buy your book and never read it. I prefer that people come to me because they feel my work has helped them to grow in some way."

Nevertheless, she, Cornel West, Henry Louis Gates Jr., and a few others now find themselves being hailed as "the new Black intelligentsia." But Dr. hooks is leery of being pulled into what she calls "the fame plantation" of Black intellectuals. That leeriness may explain why, in spite of her cult status among students and feminists, so many people still have to ask: "Who is bell hooks?"

Dr. hooks, forty-three, describes herself as a "seeker on the

path." She is that rare thinker who can flow back and forth between discussions on postmodern feminism and Tupac Shakur. She is both a voracious reader and a keen observer of popular culture—responsibilities she takes very seriously. It's all part of her ultimate goal: to look beyond academe's ivory tower, to reach the minds of the people, to find the truth.

KEVIN POWELL: You took your name from your great-grandmother, and your writing often draws on early family life. What are the strongest impressions from your childhood?

BELL HOOKS: Growing up in racial apartheid really has affected me. The world we grew up in was so segregated. I was raised in Hopkinsville, Kentucky, with five sisters and one brother. It was a traditional Black, patriarchal Southern home. My brother didn't have six sisters; he had six slaves. On one hand, it was this male-dominated household, but it was also rich in "sister bonding" between females.

POWELL: When did you start writing?

HOOKS: I started writing poetry when I was ten or eleven. We used to have these talent shows to raise money. People forget that segregated Black schools didn't get the money to buy things they needed. So there used to be all these fundraising events. From the time we were growing up, we would be told, "Get up and use your talent; do what you have to do."

My talent was acting out and reading poems, so I would get up and do dramatic monologues. I'd read "Little Orphan Annie" by James Whitcomb Riley and other kinds of poems. You know, it was very deep to grow up in an environment where that sense of performance was so immediate to everyday life. If there was nothing good on TV, then we would cut off the TV and do our own shows.

That whole legacy of performance in traditional Black folk culture is so important. Think of the great Black comedians like Richard Pryor. People coming into an awareness of Richard Pryor now, after his traumatic illness, can forget what an incredibly powerful thinking comedian he was. There was so much respect in traditional Black folk culture for the art of storytelling, and making people laugh, and making people feel something.

POWELL: What do you think of Black comedians today and their use of profanity?

HOOKS: I myself don't have problems with the cursing, 'cause we've always had cursing in our storytelling traditions. It's when you rely on that as the only source of power, then you really have a breakdown in the notion of your performance as art. The roots of Black performance art have been the poor and the underclass, folks who had to fashion a world of creativity out of what they possess: their voice, their body. When you take that level of performance art and you try to turn it into a commodity that's basically trying to reach a more materially privileged body of people—in many cases, that crossover audience of White people—then what can be construed as funny becomes radically different.

A lot of things that are considered amusing in traditional Black life, when you try to transpose them in a way that makes them available to everyone in the culture—cross-race—you lose a lot of the nuance. For the most part, when White people encounter opposition to the ethics of racism, they don't understand it, or they understand it most immediately as a threat and reject it. The colonizer is always fascinated by the colonized in the act of resistance, as long as they feel the resistance is not going to be complete. So it's like part of a sadomasochistic dance.

POWELL: What do you mean?

HOOKS: The mass media always wants to highlight sadomas-ochism as being about sexuality, but there's hard-core sadomas-ochism in the politics of everyday life. Particularly in Black/White relations, we see this very sadomasochistic orchestration of power. Think about how the Sam Jackson character, Jules in *Pulp Fiction*, is still in so many ways a servant to the power-ful. Though he has this powerful voice of authority and reason and understanding, he's made to wear this ridiculous wig. Even when he's giving his most profound statements, the wig is al-ways suggesting somehow that you can't take those statements too seriously.

POWELL: What would the response be if a Black director made a film like *Pulp Fiction*?

HOOKS: One of the things I said immediately after seeing *Pulp Fiction* was that if that rape scene—the homosexual S&M scenario—if that had been a John Singleton film, a film by Matt Rich, or by Spike Lee, I feel like gay White people would have been out in droves to call out the homophobia in that scene. There's nothing particularly intriguing about that scene; it just serves as straight fascist gay-bashing, a reminder that some straight Black men and straight White men can bond together in their homophobia. That's not an interesting truth; that's a tragic old truth that we should be dismantling.

I think that's one very clear example of how Tarantino has been figured as kind of a Great White Hope in Hollywood. He can do scenes that people will try to bring some sophisticated read to, but which are finally not sophisticated. There's a way in which a straight White man like Tarantino appropriates and simultaneously disses the best of gay subculture, as well as the best of a certain kind of African American vernacular. He's the ultimate cultural bandit.

POWELL: A lot of people who praised Tarantino's first film, *Reservoir Dogs*, are quick to criticize so-called gangsta rap.

HOOKS: I think *Reservoir Dogs* was infinitely more challenging than *Pulp Fiction*. It was on the level of Ice-T's "Cop Killer" in that it wasn't just a glorification of killing but was meant as some kind of social commentary and critique. What's interesting is that when a White boy on the edge does this, people are more willing to see it as having a complex theoretical base than when it's done by young Black men. There's no sense that there's any level of complexity in the music of an Ice Cube or an Ice-T. It's just like, "Oh, they mean go right out and shoot cops. They don't mean think about issues of control and repression and fascism." The greatest thing about Ice-T publishing his book *The Ice Opinion* was his forcing people to see that there is thought behind what we're doing. We're not just putting shit out there like whatever comes to our head.

POWELL: You say "we" as if you identify strong with these rappers.

HOOKS: I think all the artists who use the Black vernacular in this society understand that, to White minds, the Black vernacular has always been associated with the idea of being stupid. I guess I feel like part of my mission as an artist—this is what binds me culturally to an Ice Cube and even a Snoop Doggy Dogg—is understanding the beauty and the aesthetic complexity in the vernacular. In the minds not only of Whites but of privileged-class Blacks, vernacular culture is seen as lacking complexity and depth. Even though Black folks like Henry Louis Gates will step up in defense of "vernacular culture," the way they mount their defense has this patronizing aura, like, "We know better than those down-low Black people what they

really mean, and we can be the mediators between them and the dominant White culture."

POWELL: In your book *Outlaw Culture*, you use the term "urban primitivism" to discuss so-called gangsta rap. Could you comment on the attacks that have been leveled against that Black art form?

HOOKS: People really don't want to acknowledge that some people act as though the sexism and misogyny of Black men is more virulent, more horrific than the sexism of any other group of men. This has been happening, I think, because when White women began to engage in contemporary feminist thinking, they hadn't changed their racism in any way. So they necessarily focused on Black men as the ultimate expressions of patriarchal rage. Even today, I see this sort of reign of White women like Camille Paglia and Naomi Wolf. They embody certain kinds of radical feminist thought—sometimes. But they're also very reactionary with their bottom line.

It just appears that an elaborate form of scapegoating is taking place in many of the controversies around violence and misogyny in rap. It's almost an unbelievable irony that sexist, misogynist Black preachers would act as though they are denouncing rap in the name of some kind of feminist standpoint. I keep saying that the Black bourgeoisie really wants this pristine, clean cultural landscape where there wouldn't be any sort of street language, street culture, etc. Many of the Black critics of gangsta rap are not interested in critiquing patriarchy or sexism. They're really interested in checking Black folks who aren't worried about whether White people see them as "jungle bunnies."

POWELL: What's the difference between the cultural expression of your generation and the hip-hop generation?

HOOKS: Today's youth say, "We are not concerned with how White people see us. We feel the fucking planet is doomed anyway, so our real issue is to be however we want to be." And I think an older generation of Black people don't know how to respond to that. Because that's an assertion of subjectivity that Black people have not traditionally had in this culture—which is to say, "I don't care how White people see me, because I don't feel that I have a future in White culture anyway."

POWELL: Is that one reason for the popularity of gangsta rap?

HOOKS: Well, gangsta rap is not one-dimensional. One part that is very compelling, to young people particularly, is a certain notion of resistance to authority. But another part of it is totally invested in capitalism. There's also a tension in gangsta rap between a solidarity based on race and the typical gangsta mentality of, "If you fuck with me, and I need to, I'm gonna blow you away." What we see in Tupac's shooting is how the gangsta mentality actually disrupts racial solidarity. Those other young Black men who want to go out and destroy this talented young Black man aren't operating from the ethos of racial solidarity that has been a tradition in rap.

That ultimate power over life and death is so much at the heart of masculinity in this culture, and feminism has done nothing to change that. You prove the depths of your manhood by your willingness to go down in struggle—whether it's in a pathetic fight with a friend over a bag of potato chips or whether it's in going to another country and shooting other people in the name of patriotism.

POWELL: Talk to me about popular representations of Black women, whether in rap or otherwise.

HOOKS: Nobody wants to admit the depths of our culture's

hatred of Black women. And ironically, that hatred is not rooted in the conventional stereotypes of Black women as betrayers. For example, if we take a film like Haile Gerima's *Sankofa*, the betrayal of Black culture is signified through the body of the Black woman—through her rape/breeding with the White man. But in the actual history of Blackness in America, we see Black women always at the forefront of resistance struggles—not in acts of betrayal but in acts of defiance.

Traditionally, the image of Black women fucking White men has been that of prostitutes. Can we really say a Black woman turning a White trick is engaged in any kind of betrayal that benefits her? Or is it in fact a symbol of powerlessness, of being so completely victimized within a certain kind of structure that it's pathetic?

POWELL: But then you have a few Black women who seem to be backing the power structure, like an Oprah Winfrey . . .

HOOKS: Oprah Winfrey is, to me, a very tragically successful Black woman. She's not unlike Madonna in that, to some extent, she became successful by working a lot of her own dysfunctional personal tropes. And the fact is, if they become part of your popularity, then you can't ever "get well" because people are too invested in your not being well.

Oprah's problem is addiction to fame and stardom. The same thing has happened to other icons, like Michael Jackson. These people are rich beyond belief. There's no excuse for them not taking some time off and getting themselves together. I think the message we are given through a popular icon like Oprah Winfrey is that Black people get to the top and stay on top only by sucking the dicks of White culture.

POWELL: A lot of White people would say, "How could you say those things, bell? Don't you see there's a constant attack on Black people who are 'successful'?"

HOOKS: I think we have to distinguish between attacking Black folks and constructive criticism. We keep this glass cage around successful Black people, like we have our zoo—you know, "Successful Black People Zoo." Then we're really not talking about freedom at all; we're not talking about breaking through the paradigm of colonization. We're just upholding that system if we say, "Don't criticize."

POWELL: Why do you think so many Black people automatically support a Mike Tyson, a Michael Jackson, or an O.J. Simpson when they are accused of wrongdoing?

HOOKS: I wouldn't even say it begins with a Mike Tyson. Let's talk about Clarence Thomas. Mike Tyson and O.J. Simpson were two Black men who came from the wrong side of the tracks and were always ambivalent about success and their own identities. But Clarence Thomas was educated within the White system in this society. Why would Black people so unequivocally give support to a Black man who clearly does not support the interests of Black liberation? It's almost like Black people have been *duped* into thinking that Black masculinity is not nuanced or complex.

It's a Black culture that can't see a difference between Malcolm X and Farrakhan. One of the deepest differences between them is that Farrakhan is completely pro-capitalist. Part of why he can be less of a threat to the American government and the American way of life is his total investment in the free enterprise system. Malcolm X was really calling that system into question and allying himself with global struggles against imperialism and colonization.

To me it means we have internalized racism to the degree that all we see is Black skin—like, "Oh, there's somebody in trouble. They've got black skin . . ." Of course, on a deep and

profound level we sympathize with O.J. Simpson, with Michael Jackson, with Mike Tyson, because their woundedness, on the battlefield of race, is our own collective woundedness. We know that O.J. Simpson is conflicted about his identity, about being Black, self-loving—that's our primal conflict in White supremacy. To say you identify and sympathize is not to say that you condone their actions—or the crimes they are alleged to have committed. It is to say we understand what might be some of the dysfunctions that lead these men to irrational, insane behavior.

POWELL: What do women like Anita Hill, Desiree Washington, and Nicole Brown Simpson represent to you?

HOOKS: I think it does not diminish the way these women were victimized to say that they were also blindly invested in the system that hurt them. They believe in sexism. If we read Faye Resnick's book and take it to be any level of truth, Nicole Brown Simpson is not this woman who opposed sexism or racial stereotypes. She invested in the racial stereotype of the Black man as the big dick, the more sexual being. She then became a victim of that very system she bought into.

I think we have to stop seeing women solely as victims and also see women as people who make political choices. Some people like to say that Anita Hill and Desiree Washington were radicalized by the process of what happened to them. I'm interested in a world where women become radicalized *before* we are victimized.

POWELL: What do you think about the current state of Black leadership?

HOOKS: I personally feel that the crisis of Black leadership has to do with the continual investment of Black people in sexism. When we say that there are no leaders, what we mean is that no

charismatic male leader has captured the collective imagination of Black Americans. When are we going to embrace charismatic *female* leaders? We can talk about Angela Davis as a political icon, but never about her asserting herself as a leader. Malcolm X led more Black folks to consider leftist politics, but this is not the fault of an Angela Davis; this is the fault of sexism in Black life that does not appreciate her legacy and does not require of her that she go further in the struggle. And I would say the same about so many other powerful Black women—people like June Jordan, who have the critical thought and the charisma and the political vision. But Black people have not looked into these individuals.

White culture increasingly determines who Black leaders are going to be by giving mass media play to those leaders. To some extent, even Farrakhan has got the USA stamp of approval. Once White mass media started putting his image out there, they were sanctioning him as a leader in a way that they haven't really chosen Black female leaders. Jocelyn Elders is a leader, but are we as Black people out in the streets defending her, asking her to become our new leader of the NAACP, asking her to be our visionary? The fact is, the moment Black people give up on our sexism and take advantage of the incredible leadership potential in Black women, we can go forward and have a renewed Black liberation struggle.

Right On
Originally published in *Vibe*
August 1995

I n his 1980 book *The Third Wave*, Alvin Toffler (one of Newt Gingrich's buddies) spoke of the "crack-up of the nation," asserting that as our country's ruling class tightened its economic belt, regular Americans would feel the pinch and various blocs would arise, expressing—sometimes in extreme ways—a mass sense of alienation.

So you have to figure that the Oklahoma City bombing was merely the *first* climax of a story line being created by the rhetoric of the right. Capturing the killers is not the issue; what is the issue is that the bombers—along with the rise of right-wing militias, Newt Gingrich's Contract with America, Charles Murray and Richard J. Herrnstein's *The Bell Curve*, and the Rush Limbaughs and G. Gordon Liddys of the land—are part of a movement bent on casting White men as victims. They didn't need a bomb to declare war on welfare mothers, affirmative action advocates, illegal immigrants, the hip-hop nation, and anyone else whom they perceive as roadblocks to their "American way."

But by choosing to promote intolerance rather than understanding, we're left at the mercy of those who can, and will, redefine American "democracy." Consequently, Blacks and Whites will continue to eye each other suspiciously, straight people will continue to fear and harass gay people, the rich will continue to get richer and the underclass will continue to balloon, Americans will continue to distrust "foreigners," men will continue to blame women for their problems, and many of the social

and civil gains of the past twenty-five years will continue to be chipped away.

That the right refuses to acknowledge its contribution to the tearing of America's social fabric is not surprising. So long as its rhetoric stirs up an audience, more tragedies will come. As always, it is not until "the chickens come home to roost" that people will finally realize that finger-pointing is divisive—and deadly.

Colin Powell: Generally Speaking

Originally published in *Vibe*
November 1995

C olin Powell, fifty-eight, the four-star general who retired in 1993 as chairman of the Joint Chiefs of Staff, marches to his own beat. Currently on a national book tour pumping his memoir, *My American Journey*, Powell is also, in his own words, the first Black to be seriously considered as a presidential candidate who is not simply a "protest vote." Unlike most politicians, Powell isn't afraid to speak his mind, as evidenced by this, his first print interview in two years.

KEVIN POWELL: The first question I'm going to ask is rather obvious: Are you going to run for president?

COLIN POWELL: And you really think I'm going to answer? [*Laughs*]

KEVIN POWELL: I was hoping . . . Powell to Powell. [*Laughs*]

COLIN POWELL: Just between me and you, huh? I have spent the last two years traveling around the country learning about issues, and after my book tour is over—October, November—I will sit down with some close friends and with my family, and see how best I can serve the nation. It might be in politics, it

might be in charitable or educational work, it might be an appointed office. Unlike most other candidates, politics is not my passion or profession. My thing was the army. But so many people are encouraging me that I will think about it very hard and pray on it with my family.

KEVIN POWELL: But you've been a White House Fellow. You rose through the Carter, Reagan, and Bush administrations. You've been around politics for the last twenty-three years at least.

COLIN POWELL: I've been around politics for a long time. And I've seen it at the very highest level. That does not make me a politician. In fact, even though I worked in the West Wing of the Reagan White House for two years in a very sensitive position, not one person in the Reagan White House will tell you today whether they think I'm a Republican or a Democrat.

KEVIN POWELL: Why is that?

COLIN POWELL: I was an active-duty military officer who lived by a code that says you never do anything that reflects a partisan political view. So I never registered either as a Republican or a Democrat. I always voted for the best man. It was a tricky act, but I pulled it off.

KEVIN POWELL: Could it be said then that you were a true politician?

COLIN POWELL: I'm pretty good at solving problems. I've been pretty good at presenting cases. I'm pretty good at fighting with adversaries but not creating enemies, and I'm pretty good at fighting with friends without converting them into enemies. If that is what you mean by politics, yeah, I'm pretty good at that.

KEVIN POWELL: Where did you learn these negotiating skills?

COLIN POWELL: I get these questions from lots of young people: *What's the secret to success? What was the most important thing that ever happened in your life? What was your greatest failure? Who was your role model?* Life isn't like that. Everyone I ever ran into influenced me in some way. Some more good than others, some very, very much worse than others. I watched people I admired and people I didn't admire to see what they were doing right and doing wrong. So I had hundreds of role models. Don't think that there is some star that you can suddenly hitch your wagon to that's going to pull you up.

KEVIN POWELL: How did your roots form who you are?

COLIN POWELL: My family and my roots meant a great deal to me. A warm, close, typically West Indian family with cousins running in and out. A series of expectations were conveyed to their children: You will get an education. You will get a job. You will do better than we did. And you will not shame the family. Now, you got any questions? All the things that you hear people talk about in terms of family values—even though we were poor in the South Bronx, we were all there.

KEVIN POWELL: You were just an average student in college, correct?

COLIN POWELL: Yeah. I was smarter than I realized, and I also learned more than I ever displayed to the teachers at the City College of New York. I was a youngster without a great deal of direction through high school, and it was only when I hit ROTC in college that I found something I really loved and did well. I wasn't a great athlete. As a matter of fact, I was a pretty bad

athlete. I flunked math, calculus, and physics. But thank heavens they counted ROTC toward your passing grade, so I was able to graduate.

Every young person should always be searching for something to do in life that they enjoy and they can do well. Money is always a concern, but it's not everything.

Whenever someone becomes a potential candidate for president, people start picking apart their character. People have said, "Well, he worked for Reagan, so he's one of them. He's some kind of Tom." But the next thing, they find I'm down at some Black school, speaking to kids.

KEVIN POWELL: How do you react when you hear someone say things like that about you?

COLIN POWELL: Their problem, not mine. I have always been proud of my Caribbean and African roots. I have never tried in any way to suggest that I wasn't part of the Black experience and the Black community. I manifested it through constantly talking about the Black military experience in the United States, which is a unique kind of experience. It's the only profession that we've been able to participate in continuously for 250 years.

So I have never shied away from my origins, but I have also told youngsters, "We're Americans. We're not Africans and we're not Jamaicans. We have to live in this country in this time." While I am proud of being an Arawak Indian and West African and Irish, Scottish, and every other thing, and while I want to know about those roots, I also want to know about the roots of our democratic system.

KEVIN POWELL: I read a survey recently that said fewer African Americans know who you are than White Americans.

COLIN POWELL: It doesn't trouble me particularly. I work in

an environment that is not that well known to all African Americans. There's limited penetration of the media in the African American community. I wish that were not the case, but it is.

KEVIN POWELL: Do you ever feel like you're performing a balancing act?

COLIN POWELL: I simply refuse to believe I have to perform a balancing act. Ask me what I am and I'll tell you. Ask me where I came from, I'll tell you. Ask me to deny that background, and I won't. But any job you give me, I will do it to the best of my ability. Let others judge as to whether I'm too White, I'm too Black, I'm too European in my thinking, or I'm not traditional Afrocentric. I can't spend time on that. I just gotta do what I think is right, and go with my instincts and training.

KEVIN POWELL: Hypothetically, if you became president, what could you bring to this country?

COLIN POWELL: One of the reasons I am this political unknown is because both parties appeal to me in some ways. I am very Republican in my economic thinking. I am an absolute believer in free-market economics. So I would do anything to keep businesses growing, to allow people to make as much money as their talents and hard work will let them. The government should do little more than make sure it's all being done honestly so that, in case greed starts to take over, workers are not being exploited. But after that, I think the government should keep its hands off.

Having said that, I also realize that government does have an important role to play in taking care of citizens who are very needy—those who are losing faith, losing hope. Government has to play a role when the rights of citizens are being abused and there's nobody to stand up for those citizens. I certainly have

been a beneficiary of that. So, with respect to social issues, I start to sound like a Kennedy Democrat.

KEVIN POWELL: You come from an immigrant family. What's your position on immigration?

COLIN POWELL: If immigration is illegal, it ought to be stopped. I think the nation has benefited over the years by having a flow of new blood, new citizens, new culture, new color, come into the country. But there are practical limits to what we can absorb. And if we have laws, they should be obeyed. So I think we should do whatever is necessary to seal our borders to illegal immigration so that we can give all the advantages necessary to legal immigrants.

KEVIN POWELL: What about affirmative action?

COLIN POWELL: My view, and I think the view of most Americans, is that affirmative action has been good for the country. It's easy to talk about: "Hey, climb up by your own bootstraps." But if you got no boots, what's the point? All you're doing is handing people rhetoric. Affirmative action was designed to put in place certain preferences to do away with preferences that existed for two hundred years. It's not as if we invented preferences. Preferences for White people caused affirmative action to come in after the great civil rights legislation in the '60s.

But if some of these programs have gotten out of whack and are nothing but pure quotas that serve no social purpose, then I think we ought to get rid of them. The American people are willing to support affirmative action to make sure there's a level playing field. But we're not there yet. It was only two years ago that six Secret Service agents, dressed in nice suits, all college graduates, preparing to spend the day guarding the president of the United States, went into a Denny's restaurant in Maryland

and weren't served. Don't tell me that we're color-blind. It isn't there yet.

KEVIN POWELL: Why do you think so many people want you to run for president?

COLIN POWELL: Because they're unhappy with the current political scene. People have a deep sense of anxiety. They don't like what they see in Washington, they don't like the screaming and shouting. The president has some serious character problems that he hasn't been able to shake—Whitewater and other things. I'm not making a judgment. I'm just saying they're there.

KEVIN POWELL: You were decorated in Vietnam, and you directed Operation Desert Storm as well as the US "invasions" of Panama and Somalia. Do you ever sometimes think to yourself, *My God, war is horrible?*

COLIN POWELL: War *is* horrible. People ask, "Are you a hawk or a dove?" I don't get paid to be a hawk or a dove. I get paid to provide the best military advice I can to my civilian leaders, and to accomplish their political objectives in a way that minimizes the loss of American lives in combat. We know how to die in combat, but we don't like to die for unclear purposes. We don't like to die 'cause some columnist is excited. We don't send our young people in to die because Congress has been screaming up on the Hill. We send them in for clear purposes, because they've got parents.

KEVIN POWELL: Have you been back to your old neighborhood recently?

COLIN POWELL: I was in the South Bronx two weeks ago with Barbara Walters. I walked right on my street and the years just

peeled back. I felt like I was a kid again. I even bought Barbara Walters a piragua. Do you know what a piragua is?

KEVIN POWELL: Those icies?

COLIN POWELL: Yeah. Scraped ice with syrup. Then I took all the cops from Fort Apache to White Castle for hamburgers. But there are pockets of despair. There are youngsters there who do not have the kind of family I had. They are parented by a woman with no husband. Either there never was a husband or the husband's in Rikers Island, or the husband can't get a job.

KEVIN POWELL: Could you have imagined finding yourself in this position thirty years ago?

COLIN POWELL: Not at all. Along with the role-model question, I get this question: "Did you ever dream that you'd be chairman of the Joint Chiefs of Staff as a kid?" There I was in the South Bronx, I didn't even know what the Joint Chiefs of Staff was. All I knew was I always tried to do the very best I could. Always getting myself ready for tomorrow, thinking about the day after, dreaming about the future.

The unique thing about this situation I find myself in—no matter what I do, whether I go into politics or not—an epochal event has occurred. That America would seriously consider a Black man as the president of the United States. Not as sort of a protest vote that comes out of the civil rights community—you know, not like Jesse or Shirley Chisholm. To think that we have reached a point where it's possible for an American who is also a Black American to be on the cover of magazines, to be interviewed and taken seriously—that, in and of itself, should tell every young person in America that there is nothing you cannot set your sights on.

And don't forget, there is no other place on the face of this

earth—no country, no political system, no economic system, no social system—where these kinds of achievements are [more] possible than in the United States of America. So get mad sometimes, but it don't get no better than this. Is it perfect? No. Does it have some rough spots? Yeah. And what is our challenge? To fix it. But don't give up. It's the best there is.

Live from Death Row

Originally published in *Vibe*
February 1996

But some man will say, How are the dead raised up?
And with what body do they come?
—1 Corinthians 15:35

No one can just drop in on Death Row Records CEO Marion "Suge" Knight Jr. without feeling the magnitude of his reputation. No one.

On a cool Southern California evening, I arrive to see him at the Can-Am Building in Tarzana, a thirty-minute drive north of Los Angeles. I'm greeted by a tall, stone-faced, caramel-colored man with a walkie-talkie and a black windbreaker inscribed *SECURITY*. Rather than letting me into the tiny lobby area, he tells me to wait outside while he alerts someone within the single-story edifice that Suge has a visitor.

The budding legend surrounding thirty-year-old Suge Knight is such that damn near everyone—from fellow journalists to former and current Death Row employees all the way to a shoeshine man in West LA—warned me that Suge was "the wrong nigga to fuck with." The mere mention of his name was enough to cause some of the most powerful people in the music business to whisper, change the subject, or beg to be quoted off the record.

This is an especially hectic time for Knight and Death Row, whose "keepin' it real" mentality has the industry all shook up. Tha Dogg Pound's controversial debut album *Dogg Food*—the breaking point in the relationship between Time Warner and In-

terscope Records, Death Row's distributor—was finally released last Halloween and shot to number one on the pop charts. As Snoop Doggy Dogg faced a murder charge in LA, Knight secured a $1.4 million bond to bail Tupac Shakur out of prison in October and signed him up (both to Death Row Records and Knight's management arm). Shakur has been working feverishly on his Death Row debut—a double CD all written since Shakur's release, titled *All Eyez on Me* (twenty-eight cuts including a duet with Snoop called "Two of America's Most Wanted")—partly because a return to prison still looms, pending appeals.

Meanwhile, work continues on projects for singers Danny Boy and Nate Dogg, and rappers the Lady of Rage, Jewell, Sam Sneed, and others yet unheard of—to say nothing of the artists for whom Knight now "consults," including Mary J. Blige, Jodeci, and DJ Quik. Death Row is also backing record labels headed by Snoop (Doggystyle Records) and Tha Dogg Pound (Gotta Get Somewhere Records). Plus there's Knight's new Club 662 in Las Vegas and the vision of Dr. Dre directing movies for Death Row Films.

All these things are on my mind as I'm being frisked in the lobby of the Can-Am Building, now the permanent studio for Death Row, where talents as diverse as Bobby Brown, Harry Belafonte, and Barry Manilow once recorded. Around-the-clock protection is provided by a group of off-duty Black police officers who work in Los Angeles. While Death Row isn't the group's only client, it's the biggest. According to the guard at the reception desk, "We're better security because we're all licensed to carry guns—anywhere."

Another tall, muscular Black man escorts me back to Suge's office—the building also contains two state-of-the-art studios, a gym, and a space where Suge often sleeps. The man opens the door, and I'm struck by two things: a big, light-brown German shepherd rolling on the floor, and the fact that virtually everything in the room—the carpet, the cabinets, the sofa and match-

ing chairs—is a striking bloodred. I look at my escort; he reads my facial expression and says nonchalantly, "That's Damu. He won't bother you. He's only trained to kill on command." On that note, I step gingerly into Suge Knight's office.

Knight's imprint is all over: from the sleek stereo system to the air conditioner (set way too cold) to the large-screen TV that doubles as an all-seeing security monitor. Right in front of his big wooden desk, outlined in white on the red carpet, is the Death Row Records logo: a man strapped to an electric chair with a sack over his head. I was told by another journalist that no one steps on the logo. No one.

At six foot four, 315 pounds, sporting a close-cropped haircut and a neatly trimmed beard, Knight strikes a towering pose. When he sits down to face me, with Damu (Swahili for "blood") now lying by his feet, you can't help but notice the huge biceps itching to bust through his red-and-black-striped shirt. Muscle, say both his admirers and detractors, is the name of Knight's game. Speaking with a syrupy drawl, Suge (as in "sugar") details the original mission of Death Row Records.

"First thing to do was to establish an organization, not just no record company," he says, his eyes looking straight into mine. "I knew the difference between having a record company and having a production company and a logo. First goal was to own our masters. Without your master tapes you ain't got shit, period."

As Knight speaks of Dr. Dre's *The Chronic*, which laid the foundation for Death Row in 1992, and Snoop's solo debut, *Doggystyle*, which proved that Death Row was more than just a vanity label, I can't help but notice how utterly simple and ghetto—in the sense that the underclass has always done what it takes to survive—his logic is. Ain't no complicated equations or middle-class maneuvers here, just, according to Knight, people getting what they deserve. And never forgetting where they come from.

"We called it Death Row 'cause most everybody had been in-

volved with the law," Knight explains. "A majority of our people was parolees or incarcerated—it's no joke. We got people really was on death row and still is." Indeed, there is no way to truly comprehend the incredible success of Death Row Records—its estimated worth now tops $100 million—without first understanding the conditions that created the rap game in the first place: few legal economic paths in America's inner cities, stunted educational opportunities, a pervasive sense of alienation among young Black males, Black folks' age-old need to create music, and a typically American hunger for money and power.

The hip-hop nation is no different than any other segment of this society in its desire to live the American dream. Hip-hop, for better or worse, has been this generation's most prominent means for making good on the long-lost promises of the Civil Rights Movement. However, the big question is, where does this pull-yourself-up-by-your-bootstraps economic nationalism end and the high drama that hovers over Death Row Records begin?

The music industry thrives on rumors, and Death Row is always grist for the gossip mill. Stories run the gamut from Knight and his boys using metal pipes in persuading the late Eazy-E to release Dr. Dre from Ruthless Records, to former Uptown CEO Andre Harrell being strong-armed into restructuring Mary J. Blige's and Jodeci's contracts, to an alleged beef between Knight and Bad Boy Entertainment CEO Sean "Puffy" Combs, which some trace to the shooting death of one of Knight's close friends last October.

That incident, some say, has fueled a growing East Coast vs. West Coast battle, and—so go the rumors—has led to reported threats on Combs's life. "I heard there was a contract out on my life," says Combs. "Why do they have so much hatred for me? I ask myself that question every day. I'm ready for them to leave me alone, man."

In an interview in last April's *Vibe*, Shakur suggested that Combs, the Notorious B.I.G., Shakur's longtime friend Randy

"Stretch" Walker, and others behaved suspiciously immediately following Shakur's shooting in New York on November 30, 1994. Exactly one year to the day after Shakur's shooting, Walker was murdered execution-style in Queens. (When contacted by phone after the murder, Shakur offered no comment.)

The drama had already intensified when Knight bailed Shakur out last October and brought him to Death Row. Shakur's "relentless" new double album for Death Row includes a track featuring Faith—one of Combs's artists and Biggie Smalls's wife—titled "Wonder Why They Call You Bitch." According to one source, "Tupac and Faith are now very, very close." ("Me and Faith don't have no problems," says Shakur. When asked about their relationship beyond the studio, he replies, "I ain't gonna answer that shit, man. You know I don't kiss and tell.") While Knight has said repeatedly that he wants Death Row to be "the Motown of the '90s," the label's history is unfolding more like an in-your-face Martin Scorsese film than Berry Gordy's charm-school approach.

I ask Knight about all the rumors. He shifts his weight in his chair and bristles: "When you become the best, it's more rumors, it's more people want to stop you, 'cause everybody want to be number one."

"Can we talk about any of these alleged incidents?"

"Say what you want to say."

I then recount my understanding of the Andre Harrell story as Knight stares at me. Before long, he's flipped the script, asking me what I would do if I wasn't receiving a fair deal.

"You should get the best deal you can get in this business," I respond.

Knight edges forward in his chair, proud he got me to agree. "See, people got this business mixed up," he says. "They want to go and talk about a person who fixin' to come and help you. They don't say nothin' about the motherfucker who beatin' people out they money. When you stand up for right, people should

tip they hat to you and keep movin', and mind they own business."

Not totally satisfied with Knight's response, I wonder why rappers the D.O.C. and RBX are no longer with Death Row Records, and why both have gone on record, literally, complaining of not being paid. But Knight's already defensive, and I don't want to get tossed out before I get to bring up other, more important questions.

"What about the methods you used to get Harrell to renegotiate those contracts?" I ask.

"It's like this: was you there?"

"Nah."

"Then there's nothin' to talk about."

What Knight will talk about is how important it is for him and Death Row to stay rooted in the streets. The youngest of three children and a proud native of working-class Compton (where he still keeps a house), Knight was a star defensive lineman in high school and at the University of Nevada at Las Vegas before entering the music business in the late 1980s. It's not clear how he got into the game—some say he was the D.O.C.'s bodyguard during the N.W.A days, while Knight maintains he started a music publishing business that earned a small fortune off Vanilla Ice's smash 1990 debut. Whatever the case, few individuals have as much drive as Knight: "Ghetto politics teaches you how to win and really be hungry. I never been the one who wanted to work with nobody. 'Cause I think if a motherfucker get you a paycheck—listen to how it sound, *paycheck*, like they paying you to stay in check. Can't nobody keep me in check."

Time Warner couldn't. It bowed to political pressure and announced it was selling its 50 percent interest in Death Row's profitable distributor, Interscope Records. Self-appointed gangsta rap watchdog C. DeLores Tucker couldn't. She may have helped get Interscope dropped, but she had no effect on Death Row's progress. In fact, at one point she met with Knight to get a piece of the action. He turned her down.

Despite all the community outreach Suge Knight does—the lavish Mother's Day dinners for single mothers, the turkey giveaways at Thanksgiving, the Christmas toy giveaways for Compton children—he has to know he puts fear in some hearts, that his I-don't-give-a-fuck persona unfurls itself long before people ever meet him in the flesh. Hip-hop has always been about being straight up, about being skeptical of the motives of the generation ahead of us, about creating shields (or myths) to protect our world from outsiders—Bob Dole, William Bennett, C. DeLores Tucker—who seek to come in and dominate us. With four-year-old Death Row Records as his sword and an aura Al Pacino's *Scarface* would be proud of, Suge Knight epitomizes that mindset—but at what cost?

Listen to Knight summarize his modus operandi: "Black executives, they get invited to the golf tournaments. I don't give a fuck about all that. I'm not gonna play golf with you. When you playin' golf, I'ma be in the studio. While you trying to eat dinner with the other executives in the business, I'ma be havin' dinner with my family, which is the artists on the label." He pauses to emphasize his point. "Without your talent, you ain't shit."

Talent is something thirty-year-old Grammy winner Dr. Dre, né Andre Young, has in abundance. On a different day in the Can-Am Building's studio A, hip-hop's most sought-after producer is waiting for Tupac to show up and continue work on his new album. The Compton-born cofounder (with Knight) and president of Death Row, Dr. Dre has sold fifteen million records in the past decade. Six foot one, two hundred–plus pounds, Dre wears a beige Fila outfit, brown Timberlands, and a gold Rolex saturated with diamonds. If that isn't enough, a chunk of diamond and gold glitters on one of his fingers. Those adornments aside, I'm surprised how soft-spoken and shy the baby-faced Dr. Dre is in person, his eyes avoiding mine for much of the interview. To break the ice, I ask about the World Class Wreckin' Cru, his first group back in the early 1980s.

"Wreckin' Cru was a DJ crew. They used to call it that because it was the guys that came in after the party was over and broke down the equipment," Dre says, leaning closer to my tape recorder as he warms to the topic. "We eventually made a record, and we had the costumes on and what have you. Back then, everybody had their little getups, you know, like Soulsonic Force, UTFO." Dre laughs at the memory. "That shit haunted me, but you know, I ain't ashamed of my past."

Dre grew disillusioned with the Wreckin' Cru's style and teamed up with a teenage rapper named Ice Cube. They performed live at clubs and skating rinks. "We used to take people's songs, you know, and change them and make them dirty. Like 'My Adidas' was—" Dre laughs hard from the gut up. "Cube had this thing called 'My Penis.' We rocked it, and people would go crazy. So we just took that and started making records with it. And with me being a DJ, I used to sit in the club during the week and make up beats just to play in the club. I would take somebody else's song and recreate it and make it an instrumental. So that's how I basically got into producing."

Eventually Dre decided to form a group, but he needed a financial backer. In 1986, he met Eric "Eazy-E" Wright, a former drug dealer and fellow Compton resident looking to pump his money into something legal. Dre produced an Eazy single called "Boyz-N-The Hood," and it was on. "We hustled the record every day for eight months," says Dre, "riding around in a jeep, selling it from record store to record store ourselves."

DJ Yella, an old Wreckin' Cru partner, joined Dre, Eazy, Cube, MC Ren, and short-term member Arabian Prince to form arguably the most influential rap act ever. N.W.A's 1989 landmark, *Straight Outta Compton*, introduced an entire nation to urban blight, West Coast style. The album, produced largely by Dr. Dre and released on the underground label Ruthless Records, went double platinum with virtually no radio play. Dre says he and Eazy started Ruthless, although it was Eazy and Jerry Heller—a

middle-aged White man who'd previously worked with Elton John and Pink Floyd—who gained credit for building America's first multimillion-dollar hard-core rap label.

Despite his meteoric success, Dre grows bitter when describing the disintegration of Ruthless Records and his relationship with Eazy-E. "The split came when Jerry Heller got involved," he recalls. "He played the divide-and-conquer game. He picked one nigga to take care of, instead of taking care of everybody, and that was Eazy. And Eazy was just, like, 'Well, shit, I'm taken care of, so fuck it.'"

When I reach Heller later by telephone, he reluctantly admits that Dre "was probably right. You know, Dre was a producer and a member of the group," he says. "Eazy was interested in being Berry Gordy, so more of my time was spent with Eazy."

During the production of N.W.A's *Efil4zaggin* album, Dre decided he wanted out of his contract. He almost spits out the recollection: "I was gettin' like two points for my production on albums. I still have the contracts framed." Dre adjusts his Rolex. "I'm not no egotistical person. I just want what I'm supposed to get. Not a penny more, not a penny less."

That's where Knight came in. "Suge brought it to my attention that I was being cheated," he says. "I wanted to do my own thing anyway. I was going to do it with Ruthless, but there was some sheisty shit, so I had to get ghost."

Exactly how Knight helped Dre "get ghost" depends on whom you ask. When I mention to Jerry Heller that Knight maintains he's never threatened or beaten up anyone to make a gain in the music business, Heller cracks an eerie laugh reminiscent of Vincent Price's on Michael Jackson's "Thriller," then says, "I would say he's taking poetic license."

Dre gives Knight credit for coming up with the plan for Death Row in 1991. He assures me he and Knight are "50/50 partners. You know, me and Suge, we like brothers and shit." These two buddies figured Dr. Dre's name was bankable enough

to start a record label and get a distribution deal, but unbelievably, there were no takers at first. Finally Interscope took a chance and Death Row (the label was going to be called Future Shock, after an old Curtis Mayfield single, until Dre and Knight purchased the more dramatic handle from one of Dre's homeboys) has become the most profitable independently owned African American hip-hop label of the 1990s.

Death Row's first release, *The Chronic*, dissed Eazy-E and Jerry Heller numerous times. But when conversation turns to Eazy's death from AIDS last March, Dre grows solemn: "I didn't believe it till I went to the hospital." He sighs, rubs his chin, and collects his thoughts. "He looked normal. That's what makes the shit so fuckin' scary, man. But he was unconscious, so he didn't even know I was there." Obviously, adds Dre, the ensuing battle over ownership of Ruthless Records will affect Eazy's seven children. "That's who's really going to suffer from this. We were talking about doing an N.W.A album and giving Eazy's share to his kids."

Dre's words stop suddenly. He's looking off somewhere, palming the back of his neck, perhaps reliving all the years of his life, personal and public: the Wreckin' Cru, N.W.A, his run-ins with the law, Death Row, all the awards and accolades, the offers to produce superstars such as Madonna, his and Ice Cube's long-awaited *Helter Skelter* album, Snoop's trial . . .

I pull Dre back into conversation by asking, "Would Death Row exist without you?"

His expression becomes blank, then he begins to speak but stops himself and thinks for a moment. "Wherever I am, whatever I do is going to be the bomb shit. And people are going to benefit from it. I dunno, there might be another Dr. Dre out there somewhere." He laughs uneasily.

I ask him about his greatest fear.

"I'm not afraid of anything at the moment," he replies. "Actually, I'm afraid of two things: God and the IRS." He laughs

again. "That's it. You know, I get butterflies every time a record comes out. I'm like, *I hope people like it. I hope people buy it.* But it's never no serious fear."

What matters most to Dr. Dre is the digestion and creation of music. "A lot of times when I'm at home kickin' it, I don't even listen to hip-hop," he says. "I listen to all types of music." (He promises Death Row ventures into rock, reggae, and jazz.) Pushing forward in his chair, Dre, who's recently taken up the trumpet, taps his fingers on his left knee excitedly. "My personal opinion is, the '70s is when the best music was made. Some motherfuckers had orchestras! Had string sections and they'd have to sit there and orchestrate a song. And put some vocals to it. So they really got into it. Curtis Mayfield—that motherfucker was bad as shit. Isaac Hayes, Barry White, y'knowhumsayin'? Them brothers was in there doing it."

Out in the crisp air of El Mirage Desert Dry Lake Bed (a grueling hundred-mile trek north from Los Angeles) stands the $600,000 video set of "California Love," Tupac's phat first single (co-rapped and produced by Dr. Dre) from *All Eyez on Me.* The video, directed by Hype Williams, is loosely based on the flick *Mad Max*: Helicopters fly overhead, dirt bikes kick up sand, and everyone in the shoot—including Tupac, Dre, comedian/actor Chris Tucker, and a plethora of male and female extras—is wearing black leather shirts, vests, gloves, hats, and pants with metal spikes. Desert dust coats their faces, hands, and arms.

I haven't spoken with or seen Tupac Shakur since our Rikers Island interview last January. I make my way to his trailer and knock. The door swings open, releasing a powerful gust of chronic smoke. There he is, the big eyes shining brightly, the smile still childlike and broad as an ocean, his exposed muscles—probably due to his eleven-month bid—bigger than ever.

As Shakur is whisked away to a TV interview, I ask, "What do you think about this whole East Coast vs. West Coast thing?"

Tupac smiles that wicked smile and says, "It's gonna get deep."

What is even deeper is the way the word *family* has been mentioned by everyone associated with Death Row, including newcomers like teenage R&B singer Danny Boy and rapper/producer Sam Sneed. In this often cruel and unjust world, it can't be argued enough how important it is to have people who've got your back. To have, as we say, "fam with ya." Shakur's journey—from Harlem and the Bronx to Baltimore to the Bay Area to Los Angeles to Atlanta and back to New York and now back to Los Angeles—has always been about that need for family.

A few weeks later I speak with Shakur via telephone. "The family part, to me—I'm not gonna be corny and be like, 'Everybody on Death Row love each other,'" he says. "It's not like that. Nobody has beef internally. And if we do, we handle it internally. More than a family, Death Row, to me, is like a machine. The biggest, strongest superpower in the hip-hop world. In order to do the things that I gotta do, we gotta have that superpower. Now we gotta expand and show exactly what a superpower is.

"At Death Row, I don't have to worry about embarrassing nobody or standing out or doing something they don't want me to do. I'm still Tupac. At Death Row, I got my own shit. I'm independent. But this is the machine that I roll with.

"As for me and Suge, right now—as of today—we're the perfect couple. I can see this is what I've been looking for, management-wise. He rides like I ride. With Suge as my manager, I gotta do less. 'Cause before, niggas wasn't scared of me. So I brought fear to them. Now I don't have to do all that to get respect. 'Cause motherfuckers is scared shitless of Suge. I don't know why, 'cause Suge's cool. A lot of cowards are trying to make it like Suge's the scourge of the industry. All Suge's doing is riding. Making it so rappers can get what they due."

Back at the video shoot, as another TV crew tapes him, a hyper Tupac spreads out a stack of hundred-dollar bills just

handed to him by Knight, who stands in the background talking on a cellular phone. "This is why I signed to Death Row," says Pac to the cameras, "right here."

Shakur's antics hit me as poignant because—perhaps unwittingly—he's playing right into the hands of people who view rappers as foulmouthed, money-sex-and-violence-crazed lowlifes who are poisoning America's youth. Of course, one of the beauties of the hip-hop generation is that we really don't give a fuck what "outsiders" think about us. But in not giving a fuck, in having no agenda but our own selfish needs, are we ultimately fucking all the people (family, real friends, ardent supporters) who see us as representative of dreams so often deferred?

I'm still pondering this a week later at the Los Angeles County Criminal Court Building. The washed-out, gray nineteen-story structure looks as intimidating as any other courthouse, but this one is notable for its famous defendants: O.J. Simpson, Heidi Fleiss, Michael Jackson. I'm here to witness the *People vs. Calvin Broadus* (aka Snoop Doggy Dogg) murder trial.

On the ninth floor, in department 110, room 9-302, Judge Paul G. Flynn is presiding over jury selection. Some five hundred prospective jurors have been interviewed, and eleven have tentatively been agreed upon by the prosecution and defense. While the search for number twelve continues, my eyes are on Snoop and his codefendant McKinley Lee—the accused triggerman—a dark-skinned young man with a shiny bald head and a thin goatee. In the interviews, Rodney King and O.J. Simpson come up often, as does the issue of race.

While Lee pays close attention, especially to questions about potential jurors' views on rap music, Snoop, his permed hair pulled back into a bun, hunches over a legal pad, scribbling, looking up only when his lawyer David Kenner whispers into his ear.

During the lunch break, Snoop leaves the building with his bodyguard and friends (he's free to walk the streets because

Knight bailed him out). Meanwhile, Kenner, a short cock-diesel man with jet-black hair, offers that Lee and Snoop acted in self-defense in the fatal shooting of Philip Woldemariam in August 1993. If convicted, both men face life imprisonment.

Kenner, who represents Death Row on both entertainment and criminal matters, insists that "Snoop Doggy Dogg is not on trial here; Calvin Broadus is. When you reach to a performer's interviews or their songs, and try to extrapolate from that perceptions that you want to draw about the real person, to me it would be no different than saying Arnold Schwarzenegger is a cold-blooded murderer because of his last movie."

That point aside, Kenner expects the prosecution to bring Snoop's lyrics, videos, and interviews into evidence. Several people who have had contact with Snoop over the past three years, including this writer, have been subpoenaed as material witnesses. Just a few days earlier, charges against a third co-defendant, Sean Abrams, were dropped. Kenner also asserts that serious questions of missing evidence have yet to be answered.

Returning just before proceedings resume, Snoop, as raw-boned as ever in a dark-green double-breasted suit, pauses to speak with me. "I'm straight, you know," he says, picking at the strands of hair cupping his chin. "Everybody's praying for me, and I want them to continue to pray for me."

I ask Snoop if he feels rap music is on trial. His eyes meet mine and narrow. "Yeah, it is. I can't really speak about it, but listen to me, it is."

What about critics who say this trial shows what rap music is all about—violence?

"It's God, giving us obstacles to get through," he replies. "He puts everybody that's successful through obstacles to see if they'll maintain and become successful years down the line. So I'm ready for whatever."

"What do you say to people who look up to you as a hero?" I ask him.

"Keep God first. Visualize a goal and try to reach it, and if you can't reach it, find something else other than the negative. Because that negative is a long stretch behind the wall—trust me."

There's no ignoring the violence pervading hip-hop culture. Particularly when it seems to be reaching up to executive levels. In my interview with Suge Knight, I ask him about the murder in Atlanta of his close friend. Does he really believe Puffy Combs, the biggest hitmaker on the East Coast, actually had something to do with it?

Unnerved by the question, Knight changes the subject, and it isn't brought up again. However, when it's clear the interview is over, he says he has some things he wants to discuss with me.

For the first time that evening, Damu the dog rises up off the red carpet and turns in my direction. "I didn't like them questions you was asking me about the dead," Knight says, anger curling the corners of his mouth.

"You mean the questions about Eazy-E?" I ask cautiously.

"Nah, that was my homeboy that was killed down there in Atlanta. I felt you was being disrespectful, and I don't forget things like that," Knight says matter-of-factly, his eyes boring into mine.

As Knight lectures me, the possible seeds of this supposed feud between he and Combs come to mind: Tupac Shakur wondering in *Vibe* last year whether Combs and Biggie Smalls may have known something about his being shot; rumors (strongly denied) that Shakur was raped in jail; Knight publicly dissing Combs—"You don't need no executive producer who's all over your record and in the videos"—at last year's televised *Source* Awards in New York; and finally, the murder of Knight's buddy in Atlanta.

The Atlanta story, according to eyewitnesses, goes a little something like this: So So Def Recordings CEO Jermaine Dupri had

a birthday party, which Knight and Combs attended. Later, both showed up at an after-party at the Platinum House. An argument started outside the club, and Knight's friend was killed. According to Combs, Knight turned to him after the shooting and said, "You had to have something to do with this." Given the high profiles of both Knight and Combs, it's ironic that there was barely any mention of the incident in the media.

Interestingly enough, both Knight and Combs are on record denying there's a beef. Knight: "For what? I'm a man. How does that look for me to go and have a beef with another person who's not a threat to me?" Combs: "I'm not a gangsta, and I don't have no rivalry with no person in the industry whatsoever. The whole shit is stupid—tryin' to make an East Coast/West Coast war. East Coast, West Coast, Death Row, Def Jam, or Uptown, I feel nothing but proud for anybody young and Black and making money. [Some people] want us to be at each other, at war with each other. Acting like a bunch of ignorant niggas, y'know what I'm sayin'?"

But there's no denying that tension's in the air. Some folks say it's the start of a hip-hop civil war. I remember Dr. Dre saying, "If it keeps going this way, pretty soon niggas from the East Coast ain't gonna be able to come out here and be safe. And vice versa."

Back in the office, when Knight feels he's gotten his point across, he and Damu turn and head over to his desk. I rise slowly, then exit.

Out in the night air, I sigh hard. This has not been an easy article to deal with. Too many people have warned me about what to say and what not to say, and that, to me, is not what hip-hop is about. But then again, it's 1996 and shit is thick for Black folks. When a people feel like social, political, or economic outcasts, it gets easier to consider taking one another out—even over the pettiest beefs—in the name of survival. Not even journalists are immune to this logic.

The tragedy here is that two of the most successful young Black entrepreneurs ever could possibly end up hurt or dead over God only knows what. As *Vibe* went to press, there was talk of involving people such as Minister Louis Farrakhan or Ben Chavis in an effort to get both sides to make peace. The future of hip-hop may ultimately depend on such a meeting.

How long Death Row Records will live remains to be seen. But like a true player setting his rules for the game, Knight predicts, perhaps not recognizing the double meaning of his words, "Death Row's going to be here forever."

Ready for the World:
Dream Team III
Originally published in *Vibe*
August 1996

Right now, basketball is like Beatlemania . . .
—Grant Hill, Dream Team III member

And that is exactly what I was thinking this past February as I stood outside the automatic front door of the posh Marriott Rivercenter Hotel in downtown San Antonio, the site of the National Basketball Association's All-Star Weekend celebration. I came to this mega-sports event (second only to the Super Bowl in the amount of celebrities attending and rump-shaking parties) to observe and interview players selected for the US Olympic basketball team— aka Dream Team III.

There was no doubt that this squad—Charles Barkley, David Robinson, Grant Hill, Scottie Pippen, Shaquille O'Neal, Anfernee "Penny" Hardaway, Hakeem Olajuwon, Mitch Richmond, Glenn Robinson, John Stockton, Reggie Miller, and Karl Malone—would win the gold medal as their predecessors had. That was pretty much a given. The question was, how much would this latest packaging of NBA talent further the goal of maintaining a global hunger for the sport, its stars, and its merchandise? And where did this mass-marketed phenomenon come from in the first place?

But before you can ask any questions, you gotta get your ass in the joint, and even with a press badge, matters were thick.

A mighty multiracial throng packed the front entrance of the hotel, awaiting the sight of a basketball player—any basketball player. Just the mention of, say, Hakeem Olajuwon whipped the onlookers into a frenzy, their motion propelled by the sheer possibility of spotting one of their heroes. When Olajuwon's seven-foot frame actually appeared from an elevator, beefy, no-neck security men parted the sea of worshippers so the Nigerian-born superstar, grinning sheepishly, could push his way to a black limo outside.

Just as I was nudging my way toward Olajuwon to get a closer look, a gaunt, ponytailed White girl in a San Antonio Spurs sweatshirt with a Polaroid in one hand and a photo of Charles Barkley in the other smashed right into me, shrieking, "Oh my God, I touched him! I touched his hand!" She then vanished into the hysterical throng.

But it wasn't just the heads wearing NBA paraphernalia or the latest, greatest pair of Nikes that caught my attention. It was the different types of people who stood there—Black, Brown, Yellow, and White, with some faces painted in team colors—waiting, wondering, cameras ready, pens and scraps of papers nervously moving between moist fingers. This group—the middle-aged businessmen with expensive double-breasted suits; the local homeboys wearing glow-in-the-dark gear; the strikingly beautiful Black women with their butt-gripping shorts, painted lips, bare stomachs, and asymmetrical hairstyles; the older, more conservatively dressed Black women who could easily have been some of the players' moms (or not); the plain-Jane housewives trying to keep track of their hyperactive children; and the young White men and women who affected hip-hop attitude—confirmed (if there were any lingering doubts) that basketball has replaced baseball as America's national pastime. Such mythologized Black men as Michael Jordan and Shaquille O'Neal are as big as Elvis and the Beatles put together.

* * *

"In the early 1980s, people were talking about America not accepting a Black sport," says Russ Granik, deputy commissioner and COO of the NBA. "I was here with [NBA commissioner] David Stern when things weren't so good. Back then, there wasn't much focus on how the game was presented. And TV coverage wasn't great at the time."

What had always been great, though, was the NBA's talent pool. The 1970s alone produced legends like Kareem Abdul-Jabbar, Julius Erving, Pete Maravich, Rick Barry, and Walt Frazier. But only die-hard fans followed these stars—it was usually football and baseball players who received the big endorsement deals. Larry Bird and Magic Johnson entered the league in 1979, finally giving the NBA two ready-for-prime-time players. The college rivals had gone head-to-head in that year's NCAA championship game (Indiana State vs. Michigan State), and as pros, their contrasting styles of play and skin color made the rivalry even more intense. Then, in 1983, a collective-bargaining agreement that guaranteed players 53 percent of league revenues opened the NBA up to new marketing strategies. David Stern, a lawyer and businessman, borrowed heavily from pro football's playbook. Kids in the 1970s wore O.J. Simpson's number 32; now they wear Michael Jordan's number 23.

Even as the league got Blacker and Blacker—it seemed that Bird's Boston Celtics were the only "White team" around—the NBA and its unofficial minor league, college basketball, began to achieve tremendous growth in attendance, television deals, corporate support, and celebrity cheerleaders (Jack Nicholson, Spike Lee, Woody Allen, Whoopi Goldberg, Bill Murray, Jerry Seinfeld, and Oprah Winfrey, to name a few). When Michael Jordan struck his now historic deal with Nike in 1985 and began appearing in commercial after commercial—ultimately becoming as popular, according to one poll, as Jesus Christ—the floodgates were opened for America to accept this "Black sport"

and spread it like a religion across the globe. (The NBA has been opening its season in Japan every other year since 1990. Preseason games have also been held in England, France, Germany, Italy, Spain, and Mexico.)

"Basketball," says Grant Hill by telephone, "regardless of what color you are, is just an exciting game. I look at the other sports and they just don't have what basketball has. There isn't a wasted moment on the court. Plus, the way they market Michael Jordan or Shaq—these are people who are interesting to everyone." That crossover appeal wasn't lost on the International Basketball Federations (FIBA). In 1989 the organization voted to allow professional players to compete in international competition, paving the way for the colossal franchise now known as the Dream Team.

Says Granik, "The feeling around the rest of the world was that basketball was never going to reach its full popularity and the players weren't going to develop to their fullest potential unless they got to play against the very best people. So," he chuckles, "they don't mind losing."

Though Granik and others deny it, the US's elimination in the 1988 Olympic semifinals (resulting in its first-ever bronze medal; the US refused to accept the silver medal it won in '72 due to a controversial call in the final game) must have played a part in the rise of the Dream Team. Not only would the US regain its throne—it had won nine gold medals and had an 85–2 record since men's basketball became an Olympic sport in 1936—but it would also do so in the manner of a powerful nation overwhelming the opposition with awesome weapons of war. Or as Charles Barkley aptly described the first Dream Team, "We're like a group of Freddy Kruegers."

The birth of Dream Team I unleashed a huge media blitz. The press sucked up every detail, including Barkley's ignorant comment about elbowing a bony Angolan player because "he might

have a spear hidden somewhere." Instead of staying with the other athletes in the Olympic Village in Barcelona, the twelve American basketball players and their entourage had a brand-new hotel all to themselves. (Speaking by car phone from a limo after shooting a Dream Team III commercial, Barkley says he has "no regrets" and responds to all critics: "The press was jealous of the Dream Team. They always talked about the hotels we were staying in and made a big deal about it. And Americans hate you if you're popular.")

At least twelve companies spent upward of twelve million dollars in promotion and advertising to highlight their connection to the 1992 Olympic squad. Dream Team jerseys, mugs, hats, and posters were omnipresent. Though Granik insists that "the Dream Team itself is not hugely profitable," the NBA continues to assist USA Basketball in the promotion of all international events. It invests its resources with the hope that new TV and merchandising markets will continue to open up. But there is no denying that sports and big business got crisscrossed when Michael Jordan and five other Dream Teamers who wore Nike (a sneaker named for the Greek goddess of victory) balked at appearing at the medal ceremonies because Reebok—Nike's staunch competitor—had outfitted the team. So after demolishing their opponents by an average score of forty-four points, Jordan and his fellow Nike clients (as well as players under contract to other shoe companies) took the medal stand and rolled back their collars to obscure the Reebok emblem. Jordan, the epitome of basketball's surge into the global consciousness, smothered the Reebok name with the American flag.

The financial bonanza of Dream Team III is sure to be even greater than the original version. Nike and Reebok have designed footwear especially for this competition, and corporation after corporation has somehow connected itself as an "official sponsor" of Dream Team III. A television audience estimated at two-thirds of the world's population will soak up the fastest-

growing sport of the 1990s and, inevitably, will want to buy anything and everything associated with this sensation. The fact that Charles Barkley was selected again for Dream Team III after saying four years ago, "It was a once-in-a-lifetime thing, and they should give someone else a chance to enjoy it," says much about the economics of the game. "The NBA came back at me and asked me again," Barkley explains. "I said yes because Atlanta is close to my home state of Alabama. It'll be more relaxed and more fun this time, being home."

"There is a business side to it," says Grant Hill, "and that may be in part why Barkley was named to the team. There's a lot of personalities involved, a lot of selling of the game. A lot of selling of the NBA. I think all the success of Dream Team I really grabbed the attention of the world. Dream Team III is expected to take it to the next level."

"I'm like the Rodney Dangerfield of basketball," says Dream Team III head coach Lenny Wilkens. "I'm the best kept secret in the NBA."

Wilkens has won more games than any other coach in the history of the National Basketball Association, but hardly anyone acknowledges it. Whether that has to do with the fact that Wilkens is one of the NBA's few Black head coaches, he will not say—at least not directly. What he will discuss is the task that faces him as he directs, in his words, "the finest athletes in the world."

Wilkens was a star player himself during the '60s and '70s. Today, he's a fiftyish, six-foot-one, beige-complexioned man with an infectious smile, a well-coiffed salt-and-pepper Afro, and a laid-back disposition. I spoke with him at the Embassy Suites hotel in Secaucus, New Jersey, on a Sunday morning before his Atlanta Hawks—who went on to be eliminated in the second round of the playoffs—played the New Jersey Nets.

"I have players I would never have had the opportunity to coach before," says Wilkens. "Being an assistant coach for

Dream Team I was a good learning experience for this, because we had to juggle so many incredible players in and out of the starting lineup, you know, make sure people got their playing time in. I felt [Dream Team I head coach] Chuck Daly and the rest of us did an amazing job."

But the infamous Dream Team II was another story. Featuring players like Derrick Coleman, Shawn Kemp, Larry Johnson, and Dominique Wilkins, the athletes who represented the US in the 1994 World Championships in Toronto weren't considered to be basketball ambassadors on the order of Magic or Bird or Mike. Although they won the gold medal as convincingly as Dream Team I had, Dream Team II left a lasting impression that NBA players were a bunch of trash-talking egomaniacs.

"I wasn't there in 1994," says Wilkens rather testily. "I know nothing about it. In '92 we had a lot of legend-type players. I think this team will be as versatile as that team was." But then he adds, "If you are going to talk about athletes' behavior, you have to also talk about society as a whole. Because everything has changed, not only in sports. We have a lot of kids that come from single-parent families. The family ties are not as strong as when I was growing up. That is rampant in society."

Translation: ready or not, the hip-hop generation has made its way into professional basketball, and some of them are as good as or better than the players selected for Dream Team III. But business is business, and Shawn Kemp, dope as he is, isn't anybody's first choice to represent the USA. When he grabbed his nuts while hanging on the rim in '94, the ensuing criticism made it clear that street flavor of that nature was not desirable.

"Because it's become more of a business now," says Barkley, "players have to keep it in perspective. It's the NBA's fault, because they made everybody coming into the league a star immediately. Every guy acts like a prima donna. In the old days, you had to prove you were a star by making the All-Star team five or six times first."

If you analyze the roster of Dream Team III, none of the players—notwithstanding Shaq's postdunk grimaces and Barkley's outbursts (which, for whatever reasons, NBA bigwigs and the media tolerate)—are as hard-core as most of the NBA's young guns. Dream Team III is a nice mix of old and new, for sure, but it's also relatively safe.

Russ Granik is straight-up blunt: "When we picked the team in '94, we didn't stop to take into account enough the character of the individuals being picked, and went just on talent. That taught us a lesson."

Back at the All-Star practice session in San Antonio, fans were going bananas in the stands as Michael Jordan cut and slashed to the basket, Reggie Miller shot his trademark three-pointers, Shaq dunked over Patrick Ewing again and again, and first-time All-Star Juwan Howard absorbed the ribbing of Alonzo Mourning and Scottie Pippen. As the session ended, the PA announcer said, "The East players will remain on the court for fifteen—" Before the sentence was completed, Mike, Shaq, and Grant, three of the most talented and visible athletes on the planet, were besieged by photographers on stepladders, TV cameramen banging one another for position, and overbearing, impatient writers shouting questions.

Standing just outside of Shaq's orbit, I heard a meek voice pleading, "Mister, please mister, could you just tap Shaq on the shoulder? Please, mister, please." When I realized I was the "mister" in question, I turned around to see a diminutive, middle-aged Chicana clad in an Orlando Magic jersey and waving a Magic banner, tears running down her cheeks. The hoop-hero-as-god syndrome was definitely in effect.

In 1996, twenty-four-year-old millionaire/hoopster/rapper/product pitchman/movie star Shaquille O'Neal (with his Superman tattoo) is a modern-day Hercules. He doesn't need the Olympics to be an Olympian.

The bedlam was upped a notch when the West All-Stars, led by hometown favorites David Robinson and Sean Elliott, took the court. The East players, notably Miller, O'Neal, Pippen, and Hill, accommodated every interviewer, including the foreign press. Michael Jordan, relentlessly sweated by the media even when he attempted to leave for the locker room, was a ghost.

As Shaq was trying to leave, an Orlando Magic PR rep grabbed him so I could ask what being on the Dream Team meant to him. "It means a lot," he said dryly, as if he'd delivered this answer many times before. "It's an honor to my family and to my country. I'ma just go out and show a lot of sportsmanship and, you know, be a class individual. And just try to bring home the gold medal. I don't believe in pressure. But Dream Teams I and II set such high standards that we must follow."

I made my way across the floor to where David Robinson was being interviewed by a Costa Rican reporter. Robinson, an original Dream Teamer and born-again Christian hailed universally as one of the NBA's best role models, was struggling with his Spanish. When I passed him a question about Dream Team III's chances of duplicating Dream Team I's success, he got open: "I'm sure it'll be real dominating, 'cause of the type of players you have. Me and Hakeem come out, and Shaq and Karl Malone come in. All we have to do is go out and play."

A few feet away, Olajuwon was being quizzed about his favorite foods by a Dutch television crew. "I like jollof rice," he said, obviously distracted by the whirl of action around him. "Sweets? Uh, I like, uh, apple pie. And ice cream."

I asked Olajuwon, who became a US citizen in 1993 and thus eligible for the Dream Team, what the opportunity meant for him. He said, "I feel honored," before being pulled by the arm to another camera crew.

Reggie Miller, who also played on Dream Team II, was a bit more profound: "My first dream and wish of playing in the Olympics is when I saw my sister Cheryl [a star player at the

University of Southern California] accept the gold medal around her neck in the 1984 Olympics. Being in the Olympic Village and seeing the athletes walk around, just the unity among everybody. That's what I kinda wished and hoped for."

I asked Reggie if Dream Team III is a shoo-in for the gold. He frowned.

"We're never going to underestimate our opponents. You've got Vlade Divac, Dino Radja, Toni Kukoč, Detlef Schrempf. These guys have played in the NBA and they've gotten the experience, and they're taking that back to their countries and making their countries automatically better. Everyone thinks it's going to be a cakewalk, but we're gonna be prepared like we're going into an NBA Final."

Dream Team veteran Scottie Pippen admitted that there's pressure: "Every team that went to the Olympics and didn't come back with the gold medal, you remember them. You remember those years when the US lost at the Olympics. And I don't want to be a part of that group that didn't win an Olympic gold medal."

If there's any single thing I got from All-Star weekend and all the research I've done and all the people I've interviewed, it's this: basketball—a sport that was invented by a White dude named James Naismith in 1891 but molded into a gravity-defying art form by Black men from America's urban centers—is the ticket out for so many people, economically, spiritually, psychologically, and recreationally.

More than any other sport, basketball is a reflection of the high-tech, fast-paced world that we live in—postmodern athletes breaking and bending rules all the time, like new gadgets popping up to take things to another level. The Dream Team is the NBA raised to the level of virtual reality, like a dope new Sega cartridge. Whether you're a kid from the ghetto or Jack Nicholson, you love this game.

It is no coincidence, for example, that a record thirty-five college underclassmen and three high schoolers decided to enter this year's NBA draft. Many of them cited increasing financial pressures for their decisions and now carry the burden of fulfilling dreams for themselves, their families, and all the kids in America's inner cities who will never make it from the playgrounds to the big time. Just like their rap brethren, today's young B-ballers don't have time for playing by someone else's rules. The "get money" mentality reigns supreme, even if that means sacrificing a college education, or maybe in the future a high school one.

But I'm not gonna fake the funk: there is a certain pleasure in noting that America's Dream Team is largely peopled by brothers, even if they do appeal to all colors. And that, perhaps, is the ultimate beauty of the Dream Team—it can be anything you or I want it to be.

What else are dreams for?

The Breakdown

Originally published in *Code*
December 1999

And we are programmed to self-destruct
to fragment.
—Jayne Cortez, "There It Is"

Afew short years ago, I wanted to end my life. Suicide, yeah. You see, there is nothing worse nor more humiliating than to move to a metropolis like New York, become a writer both prolific and known during your very hip twenties, then lose it all—your cushy magazine job, your phat apartment, your instant access to money—by the age of thirty. I suffered through this period privately, telling a small knot of comrades of my predicament, while feigning sanity to others. That I am able to write this essay is testament to how far I have come since falling so low. I am not remotely confident where to start other than to quote F. Scott Fitzgerald who said famously, "All life is a process of breaking down."

Like Fitzgerald's roaring 1920s, the naughty '90s were my time to live and play irresponsibly. Upon moving to upper Manhattan—Harlem—from Jersey City, New Jersey, my hometown, in August 1990, I wrote in my diary, somewhat egotistically and in spite of my few years of toiling in obscurity as a freelance news reporter, that I wanted to be remembered as one of the best, and best-known, writers of my generation. As the elders say, be careful what you ask for.

Two years after my unheralded arrival on Manhattan's

shores, I would be drafted to costar on MTV's hugely popular docu-soap *The Real World*, and soon thereafter I found myself writing the cover story for a new magazine founded by Quincy Jones named *Vibe*. I had become a staff writer with a national byline and face recognition at twenty-six. I wore this freshly minted notoriety akin to how a homeboy wears his straight-outta-the-box Timberland boots. I admired it in the mirror. I scrubbed that notoriety regularly. I deemed my self-generated franchise better than anyone else's. And I got caught up in the hype of the entertainment industry: the fluffy parties, the air kisses, the synthetic let's-do-lunch rhetoric, the rubbing of slippery elbows with icons like Spike Lee, Tommy Hilfiger, General Colin Powell, and many, many others. At *Vibe*, the demand to produce articles like a well-oiled machine wore on me. I binged on liquor to keep the motor going; I drank more liquor to make it stop. I did not take a legitimate vacation during my four-year association with the glossy. I felt guilty for thinking of one, and I found myself becoming an insomniac who slept by inhaling loads of liquor or alcohol-laced NyQuil.

Then, in May 1996, I was fired.

In the nature of these things, my firing was the twin two-edged sword to my hiring. When I started at *Vibe* it was a magazine that promised to boldly, beautifully showcase the journalistic element of the culture I lived and breathed, which I'll roughly define by that elusive term of art: hip-hop. But almost from the start it betrayed the source of its power. Many of us people of color at this ostensibly urban people-of-color magazine were miffed that management could never seem to find "qualified" Black editors. Moreover, it bothered us that while the colored folks—chiefly the mostly female cadre of editorial assistants—carried workloads comparable to those of the White men at the monthly, the salaries and perks were hardly in the spirit of egalitarianism. Among ourselves, at the water cooler, outside the

office during lunch breaks, or even within earshot of some of our White coworkers and superiors, we began mocking the *Vibe* headquarters as "da plantation," because, as coarse as it sounds, we felt like the latest in history's line of slaves, picking the cotton only to watch the masters reaping the profits from our labor.

This wasn't the way it was supposed to be. We were supposed to be a chic, multicultural collection of the best and the brightest, inventing a way to *do* hip-hop in words on the pages of a glossy national magazine on a weekly basis. That's what Quincy himself promised at the magazine's launch (geez, how rapidly I figured out that Q may have been the founder, but it was not him running things day to day). But the scene lost its sexy allure—with a quickness—once it became plain as the African nose on my face that *Vibe*, for all its freshness, was run the old-fashioned way, by a strictly enforced racial hierarchy with White male editors at the top, including a grumpy old dinosaur that Time Warner (the original owner of *Vibe*) deposited as the editorial "consultant" for the magazine. But this stifling hierarchy was more than just business as usual to me; it was patently obscene in the context of the culture we were ostensibly representing, not to mention that more than a few of those White male editors were ridiculously incompetent and, we suspected, only using *Vibe* as a launching pad to "better opportunities" at mainstream White-oriented periodicals. On the other hand, for most of us Black and Brown writers, we knew damn well that *Vibe* was as good as it was ever going to get. We were committed because the magazine was more than just representative of our culture; we had started to see it as the only refuge for our professional survival.

The old dinosaur habitually marked up pieces with a pen adroit at minimizing commentary that flirted with race and racism in America. Indeed, there was a time when one could write an article for *Vibe* and after it left one's Black hands, no Black hands—not those of the editor, the researcher, the copy editor,

the editor in chief, or the consultant—would touch that article until another set of Black hands purchased the magazine. It would be years later before *Vibe* began to consistently hire editors of color, including for the post of editor in chief—a change brought about largely because of the unrest we sparked during those first years, I feel.

The potency of our sense of injustice—*my* sense of injustice—might seem silly to some, but to think of this as just one writer's problem at one magazine is to miss the larger point. Yes, this is the story of my personal breakdown, but it's also the story of the maddening endurance of White-skin privilege—even in as unlikely an arena as hip-hop—and how this persistent, insidious force worms its way into lives and psyches, forcing us to deal with it, to take a position on it, to make choices of consequence even when our judgment isn't clear. Sometimes, when we're tired from the fight, it can drive us crazy. Most of my White peers saw nothing wrong with the *Vibe* power structure, which spoke to how comfy they were in their White-skin privilege. How could I be mad at that? If your whole life has been spent on top with doors flung open for you at every turn, regardless of whether you are qualified to go through those doors or not, why on God's vast earth would you *think* to challenge something like that? For in defying that, you would be messing with the very basis of your day-to-day existence. This realization became a hot coal in my chest every time my disgust with the editorial plantation was dismissed by my White colleagues.

One of their key arguments involved conjuring the distorted legacy of integration, the hideously naive or hideously cynical notion that merely having people of different colors in proximity at the table of humanity would be sufficient to eradicate centuries of ingrained White supremacy. What is conveniently omitted is that Dr. King, the alleged architect of integration, by the end of his life was calling for economic justice (remember the Poor People's Campaign, beloved?) and was rethinking integration as

the best route for Black America, especially if it meant Blacks would remain mired in bottomless self-hatred and confusion, fundamentally powerless. I count myself among those who believe the Civil Rights Movement was about changing policies of legal desegregation, freeing African Americans to exercise their birthright of free movement in this social order without the fear of attack or retribution. In other words, to realize, without legal restraint, the full experience of human freedom. At some point in the transmitting of the civil rights narrative, the script was flipped: the hardheaded fight against segregation was swapped for the warm symbolism of integration. Over time, this symbolic integration has found its goal in the triumph of the myth of multiculturalism. But even though the colors of the rainbow can all chill together—at least in GAP commercials—they are not all sharing *in the power*. So what's the point of multiculturalism if it is reduced to folks eating each other's foods, marrying each other, having multiracial children, and proclaiming myopically that interracial relationships, be they friendships or loveships, will rid the country of its historically paralyzing racial quagmire? Or is *that* the point? As presently practiced in the majority of American circles, this kind of Happy Meal multiculturalism allows us to avoid yet again the necessity of scrutinizing, in a grab-the-collar, eyeball-to-eyeball manner, the power dynamic this country was founded on.

America *was* "multicultural" right from the very beginning, given the presence of Native Americans (the original owners of this land you call your land), Europeans, and captured Africans. America is a mulatto family, has always been, and will always be—this is neither news nor a cause for celebration. But why must the head of the household ceaselessly be a White male calling the shots? Rich White males are still the straws that stir the drink, and the rest of us are supposed to just smile and go along for the ride, content that we have employment, 401(k) plans, and health benefits. Even if we *don't* have these middle-class

accoutrements—even if we only see them on TV—we are supposed to be content that those dreadful *For Coloreds Only* signs have disappeared. But while the physical signs have come down—after much protest and much bloodshed—the signs never came down in our shared psyche. Buried in the mud of our collective brain, the wriggling worm of White supremacy, White entitlement, White power is still there.

And this was, for me, the crux of the matter. Thus, who cares if it was the same poor Black and Latino people Dr. King was attempting to help at the end of his life—the ones left behind by the gold rush of integration (oh, the contemporary Black middle class has a heavy cross to bear for its unapologetic abandonment of the Black poor)—who created hip-hop culture as a response to their alienation, their isolation, their invisibility? Who cares if these poor Black and Latino people were simply attempting to make something out of nothing, to create power for themselves, alchemizing it from the minimal resources at their disposal in their very limited and forgotten world? And who cares if these same poor Black and Latino people would, by laying their souls and their lives and their genius on the line, launch a cultural revolution that would inspire *two* American generations (and counting) and youth across the globe? If you think hip-hop does not rule the cultural world, you'd better look again. In the beginning, these wretched of the earth took very basic tools—two turntables, a microphone, spray paint and markers, cardboard from the corner store, and linoleum from their mother's kitchen floor—and hewed the four fundamental elements of hip-hop practiced by four new kinds of urban artists: the DJ, the MC, the dancer, and the graffiti writer.

I was one of those young people who participated in this thing, this energy, before it was even categorized as "hip-hop." I learned any and all inner-city dances; scratched my multifarious nicknames into my school desk, on lockers, or on walls;

mouthed the lyrics of the hot MCs of the day, flashing my hands to mark out the beat in the air; and tinkered with DJ equipment, albeit not very well. As a jazz connoisseur is passionate, I am passionate: I live and die for hip-hop culture and am a self-described hip-hop head. Hell, I *am* hip-hop, to bite rapper KRS-One's brash declaration. And hip-hop is mine. I earned it, just like a million other ghetto bastards left behind in the '70s and '80s.

I remember when only a few brave White people hung around hip-hop clubs like the Latin Quarters, Union Square, and the Rooftop, while most condescendingly dismissed it as nothing more than a passing fad. They were dead wrong. Hip-hop is what rock and roll and jazz once were: the popular American music that owns the epoch, that speaks to the spirit of the generation that gave it birth and the generation that grew up with it. And like those other, earlier art forms, this culture, too, must have mouthpieces—writers, critics, radio DJs—to track its evolutions and revolutions, describe it, analyze it, celebrate it, and try to understand it. *Vibe,* the *Source, XXL, Redeye,* the *Fader, Murder Dog*—these and other fanzines were born as a corollary of hip-hop. Don't get it twisted, yo. The media was the tail, hip-hop was the dog.

And it was this background that I brought with me to *Vibe.* Yes, I, a poor colored lad from the gutter, was elated that I had a job writing about something as natural to me as the air puncturing my nostrils. On the other hand, I also wanted more than just a taste of power because, for Christ's sake, we created this culture.

But we had no major clout at *Vibe.* I remember being told this repeatedly, primarily on those days when it was clear that I was not happy, by the White folks and the Black CEO who assiduously barked the company line: "Kevin, these business affairs are not your worry, just write." In a way they were right: I was a writer, and if a writer has any right to that title, then he or she must learn to sense deception. And I could sense clearly that

we were not being treated as equals, that we were being duped and the people doing the duping were convinced that they'd pulled the wool tightly over our eyes without us noticing.

America has a legacy of deceit masquerading as history. Conceivably we can overcome our fear of the past and actually discuss racism intimately, but first we must be willing to discuss what happened to the Native Americans and those captured Africans before, during, *and* after slavery (anybody out there down to define *reparations*?). Meanwhile, our nation of millions partakes in this grand scheme, and in the immortal, stuttered speech of the eternally battered and bruised Rodney King, we implore, lips greasy, mournful: "Can we all just get along?" We imagine that everything is swell because to begin unraveling the layers of deceit and violence and theft that brought us to this comfy present would require us to open our eyes to a singular horror and fall to our knees in shame. I recall those bare, empty stares of most of my White *Vibe* cohorts vividly. Those stares said, in effect, *We do not understand what* that *has to do with* this, *and besides, there is nothing we can do about it, and for that matter, why don't you just lighten up a little?*

Afresh the buck is passed from that generation to this generation. As we are told, as them Negroes were told in Alabama and Mississippi in the 1960s, *Go slow.* No one, beloved, is willing to carry the weight of this racial trick bag. The scenes have changed, but the scenes remain, inexplicably, the same. The innocent children assert, in unison, *By gosh, the office* is *diverse, so what could possibly be the matter?* The matter is that the natives—as in those tragically racist Bob Hope–Bing Crosby flicks—will shortly get restless. This is not about one writer, one magazine, one culture. This is about power and its consequences: who wields it and who does not?

The entertainment industry is one of the few places—along with sports, the Black church, and the drug hustle on the block—

where folks have the impression that Black people have achieved power and wealth by virtue of our stunning, swaggering over-representation and the gaudy amounts of money evidently generated. But real power doesn't necessarily follow appearance. What we have is a presence, but only if your name happens to be Russell Simmons or Oprah Winfrey or Bill Cosby is that presence accompanied by even a small amount of power. Power means the ability to say what can and cannot go in a national magazine with millions of readers, in editorials *and* in ads. Power means the ability to say which artists will be supported by a record company, how big those artists become, and why. Power means the ability to delegate the mining of America's ghettos for musical talent to desperate dark-skinned "entrepreneurs," providing them with the illusion of a label deal and corporate support, but never letting these glorified miners get their hands on the precious yield of their work—the masters—and all the while keeping a firm grip on the means of production and distribution.

Expanding the conversation, power means the ability to say what sort of textbooks are coming into the schools in your community, which, for all intents and purposes, signifies the power to determine *whose* education your children will be receiving, from what angle, and to what effect on your children's self-image. A number of these same children will one day aspire to be rap stars or some general cog in the entertainment empire and see nothing wrong with denigrating their people (and themselves) as "niggas" and "bitches" because their marvelously imaginative school system never bothered to teach them anything about American history from viewpoints other than that of the heroic Europeans and their descendants. Indeed, what other people in the history of this planet have been so miseducated that they see nothing wrong with publicly identifying themselves as "niggas" and "bitches" (under the pretext of keepin' it real)? That self-hatred is then digitized on compact disc and shipped worldwide by multinational conglomerates—Sony, Bertelsmann, Vivendi

Universal, AOL Time Warner, et alia—until the whole world can discover and emulate our self-hatred, thinking that these words manifest who we think we are. *Niggas and bitches . . .*

That is power, my friend. Meanwhile, we are expected to be content with overpriced jewelry, clothes with some designer's name emblazoned all over them, easy access to parties, book deals, guest appearances on MTV or VH1 (it is so so def to be an in-demand young Black writer these days with nothing, fuh shizzle, to say), free CDs and T-shirts, an expense account for all those lunches and dinners and trips, and a pipeline to all the liquor and marijuana and Ecstasy humanly consumable while etching another saga in the life of "the industry." But even in the haze of my drinking sprees and ego rides, I smelled a rat. Something was rotten in Gotham, and all the pats on the back and nice liberal smiles could not erase that certainty. This multicultural mecca was a vacuous hell once my heart aligned itself with my head and I saw, suddenly, a crystallized truth: I was more than just a happy darkie thrilled to have a gig. Or, as rapper Chuck D has said, maybe a bit too bluntly for the taste buds of the hypersensitive, *slavery* was a job, with work hours and a daily regimen, once you stop to contemplate that peculiar institution. Here I was, a twentieth-century slave ready to break north, but completely unable to rid myself of the mental shackles implanted by the high life of the industry.

I will not front, though: I got mad love for some of the White colleagues I had at *Vibe*—Jonathan Van Meter (he gave me my big break by hiring me), Alan Light, and Rob Kenner, among others—but I also know that they may never understand why some of us felt the way we did. How could they, in spite of whatever love they may have for individual Black people or for Black music and Black culture? I am checking for more than an appreciation, friend. I wanted to see us in on the major decision-making of *Vibe*, on both the editorial and business

sides, and I could not understand why *they* could not under-stand why we were pissed by the mirage of progress.

Is this what the Civil Rights Movement was for? To leave our Black-run institutions—our neighborhoods, our schools, our law firms, our newspapers and magazines, our banks, our insurance companies, our hotels, and so on, where we ran things, where there was some semblance of self-determination and power—so that we could be in an integrated heaven where we can't even decide what time to go to lunch? What a conundrum, as has been said by another writer in another time. All of this troubled me greatly; I knew I was trapped by the game, I began hating my job, and I became increasingly hostile toward my employers. Yes, I had had temper tantrums before: Lawd knows, up until this showdown I had often acted a fool up at *Vibe*, screaming at folks, hurling thinly veiled threats, my social skills, back then, about as refined as Bill O'Reilly's or the latest, hottest rapper with a long rap sheet. But now things were different, at least I thought so, because I figured the work I had done, the many ma-jor cover stories, the glory I had helped to bring to *Vibe*, meant I had a voice, some juice, some, well, power. I felt my feet slipping, my head sinking under the waves of my own rage. Determined to change things, the coloreds secretly planned a revolt . . . sort of. As the most visible voice at *Vibe*, I was to lead the protest. But before anything constructive could be done, I allowed the anger, the exhaustion, and the frustration to get to me, and one day I just lost it.

It was a Friday, I know that, but it's a blur in my memory no matter how many times I rerun the tape. I was in *Vibe*'s bright, modern offices, struggling with ancient problems—both within me and around me—when my words, my language felt suddenly, hideously impotent, not up to the task of navigating a solution. I felt myself crashing against the same old rocks, and that hot coal in my chest glowed brighter. Finally, I couldn't control it anymore. I cursed out several staff members—Black, White,

whomever, it didn't make a difference at that point—and I had to be physically restrained. Later that day, I was called in front of the magazine's senior staff after everyone else had gone home for the weekend and was unceremoniously terminated—told, among other things, that I was "unmanageable." I cried like a baby for nearly half an hour in front of the CEO, the editor in chief, and the senior editor, long-repressed emotions rushing to the surface. In retrospect I realize I was especially wounded that the CEO, a Black man whom I had known for years and for whom I had written at another publication he ran prior to his coming to *Vibe*, was the one who lowered the boom on me as the two White male editors sat and watched. (Yes, he was the CEO, this Black man, but he too had to answer to the White check writer above him. A few years later he would leave, making the same argument I had made: that it was wack to call *Vibe* an urban or Black magazine when the people of color there had no bona fide power, including him.) I felt like I had been professionally lynched for being "an uppity, unappreciative nigga" and that a Black man had participated by throwing the rope over the tree branch. Yes, that is how deeply it cut that it was *he* who spat the lyrics, as unsmiling as a hard-rock MC: "You are fired."

For some reason—call it my youthful naivete, call it my stupidity—I was sure I would find employment once more. I did not. I had alienated many, many people during my years at *Vibe*, and some of those individuals were now in a position to decline my job inquiries. One editor said to me, his tone dripping with venom, "I don't have time for superstar writers," and promptly slammed the phone on me. Rejection after rejection led me to believe that I had been whitelisted: *Do not, under any circumstances, have anything to do with Kevin Powell. He is arrogant, unruly, crazy, and prone to temper tantrums.* I was paranoid, thinking folks were taking potshots at me from every bend in the road and that there was an unwritten agreement among industry heads to

destroy my writing career. Meanwhile, my wild spending habits had caught up with me. I had no job, no bank account, no rent money. Because my landlord and I were feuding, I was forced to move from my apartment in the heart of the summer, in the middle of this downward spiral. When the world caves in on you, it seems to cave in from every possible direction. I begged my then-girlfriend to permit me to live with her for a few months until I got myself together. Nothing makes a man feel less like a man, if he has any pride whatsoever, than to have to ask his woman to carry him. Totally depressed, there was many a night when I would come home long after my girlfriend had gone to sleep and creep into bed next to her, reeking of liquor, cigar and cigarette smoke, and the perspiration accumulated from combing the streets of New York. How and why my girlfriend tolerated this is beyond me. I would have thrown me out.

I sank further into depression when I realized that I had to sell my massive CD collection, built over a six-year period. Four thousand CDs gone, in three hours of bargaining, for only one thousand dollars. I had no choice, because my wallet was operating on fumes. I also sold my living room set and other items, but gave my bed to a young female poet who needed one. What did I require a bed for when I had no roof to call my own? The next several months were a haze of drinking, a few therapy sessions, more drinking, and the deterioration of my relationship with my girlfriend. She would go off to work, and I would sit at home and gaze at the television, tired, perplexed, and enraged that one magazine editor after another had spurned me or that some editors expected me, after the numerous cover stories I had done at *Vibe*, to begin anew with menial assignments for what I thought was chump change. Had I been that nasty to people? Had I been wrong to protest? Or had it been the *way* I protested? I was absolutely confused and irreconcilably self-doubting. My ideals and identity—the things I was so sure of such a short time before—were all up for grabs. Who was I? As was the case for so many

of my generation, my work defined me, and—especially when I was riding a wave of success—I liked it that way. But now it was stripped away, and where did *I* begin? Or was all that I had been now gone, stolen from me by men I didn't even respect? And it was then, right there, that the spidery idea of suicide crawled, on prickly legs, into my mind.

I need to add that being one of the so-called stars of MTV's *The Real World* was the beginning, specifically, of my adult-level bewilderment. I had no clue what I was getting myself into when I was picked, along with six other cast members, to be on the first season of this now legendary TV series. It was a fluke that I had even been "discovered": I was at a 1950s-themed Midtown Manhattan restaurant with an R&B band called Joe Public, interviewing them for their record label biography (a way I made a living in those early, happier days), when a smallish White woman approached the table and said she liked our look, then asked if any of us would be interested in interviewing for this new reality-based MTV program. I presumed, unfairly, that the woman was just trying to come on to us Negro studs. But I took the woman's card because my gut told me to do so, thinking that maybe if I wound up on MTV I would subsequently be able to get some college lectures to help pay my bills. I never for the life of me thought that I would become a part of pop culture history, that this would happen in the same year that *Vibe* was inaugurated. I will not lie, either: it was a magical ride—the invite-only, celebrity-riddled parties with an apparently infinite supply of alcohol; the car service whisking me to this interview, to that press conference; the respect I got on the streets in New York City, in Los Angeles, wherever I went in the country, and abroad in London; the money, all the money that came and went buying dinner and drinks for my new "friends" every week as we members of Generation X (isn't that what the "they" who like to advisory-sticker everything young and chic dubbed us?) drowned

in the booming economy of the 1990s. It was our soundtrack, hip-hop—our mission, Andy Warhol's fifteen minutes of fame at any cost and with no shame. Our heroes were Tupac, Bill and Hillary Clinton, the suddenly ubiquitous Sean "Puffy" Combs, millionaire dot-comers, and anyone with the gumption to be their own best logo and boutique business. And our personal credo: *Tomorrow is not guaranteed, so live this day like it is your last, baby!*

It is sheer lunacy, looking back on it, to have lived like this. It was, indisputably, already an acquiescence to a slow form of suicide, an extended adolescence destined to end in death, not adulthood—a brutally abusive love affair with and fatal attraction to the worst attributes of American culture, American capitalism, American me-ism. But how could I, a little Black boy from the ghetto, have resisted any of that? Heck, how could even a wealthy little White boy from the Upper East Side of Manhattan resist any of that? The carrot on the stick is status, influence, and power—or, more accurately, the fantasies thereof. The difference between the Black boy and the White boy, more times than not, is that the White boy knows—and has been taught religiously, virtually from the cradle—that he can aspire to power on his own terms. The Black boy has to erect a fantasy island for himself. That is precisely what I did: I smeared my status in people's faces, so cocksure that others wanted what I had. Nothing wrong with that except I badly overestimated my juice, my power, until it became clear that I had neither because everything I claimed belonged to someone else.

Ergo the survivor's query: what kind of power have we got when we live in a society where our worth is measured by our notoriety and bank accounts, or, in the case of those of us who were mere satellites in this universe, our tenuous connection to those with lots of notoriety and big bank accounts? Too communally insecure to answer this gut-check subpoena, we industry brats rush to the Hamptons; we rush to Martha's Vineyard; we

frequent the trendy, exclusive lounges; we squeeze our way into the nouveau-riche restaurants where we might run into Leo or Gwyneth or Donald or Martha or Jay-Z or any other first-name-only baller/shot-caller; we drink the latest open-bar concoction (glory be, those apple martinis) from liquor conglomerates eager to reach our demographic; we do not mind being depicted as a marketing scheme, a targeted audience; we bling-bling as if we were rappers in those platinum-studded videos and do not care if we are simply journalists, spoken-word artists, publicists, hair stylists, makeup specialists, models, fashion consultants, DJs, party promoters, or just fans—the most derogatory term of all—along for the ride. For thanks to America's pornographic rapport with all things rubber-stamped "celebrity," we got the feeling (vicarious though it may be) that we are doing big things, nahmean, son? As a consequence, we live these terribly pretentious, plastic lives, runaway *and* runway children, truly, who don't want to grow up, thinking this will go on forever. But was it not the omnipotent, omnipresent Puffy who said the sun don't shine forever?

I could go on, but I bet you get my drift. I was so utterly lost that I did not know who I was, could barely recollect where I came from, rarely called my mother, and dug the fact that when my moms and I did speak, she customarily reported that someone from the neighborhood had, once more, seen me on television. Ah, her poor little son, that Black boy with the smile-scowl, had made it to the metaphorical red carpet. It has been said that America eats its young. An addendum: the young will eat themselves if given the proper utensils.

The firing from *Vibe* was a death knell for me. What does one do when the jig is up? Nothing in my life journey had prepared me to climb so high, then be dropped so dramatically low. Life was over, as far as I was concerned, and suicide—the bullet to the head, the poison to the throat, the knife to the wrist—was but a formality. What did I have to lose? Most people don't ex-

pect us Black men to live long anyhow. At least I had achieved my childhood dream of being a published writer, right? No regrets.

But something nudged me, would never allow me to swallow poison or get a gun and blow my brains away. *There must be,* I reflected on the days I was lucid, *some life lessons here somewhere.*

Ironically, I found them when I moved from my girlfriend's apartment to a space, a room, in Harlem. I was pathetically ashamed of my predicament and could not bring myself to seek temporary shelter in the Fort Greene, Brooklyn, hood where I had lived large, flossing for the masses to see. I had come full circle, back uptown, back to a room, living hand to mouth, eating at the same hole-in-the-wall soul food and Dominican restaurants as in 1990, when I had no money. Yes, the human novel lapping itself. This sort of circle confounds the most brilliant among us. At one moment the circle looks like a necessary path; at other times it appears to be a noose dangling above our heads. But in my rented Harlem room I began to find chunks of myself. My landlord was a middle-aged gay Black man, a visual artist, who would come to regard me as a son. I was frightened of life, of people, certain that everyone was fixated on getting at me. I felt like a crackhead who had gone cold turkey without my body's consent. I had been that addicted to the scene, the celebrity, the money. And now I felt undersized, broken, alone, my soul iced and chopped up by a surreal, hazardous lifestyle.

Humanity can be measured in the smallest of acts: the handshake, the smile, the curiosity about another's well-being. When humanity is downgraded to clenched fists, frowns, and a reckless disregard for the person breathing two steps to your left or right, each of us is doomed to an awfully tormented social Darwinism, the individual more important than the community, surviving alone more essential than all of us winning in concert. I say this because the man I lived with, who loved to cook, routinely left

food for me. Otherwise I would have starved, honestly. He did not know me (I had been recommended by a mutual friend), yet he prepared those plates for me, he loaned me money, he talked with and listened to me. *The men in the Harlem kitchen.* That is how I came to frame our bond as I kick-punched the rock-hard residue of homophobia in my bones and saw this amazing human being, the manliest of men I had come in contact with in a very long time. Who cared what the dude's sexual orientation was? He nurtured me the way my father had not, the way the CEO who fired me ultimately did not (I fought him for several months to get a minuscule severance package). And this man, this gay Black man, taught me more lessons about manhood than one would think possible: that one could be a man, be responsible, be kind, be loving, show love, give love, without compromising one's self-worth and dignity. The source of his power—and he was powerful—was in his own simple humanity, his wholly self-possessed life. He taught me, just by being who he was, that without knowing what I was doing, I had leveraged my manhood—no, my humanity—to forces and individuals that were not only beyond my control but were openly hostile to my survival. He did not know me from a can of paint, but he, this man, did these things for me.

I had been guilty of verbally bashing, privately and publicly, men with his sexual orientation as "fags" or "homos." This chance encounter began a reassessment, in another stratosphere, of what it is to be a man, and by whose definitions. I had been among the armies of straight fellas who routinely justify our power(lessness) by dehumanizing men we perceive to be weak or soft. It was me, indeed, who had been weak and soft from the jump, my fragile existence glued in place by the superficiality of my dependence on fame, money, and unmitigated pleasure. As I lay on my thin mattress in the African darkness of Harlem, I would fix my eyes on the ceiling, wondering how I had lost myself so easily to the temptations of the material world. And

I would shed buckets of tears some nights as the shrieks, the screams, and gun blasts of Harlem hovered outside my window like the death stench from a gas chamber. I felt imprisoned by a past I had long sought to escape. Perhaps, I reckoned, this was a reminder that no matter where you go, you can never escape where you come from. That time humbled me in a way I had never been humbled in my entire life. Things that had previously meant a great deal to me—-the magnetic trinkets of the enter-tainment industry—were suddenly meaningless.

I didn't write for a lengthy stretch, and when I finally did—a free article for a college Internet news service—it was as special as my first high-paying piece for a national magazine. And I have been writing and living, fully, since. I now reside in my own apartment, back in Brooklyn, enjoying the unfussy delights of life, like Yankee Stadium, an old movie, a Marvin Gaye song, a Keats poem. I no longer take anything for granted. People often ask, "What are you doing now?" and I beam and respond, "Just living, yo." I stopped drinking altogether when a holistic doctor told me the course I was on would lead to a badly contaminated liver. While I don't believe I was an alcoholic, I do believe I could have become one. My depression and ballooning self-hatred were entrenched in my spirit, for sure.

Nowadays I try to respect myself and other people, although I have slipped on more than a few occasions. The demons are going to be there, on your shoulder, whispering in your ear. I am still very concerned about injustices and still insist I was right about the lack of Black editors and the power struggles at *Vibe*. But the bigger lesson I gleaned from that entire crazy episode is that success defined in a material way means nothing if you are not successful at negotiating the unpredictable terrain of life and if you don't really know yourself. I will, without fail, argue that racism coupled with my unflinching working-class perspective and my bad-boy persona were major factors contributing to my downfall. Yes, each of those things did play a significant role.

But the true measure of any human being, I have come to believe, is your ability to take some personal responsibility to reverse the crack-up, the breakdown, and not be afraid to stop the cycles of self-pity, sit alone in the quiet of your own room, and stitch yourself back together. Because that self you repair is the only thing that's truly yours, the ultimate source of true power. I pray that I never sink to that point again, where life and love—particularly self-love—seem utterly useless and disposable. And I have never wanted to live and love as badly as I do right now.

"Hip-Hop Is the Most Important Youth Culture on the Planet"

Originally published in *Time*
September 22, 2000

TIME: A major museum exploration of hip-hop acknowledges its rightful place in the annals of American popular culture. But doesn't putting something in a museum also imply that it's dead?

KEVIN POWELL: No, putting something in a museum does not imply that it is dead. It implies that it is important, a crucial part of the human journey. The art of Basquiat is not dead, although he has been dead for thirteen years. The art of Bearden, Lawrence, and others is full of life because art is about life, not death. And hip-hop is urban folk art, period. And that urban folk art is about the lives of a very unique group of people, of how they made something out of nothing, and how that nothing has come to define an entire era in many ways, be it our language, our fashion, our attitudes, our art, the way we make music, and the way we do and do not communicate across race, gender, geography, and cultures.

I think the fact that the Rock & Roll Hall of Fame (the originators of this exhibition) and now the Brooklyn Museum of Art have taken on "hip-hop nation" is a mainstream institutional recognition that hip-hop is the most important youth culture on the planet, bar none. And that has been the case for some time.

TIME: Hip-hop's influence over the wider American youth culture is quite without precedent. How did it achieve this tremendous crossover appeal?

POWELL: Viewed in the context of Black music in America over the past century, there's nothing surprising about hip-hop "crossing over." Blues and jazz crossed over in the 1920s, when Whites rushed to Harlem to hear the music. In the 1930s, jazz became—for Whites—"swing." When Black musicians created something called bebop (a clear antecedent for hip-hop) in the 1940s, that too crossed over as Whites gravitated toward the language, fashion, attitude, and music of hip cats like Dizzy Gillespie and Charlie Parker. And I think most people today are clear that it was artists like Louis Jordan and Big Mama Thornton, not Elvis Presley, who created rock and roll and laid the musical foundation that crossed it over to young White people.

You can't talk about American music without talking about Black people and Black musical forms. And you cannot discuss Black music without taking into account its edginess (think of bluesman Robert Johnson, bebop innovator Charlie Parker, rocker Little Richard, soul man Otis Redding, et al.), its rebelliousness (anyone from Big Mama Thornton to Jimi Hendrix), and the fact that edginess and rebelliousness ultimately appeal to White young people as much as they do to Black young people. That and "White music" suffering slumps from time to time made the White embrace of hip-hop inevitable—has there really been anything interesting happening in rock music since the heyday of Nirvana? Not really.

TIME: Of course, this crossover success and hip-hop's current dominance of youth culture has not come without a price. What was the effect on hip-hop of its success?

POWELL: Same thing that has happened to everything else Black folks have done creatively: White folks control it and own it and we remain, for the most part, economic slaves. Pretty basic. And we become slaves to what the "market" tells us we should be buying. And the question I always ask young people when I speak at colleges, community centers, prisons, or wherever: what other people on the planet are allowed (and encouraged, from what I have seen through my many years in and around the music industry) to call themselves the equivalent of "niggas" and "bitches" on CDs that are distributed for mass consumption?

TIME: Is hip-hop the same thing now as twenty-five years ago, or has it transmuted into something quite different? How have the constitution and the borders of the "hip-hop nation" changed?

POWELL: Nothing stays the same. Remember, hip-hop was born on the heels of the Civil Rights Movement, a serious fiscal crisis in New York City and other urban areas, gang activity, etc. Since then we have been through the horrific Reagan era, the invasion of crack, guns, AIDS, and an alleged economic boom in the 1990s—"alleged" because not too many Black people I know, even the ones with college degrees, are anything more than a paycheck away from poverty. Hip-hop has documented all of this, and more. As Amiri Baraka (né LeRoi Jones) stated in *Blues People* (perhaps the most important book on Black music ever written), you can always tell where a people are at by the music they make. That means if you listen to Marvin Gaye's "What's Going On?" or Bob Marley's "Redemption Song" or Fela Kuti's "B.B.C.: Big Blind Country," you can gather what is going on with Black people at various times and in various parts of the world. Hip-hop is no different. It has evolved with the times. Now, whether or not that evolution has been progressive or regressive is another discussion entirely.

TIME: Your exhibition defines the mid-'80s to 1990 as hip-hop's "golden years." What happened after 1990?

POWELL: The "golden years," to me, simply means that was a period when hip-hop or, specifically, rap music was incredibly exciting, fresh, def, and diverse. There was no such thing as positive rap or negative rap, or so-called gangsta rap. Rap was rap: rhythmic American poetry, period. There has not been a time since when an N.W.A was as popular as a Public Enemy, or where the storytelling of a Slick Rick could fall alongside the pimp strolls of a Too Short, or Roxanne Shante was just as necessary as a Salt-N-Pepa or Queen Latifah. A lot of us cats who have lived through most or all of the history of hip-hop are the ones who proclaim that period the golden era. Why? Because we can. And because we know what we are talking about. It has nothing to do with nostalgia. It has everything to do with consistently good music. Back then I used to get excited whenever a new release was coming. This year I can count on one hand the number of hip-hop albums I have been eager to hear (Nelly, Eminem, and OutKast). The corporate takeover of hip-hop has taken away much of the creativity and genius, except for the underground stuff, and that rare album where an artist is allowed to grow and shine rather than being forced to follow a formula.

TIME: Public Enemy proclaimed hip-hop the "Black CNN," and even original gangsta rappers N.W.A said, "*It's not about a salary, it's all about reality . . .*" Does this still hold true? What's happened to the "bearing witness" side of hip-hop? And how do the more mainstream artists view those like Mos Def, Common, the Roots, KRS-One, Black Eyed Peas, etc., the acts that arise in every generation who rededicate themselves to the core values of the socially conscious rappers of the early years—are they the conscience of the hip-hop nation?

POWELL: One thing George Orwell said that I very much agree with is that everything is political, which means, to me, that Nelly or Master P is as political as a Chuck D or Common. What is missing from a Nelly or Master P is a political consciousness that would force them to question WHY they have chosen a certain path and why materialism and hedonism are more important than the conditions of their communities.

That said, hip-hop has always been Black America's CNN. That has never changed. CNN shows all kinds of news, not just "positive" stuff, and that is the same for hip-hop. And hip-hop has never stopped bearing witness. Listen, for example, to Nelly's album very closely. I have been to St. Louis several times, but his album gives the close listener, via the lyrics and the accents and the attitudes, an inside look at Black working-class St. Louis. If that is not bearing witness, I don't know what bearing witness is. A lot of people, unfortunately, expect hip-hop to be overtly political. Well, we live in apolitical times and the art created in America, by and large, reflect the times. Again, how could anyone say something "positive" if there is no consciousness (or consciousness movement, for that matter) there to provide another way to look at and absorb the world.

Also, hip-hop, in spite of being a billion-dollar business, is still the blues of the working poor. And I can say this because this is the world I come from; the working poor are just basically trying to survive from day to day. I find it very classist for people to raise the issue about positive versus negative hip-hop because the same people who raise that issue don't usually discuss the death-baiting conditions which most hip-hoppers come out of. And most cats who raise that issue don't really have much to do with the hip-hop heads they are criticizing. For example, not only am I curating this exhibit, lecturing around the country, writing books, articles, etc., I now manage a young hip-hop DJ and four young hip-hop producers because I felt it important to engage people directly rather than be an armchair critic who

ain't even trying to turn this apolitical madness around. It is safe, to me, to cling to Common (my homeboy), Mos Def (another one of my homeboys), and the other so-called socially conscious rappers. That is what the bohemians here in my Fort Greene neighborhood love to do. But I rarely see these same hip-hop bohemians in downtown Brooklyn shopping on Fulton Street on a Saturday, and I definitely don't see them walking past the Fort Greene projects on Myrtle Avenue. Which says to me there is a fear and a hatred of the working poor and their expressions. The irony of that is that cats like Common and Mos Def embrace the working poor, but a lot of their fans do not.

My basic point: It is real easy to divide hip-hop into camps. The real challenge is to understand *why* hip-hop has deteriorated from the golden era into what we have now, and how corporate interests have played a role in that, and how even the socially conscious among us are guilty of perpetuating ignorance rather than education and self-love, especially among those who need it most: Black and Latino young people.

TIME: The exhibition traces hip-hop's roots to Bronx in the '70s. But what about the Jamaican "sound system" tradition which predated those Bronx block parties, and were clearly a major influence?

POWELL: Hip-hop's roots are not Jamaican, nor Puerto Rican, nor African American, but African. It's part of the continuum of African art forms. In some traditional African societies, for example, we find the "griot," who is the storyteller or oral historian. How is that much different from an MC telling a story (think of Slick Rick, Ice Cube, or Snoop Dogg) or rhyming about the past.

Hip-hop is a collision between African American, West Indian, and Puerto Rican cultures, with the understanding that we are all African people. My point is that no matter where we were

enslaved in the Western Hemisphere, be it Jamaica, Brazil, or South Carolina, we as Black people held on to modes of speech, dance movements, and attitudes (what some call "cool") that formed the foundation for hip-hop's emergence in an African American context.

So the point of the exhibition is to give people an overview of hip-hop culture and history and, really, to encourage people to do their own homework. It is not going to please everyone, but that is the beauty of dialogue, is it not?

Part II

Part II

September 11
November 2001

Might it be, as my mother said to me on this ugly, sinful day
That the world is on its last go-round?
Hijacked wild birds strip the sky of its innocent morning breath
Steel towers crumple like playing cards on an uneven metal table
Unrehearsed screams we dare not hear leap from windows
Into the open, bottomless palms of God
I cannot stand to watch life reduce
Itself to powdery dust and soot lathering the devil's inflamed
mouth
But I am fixated on the television anyhow:
Is this what slavery was like?
Is this what the Holocaust was like?
Is this what famine is like?
Is this what war is like?
Is this how you felt, dear Mother, when King and the two Ken-
nedys were killed?
I want to stitch up the sky, deny humans the right to fly
Cry until my tears have washed hatred
From the mildewed underarms of history
And I want to say to the firemen
Ah, yes, the firemen:
Your husband, your father, your brother, your uncle, your friend
Thank you for speeding to the end of
Your time and thank you for showing us that
Courage is a soul so unselfish it would
Scale a collapsing building to liberate a stranger

Even as your blood relatives wonder if you are alive—
From the remains of this madness
I detect a heartbeat called life
From the remains of this madness
I smell an aroma called love
From the remains of this madness
I embrace a body called humanity
From the remains of this madness
I construct a dream called hope
From the remains of this madness
I will ride the wings of the deceased
Into the clouds, scribble their names on the sun
Erect a memorial to the moon, chant the blues
For New York City, then resurrect a world
Where a newborn rose will jut through the broken concrete.

Looking for America

Originally published in *SPIN*
November 10, 2004

Few will have the greatness to bend history itself,
but each of us can work to change a small portion of
events, and in the total of all those acts will be
written the history of this generation.
—Robert F. Kennedy

I have always kept an open mind, which is necessary
to the flexibility that must go hand in hand with every
form of intelligent search for truth.
—Malcolm X

I have sat in my Brooklyn apartment, quietly, for several days now, too perplexed to talk with many people, friends or not, about the American presidential election of 2004. I have read mainstream and alternative news accounts of the campaign both on- and offline, absorbed statistics and exit polls, sifted through the debates, flipped between CNN and the Fox News Channel, dodged most emails and phone calls coming my way, asking me what I thought it meant that President George W. Bush had won, that Senator John Kerry had lost. I have heard the chorus of Bush supporters say it was Mr. Bush's "faith" that led them to punch the hole, to pull the lever, to touch the screen for the president-elect. And I have heard the chorus of Kerry patrons say they feel robbed, that there must be some vast conservative conspiracy, that they are deeply trauma-

tized, in a state of shock, that they do not know what to do next, nor to whom to turn. I have spoken with my mother, who has voted in every election since she has been able to, dating back to the 1960s and the Civil Rights Movement. And who, with her sharp South Carolina accent and uncomplicated front-porch observations on the world, has always given me something to ponder. My mother, like me, is a lifelong Democrat and her sleepy response was, well, dry, nonchalant, uncharacteristically melancholy: "Boy," she said, "at least we got the chance to vote."

Indeed, Mother, indeed. But has it come to this? Where real democracy, real freedom, real self-determination, is tied, exclusively, to our right to vote? Is the vote it? Twenty years ago, when I was an eighteen-year-old first-year college student at Rutgers University in New Jersey, the vote was the thing. I was stirred by a Southern Baptist preacher named Reverend Jesse Jackson, who, after Congresswoman Shirley Chisholm had done it in 1972, was the only other serious Black candidate for president my community has ever had. Reverend Jackson implored us, young and old alike, Black, White, Latino, Asian, Native American, to keep hope alive, that we were, in fact, somebody, and we believed him, believed that our vote could, would, matter. President Ronald Reagan was reelected, in a landslide that year, and by 1988, when Reverend Jackson ran a second time for president, and came in second in the Democratic primary to eventual nominee Michael Dukakis, many of us felt that Reverend Jackson, with those millions of Rainbow Coalition votes, had the power, the juice, to manifest a new American coalition of progressive people: Blacks, Whites, Latinos, Asians, Native Americans, labor, city and country folks, working- and middle-class people humane enough to care about their neighbors to the left and right; and all those groups that had been marginalized during the Reagan-Bush years. It was, we felt back then, an opportunity to win back the soul of the Democratic Party, to have a party, an organization, that truly reflected the diversity,

the gorgeous mosaic, as former New York City mayor David Dinkins was fond of saying, of America. But, alas, and for reasons only Reverend Jackson knows to this day, a great compromise was struck, the Rainbow Coalition was allowed to wither on an ashen sidewalk in exchange for Reverend Jackson's seemingly cozy relationship with the Democratic Party hierarchy, and many of us young folks became disillusioned with politics for years to come.

I was one of those young people, at age twenty-two, who walked away in 1988, right through the Clinton years, and in spite of Mr. Clinton's youthful appeal and Kennedyesque affectations. I never stopped voting. I could not fathom that inaction as my mother chided me, habitually, that there was a time when we, African Americans, could not vote, that I had an obligation to do so for no other reason than blood, literally, had been spilled, that heads had been smashed, literally, so that I could have a semblance of citizenship in these times.

I say all of this to say it hurt me, immensely, to see so many young Americans, of various persuasions, registering to vote for the first time, volunteering for Mr. Kerry's campaign throughout America, standing in lines in some areas for up to ten hours, then having to deal with the harsh reality that their candidate had lost. It hurt me to see the tears of defeat, to hear the echoes of *Hey, it does not seem to matter what we do, nothing is ever going to change.* There is a sense of confusion, of hopelessness, permeating young America, older America, Democratic America, liberal America, progressive America. Many people believed that MTV, BET, Rock the Vote, the NAACP, the League of Women Voters, Russell Simmons, Oprah Winfrey, P. Diddy, Leonardo DiCaprio, Eminem, Michael Moore, and other popular and well-meaning institutions and icons could, and would, make a difference. Several people believed that because of the Iraq War, the horrible economy, the outsourcing of American jobs, the ugly partitions that have been erected on our soil during the Bush-Cheney years

(Black vs. White, White vs. people of color, Christian vs. Muslim, Americans vs. Arabs, poor vs. rich, straight vs. gay, and so on), that there was no imaginable way that Mr. Bush could get reelected. Many of us assumed, hoped, prayed, that John Kerry, though a mediocre candidate at best, would somehow win this election and get America back on the course of figuring itself out, for the good of us all.

But perhaps this is where the mistake began. We placed more faith in one person, Senator John Kerry, than we placed in ourselves. When Mr. Bush was awarded the presidency in December 2000, after a long and acidic fight that wound up in the United States Supreme Court, I did not, could not, read the newspapers nor watch the news for several months. I felt cheated, that a high crime had occurred. This was the sentiment of many Americans. But while we stuck our heads in the sand, the Bush-Cheney regime took root, its agenda took flight, and before we knew it a tax cut was passed that greatly benefited the rich, September 11 happened, a war on terrorism began, and we invaded, first, Afghanistan, then Iraq. Civil liberties have been eroded under the heading the Patriot Act. And over one thousand American soldiers, mainly young, have lost their lives to date. And the count for dead Iraqis is one hundred thousand, according to several reports.

So we have essentially been in reactionary mode the entire time; we being liberals, progressives, the Democratic Party. We being Americans who know that America does not belong to one particular party, to one particular ideology, to one particular race of people, to one particular history, to one particular god. And as we have been playing catch-up, the incredibly wealthy leadership of the Republican Party has pandered, so very effectively, and with the help of a well-oiled propaganda and marketing initiative, via, among other instruments, talk radio, to blue-collar, rural White Americans, in the Midwest, in the Deep South, catering to their most basic thoughts about God, religion,

and, if we are to be mad truthful, to their fears and prejudices. I was just in the great state of Ohio a couple of days after the election, and it was striking to be in areas where some of the poorest Whites lived, but there, on the windows of their homes, on their pickup trucks, stamped into their minds, was some symbol (a poster, a bumper sticker, a hunch) that Bush and Cheney were on the right side of God.

Somewhere, some time ago, the Democratic Party ceased to be the party of the people, and we have no one to blame but ourselves. We have developed very few leaders who know how to talk with and listen to the masses of Americans. We have shied away from what the party had been about, at least on the surface, during Franklin Roosevelt's tenure, and as manifested in the thoughtful dreams of Bobby Kennedy in 1968, of his brother Ted at the Democratic National Convention in 1980, and of Reverend Jackson for much of the 1980s. And we have allowed the Republicans to paralyze us with paranoia and inertia, thereby forcing us, again and again, to replicate strands of the Republican agenda rather than fulfill our mission of doing what is right, for the people, all people, all the time. I now wonder how many leaders in the Democratic Party actually spend consistent time in their respective communities, in the ghettos, in the backwoods, in the suburbs, on college campuses, in the churches, at prisons, at homeless shelters, at battered women's facilities, interacting with the people, and not just when it is time to rally the troops for votes.

I can say this because, for sure, I have been fortunate, very fortunate, these last several years, dating back to the mid-1990s, to travel America extensively as a public speaker, a political organizer, and a writer, to see life in this nation beyond my city, county, state, region, and I have visited nearly all fifty states, big cities and small towns, densely populated locales and places where I did not see another person for miles at a time. These trips have given me a very different take on America. A fuller,

more comprehensive take. While we remain a nation still embarrassingly segregated due to race, gender, class, region, religion, sexual orientation, and the like, I am also struck by the common stories of alienation, of the multitudes living on the frayed fringes of this so-called democratic nation.

There was the middle-aged White gentleman in New Hampshire I met back in January, at the tip-off to the presidential crusade, who told me he was a Vietnam veteran, that he was driving the cab I was in because there were no jobs for him, that he was on welfare and ridiculously destitute, that he felt the government had been neglectful, woefully neglectful, of Vietnam War veterans. That he was not going to vote, and, as a matter of fact, he had not voted in over twenty years. When I asked him why not, he said, with contempt at the borders of his mouth, that politicians did not care about people like him. When I asked which politicians, he muttered, "All of them."

There was the Black man, early forties–ish, in Texas, Mr. Bush's home state, whom I met only a week or so ago, who, when in his twenties during the Reagan '80s, was falsely accused and convicted of raping a White female. His jury was composed of eleven Whites, ten men, and one woman, and, sadly, in a state like Texas, with its history of sadistic racism (let us not forget that disabled Black man, James Byrd, who was tied to the back of a truck a few years back, by bigoted and demented White males, and dragged to his death), this gentleman did not stand a chance. He lost his youth, he lost his innocence, he lost chunks of his sanity while in prison for a crime he did not commit, and only the use of a DNA test exonerated him, right at the start of Mr. Bush's first term in office. This man now carries in his hip pocket crumpled copies of articles about his case, as well as a crumpled copy of his official pardon, as if he were in another time in American history where one, if Black, had to carry around his or her freedom papers to prove, without question, that one was free.

And I have mentally recorded more tales than I can recount in this space, but the point is that America, this country, our country, continues to be stuck, spiritually, emotionally, in spite of the proclamations of democracy, of equal opportunity, of being one nation under God (which god, and for whom?), of this being the greatest show on earth. If all of us are not completely free, and free in every sense of the word, then, dear friend, none of us are as free as we have been led to believe. And what, pray tell, is freedom anyhow, and what is democracy, when in the alleged most democratic nation in the universe millions upon millions of human beings wondered, and still wonder, if their vote was actually counted on Tuesday, November 2, 2004, and why, for God's sake, did some of them have to present an ID or otherwise prove why they have the right to vote in the year 2004? Is that being free, after all that has happened to make the vote accessible to anyone qualified to vote?

Well, we certainly were not free at the Democratic National Convention in Boston back in July. As happy as I was to be there, I could not help but think, far inside the marrow of my Democratic bones, that it was a charade, a hoax. There was no far-reaching vision, no expansive, humanistic agenda, no imaginative leadership, just, with the exception of brilliant speeches by Hillary and Bill Clinton, Barack Obama, and the Reverend Al Sharpton, a lot of empty rhetoric and unsophisticated retorts to the Bush-Cheney platform. It was evident to me that while the Dems had more A-list celebrities, threw better parties, allowed hip-hop, the forever controversial yet dominant culture of our day, into its sacred halls, it was all dental floss distorting the fact that we had, and have, no teeth on the left, and, really though, have been missing our teeth for some time now.

A month later I attended the Republican National Convention here in New York City and you could feel the focus, the vision, however myopic, and the battle plan. While the Dems barely spoke of faith, of religion, of spirituality, the Republicans

spoke of it every chance they got, and they monopolized the market on moral values. The perception became the reality: the right is of God and the left is of the Devil. And the Democratic Party, the liberals, the progressives, or whatever we label ourselves, have allowed the right to act as if they are more in step with God, with morality, with spirituality, with personal virtue, than we are. This is sheer lunacy, from my perspective as an African American, given that practically every movement, from the antislavery rumblings of the 1800s right through the civil rights era of the 1950s and 1960s, has been led by the spiritual leaders of my community, by individuals who had a deep belief in a higher power, no matter what we called that higher power. And we were always clear that we were on the right side of God, that religion was about liberating and uniting people, not oppressing and dividing the multitudes.

Certainly, we Americans who do not suffer from selective amnesia know something of the hypocrisy of racist White American Christians and their skill at distorting God's words to suit their needs. Let us not forget that there was a time when these very types of Christians manipulated and abused the Bible to justify slavery, for nearly three centuries. Let us not forget that there was a time when these very types of Christians turned their noses up and turned their backs on Jews as they were being stuffed into Holocaust ovens in Germany. And let us not forget that there was a time when these types of Christians, under the guise of representing the true intentions of the Lord, physically assaulted civil rights marchers, Black and non-Blacks alike, in places like Alabama (down south) and Illinois (up north).

The point, dear reader, is that much of the Bush-Cheney agenda has everything to do with fear, with playing to folks' base bigotries. The Southern White Democrats of the 1950s and 1960s (popularly known, then, as "Dixiecrats") used the race card and their interpretation of Christianity to attack the Civil Rights Movement, then slowly but surely championed a mass

exodus of the party (as Negroes got their right to vote) to become the driving force, all these years later, of those too-many-to-count red Republican states we see today. While the race card is still used, albeit in more guarded, coded language, this year the taboo topic was homosexuality, or, rather, same-sex marriages.

And what does it mean that right-wing Republicans, during an election year, can play political football with this polarizing subject, get it on the ballot in several states, while Vice President Dick Cheney's daughter, who is openly gay, is there at the post-election victory celebration, shoulder to shoulder with her lover, her partner, being photographed for the world to see? What kind of hypocrisy is that? Or, better yet, does it not suggest, we people of moral conscience, that many Americans have someone in our lives, a sister, a brother, a son, a daughter, a cousin, a friend, someone from our childhood, someone from high school or college, a coworker, a neighbor, a church member, a pastor (gasp!), who is gay, lesbian, bisexual, transgender, just as Dick Cheney does, but we are too ashamed to recognize their humanity, their existence, so terrified, in fact, to do so that the Republicans can steamroll in and make homosexuality one of the central issues on which we are deemed as spineless, and lacking in morality? Why did anyone not say, boldly, *Look, homie, Dr. King, a man of God, a Christian, a Christian minister, a Christian scholar, worked with Bayard Rustin, a gay man, who was the chief architect of the March on Washington in 1963?* Dr. King may not have agreed with Mr. Rustin's life path, but he at least respected the man's genius, the man's work ethic, the man's humanity, the man's quest for democracy, the man's right to exist. And what could be more Christian than that? And who among us is God, himself, herself, itself, that we are in a position to say what form a person's life should take anyhow?

But we on the left, as Newark's deputy mayor, Ras Baraka, has said of the hip-hop generation, need to grow up. Grow up and ask ourselves: what do we, in fact, believe in? What are

our moral values, our spiritual values? There are many Americans, in the Deep South, in middle America, who believe we have no principles whatsoever, that we believe in nothing more than having a good time. Any extreme is dangerous. That means the extreme of blind religious zealotry, but also the extreme of no boundaries, no agenda, in any form, for our lives, for this nation. Where, then, is the middle ground, where are our souls, and where is the soul of America, or are we simply destined for a certain kind of hell these next four years and beyond?

As I continue to struggle and grow in my spiritual walk, in my Christian walk, in my human walk, I am clear that I don't want to go to hell, nor do I want life in America, for any of us, to be a hellish nightmare. Nor do I believe that the four million votes that separated President Bush from Senator Kerry constitute a mandate. We need to state, emphatically, that they do not. Mr. Bush may be the president, Republicans may control both the Senate and the House of Representatives, but the struggle has only begun. Our work was not in vain. I feel we have awakened a sleeping giant, or, more importantly, the giants, the leaders, in any of us who care about real democracy, real freedom, real self-determination, real people power. The younger Americans who became passionate about politics, about life, about living, in 2004, give me hope. Hope in spite of the fact that more body bags will come home from Iraq. Hope in spite of the fact that extreme poverty is as deadly in America's ghettos as it is in any so-called third world nation. Hope in spite of the ugly divides, the intolerance, the lack of humanity we often show to each other. Hope in spite of the fact that the budget deficit will continue to force this nation to its knees, and in spite of the fact that unemployment and despair have reached epidemic levels unseen since the Great Depression of the 1930s.

Undoubtedly, I think all of us, myself included, because of Tuesday, November 2, 2004, must do a gut check, confront our personal demons (I assuredly have mine and have no problem,

none whatsoever, owning them and working through them), shovel the debris surrounding our souls, struggle against our blatant contradictions, think hard about all the unnecessary fights, arguments, petty jealousies, juvenile competitions, pathetic trips into backbiting and gossip, and ask ourselves, amid another term of Bush-Cheney, *Is this the best we can be in America? Is this what I, we, desire to be, an utterly imperfect human being, wallowing and content to be in a state of arrested development for the remainder of my natural life?*

I am not going to surrender the moral high ground, any longer, to these right-wing activists who pretend to care about the average American, and really do not. And you should cease surrendering as well, if you truly care about freedom and democracy. For if we capitulate in this arena, we will never be able to have any fruitful discussions, debates, and actions about the Iraq War, this destructive economy, the lost jobs, nor about race, gender, class, religion, sexuality, poverty, hunger, homelessness, the environment, the Palestinian-Israeli conflict, the genocidal mayhem in the Sudan, the crisis in Haiti, and every other human drama that demands our attention. And at the end of the day it should not matter whether one is Black, White, Latino, Asian, Native American, or Arab; liberal or conservative; a Democrat or a Republican; Christian, Jew, or Muslim; what should matter is what type of human being you are, what type of human being you aspire to be, and whether you have any regard, any concern, any God-given compassion, true compassion, not just lip service, for other human beings.

And what do we do with that true compassion? Well, if we did not learn any other lesson from the tragedy of September 11, 2001, we should have at least learned this: As the Twin Towers were hit by those two jumbo airliners, as those buildings came crashing from the sky to the earth, as bodies leaped from windows or were crushed beneath the force of that concrete and steel, at that very moment suddenly trivial categories like race,

gender, age, class, sexual orientation, religion, status in society, did not matter. What mattered, on that day, was how one had lived one's life, what one had done with one's life, to advance humanity, be it via the tiniest of baby steps, or via gigantic strides. That is the kind of American I yearn to meet, the kind of America I am looking for.

America did not begin as a real democracy, and in spite of the changes, the upheavals, the lives lost, the sacrifices made, we are still not there, yet. Mr. Bush and his crew need to think again if they believe, truly, that the American people have spoken. No, the last word has not been uttered, the last battle has not been waged. The freedom fighter legacy represents the America I am looking for. Freedom fighter as in Patrick Henry and Harriet Tubman. Freedom fighter as in Cesar Chavez and Fannie Lou Hamer. Freedom fighter as in the multicultural young leadership of today, of young people with names like Billy Wimsatt, Rosa Clemente, L. Joy Williams, Jeff Chang, Farai Chideya, and T.J. Crawford. Freedom fighter as in the millions of young people who voted in this presidential election, who understand, clearly, that they, we, younger Americans, are the leadership we are waiting for. What would the so-called American democracy look like if these folks had not existed, if they did not exist today?

I am looking for an America that will acknowledge, finally, its history of taking Native American land; of using free Black labor to build this nation; of treating women as objects, as invisible second-class citizens; of viewing Latinos as nonspeaking nuisances to be seen, worked to death, but not heard; of marginalizing and excluding, at different times in our history, among many others, the women, the Chinese, the Jews, the Irish, Italians; of scapegoating and isolating the Japanese and, in this new millennium, Arabs, Muslims, gays and lesbians. I am looking for an America that will acknowledge that this nation would not exist were it not for the Native American, the Blacks, the women, the Latinos, the Chinese, the Jews, the Irish, the Italians,

the Japanese, the Arabs, the straight, the gay, the liberal, the conservative, the me, the you.

I am looking for an America that respects every explanation for life, for the creator, the life-giver, the higher power, that entity some of us may refer to as God, that others may refer to as Allah. I am looking for an America that ceases to refer to itself as a Christian nation but, instead, as a nation of many faiths, or many spiritual walks, a nation that has a tolerance and a patience not just for Christians, but also for Jews, Muslims, Buddhists, Rastafarians, Yorubas, all the many belief systems that manifest themselves daily within these borders.

I am looking for an America that does not rely on celebrities, on superstars, to be the leaders of the people, but understands that the real celebrities, the real superstars, the real leaders, are the mill workers, the secretaries, the construction workers, the teachers, the layers of cables and telephone lines, the postal workers, the artists, the grassroots organizers, the bus drivers, the home health aides, like my mother, the military veterans, like my uncle.

I am looking for an America that will have the courage to abolish the electoral college once and for all, that will have the audacity to create uniform and modern voting methods across the land, that will not seek to disenfranchise the most vulnerable persons in this society from their God-given right to be free, to speak their minds without fear of punishment or alienation. I am looking for an America that will no longer attempt to teach other nations how to make democracy work until *we* get it right, and working, here at home.

I am looking for an America that will raise the minimum wage, provide more money for public school education and less for war, an America that will really rehabilitate prison inmates, that will ensure that elders, like my mother, can afford their prescription drugs and have a Social Security program that acknowledges what they have given to this country by way of labor, taxes, and endless loyalty.

And I am looking for an America where through much defeat and pain and suffering we can birth new possibilities, new ways of being and doing. We are not losers, friends, those of us who voted for Mr. Kerry, or, in some instances, against Mr. Bush. I am not, and neither are you. We who believe in real democracy, in real freedom, in real self-determination, who believe in the creative force or forces that placed us on this planet, who believe in the possibilities of humankind, in truth, in justice, in life, who believed that our efforts, our sweat, our vote, could and would count a few days ago, on Tuesday, November 2, 2004, here in America, have nothing to be ashamed of. Nothing at all. Nor should we see the reelection of President George W. Bush and the defeat of Senator John Kerry as the beginning of a great catastrophe for us, for this country. No, what we have is a beginning, a start, with necessary speed bumps along the way. But questions remain for all of us to ponder. What are we going to do to create the America, to create the world, we so desire? And are we, each of us, willing to look within ourselves for that answer?

 # Heaven, Hell, Dave Chappelle

Originally published in *Esquire*
May 1, 2006

No one can imagine what it is like to be Dave Chappelle on this very night. *No one.* Here he is, *the* comic genius of America, curbside at the aristocratic Beverly Hills hotel Raffles L'Ermitage, Hollywood's new celebrity magnet, pacing back and forth, habitually fielding phone calls and thumbing through his BlackBerry and inhaling Camel after Camel as he anticipates a ride to the 2006 Grammy Awards from Chris Tucker, a longtime friend and funnyman frat brother. Disrobed of his customary hip-hop uniform of sagging, ballooned jeans, agitprop T-shirt, tennis shoes (as they say in the Midwest), and a charcoal-black hoodie, Chappelle is wearing a brown pinstripe suit, a crisp white shirt, a coffee-colored tie, and tan leather shoes—very much resembling a young man in a courtroom awaiting his fate. And appearing very uncomfortable, as if he is in the wrong costume for a morality play in which he is the reluctant lead actor. Certainly, it is hard to say what, precisely, is running through Dave Chappelle's mind on this muggy February evening in Southern California. On the surface, at least, he is at once excited and mad nervous.

Excited because tonight, for the first time since his well-documented exit from his hit Comedy Central variety program in May 2005, the critically acclaimed *Chappelle's Show*, he will be in the midst of a constellation of entertainment heavies. In fact, Chappelle will introduce the musical tribute to Sly Stone, the reclusive soul and funk visionary who has not performed in

public since Ronald Reagan was president. Stone, as hearsay has it, had grown to despise the limelight and opted out for a less demanding life.

The irony is not lost on Chappelle, who too made himself scarce when he became unhappy with the executives overseeing his wildly popular franchise and bolted, last May, midway through the shooting schedule, to Africa. So wildly popular and cultish is *Chappelle's Show* that it has broken a number of DVD sales records, in spite of being on the air for only two full seasons to date. And *Chappelle's Show* has been called a singular juggernaut in the annals of American television comedy, a cable show up there alongside *Rowan & Martin's Laugh-In*, *The Carol Burnett Show*, *Saturday Night Live*, and *In Living Color*. But Dave Chappelle has been paying the price of the fame ticket for walking away from a deal worth upward of fifty million dollars. His every public move—on *Oprah*, on *Inside the Actors Studio*, as he bikes down Xenia Avenue in his hometown of Yellow Springs, Ohio—has been dissected, applauded, and, yeah, ridiculed; his paper-thin sanity has been questioned and shredded; his virtual body bandied about by a mosh pit of hands and handlers who've come and gone; and his rubbery soul, the one that believes very quietly yet very deeply in Allah, in the religion of Islam, has been deformed by media, fans, and the player haters. There are websites set up by Chappelle worshippers and fanatics on which Chappelle can do no wrong; and, likewise, there are sites proposing bizarre and warped conspiracy theories on why Chappelle pulled the plug on himself. It seems, these days, if Dave Chappelle merely catches a cold, it winds up in the media or on the Internet.

So it is understandable that tonight Dave Chappelle is nervous. He does not know how his peers will receive him, if at all, for he has done something that is unthinkable for the rich and recognizable: he has openly rejected the glamour, the mystique, the fast money, and the fast life. Chappelle, as he will say again

and again over the nine days I spend with him, simply wants freedom—the freedom to make art the way he feels it should be made; the freedom to live wherever he pleases; the freedom to control his own destiny, his own identity. So even something as minor as the script he has been handed to study for the Sly Stone monologue becomes a raging internal battle for him. *These are not my words. I would never say something like this. Is it weird that I am the one introducing the Sly tribute?* No, Chappelle is not going to do it. There is more pacing, another drag on another cigarette, sidewalk consultation with his publicist. *Okay, I will do it, but I will change it, improvise, make it feel natural, proudly identifying with Stone's legacy of doing things his way.*

As Chappelle rotates the script, like a diploma, between his long brown fingers and walks back and forth once more, Chris Tucker finally arrives. He is not in a limousine nor in a town car but in a bus, a great big tour bus, complete with bodyguard, television set, DVD player, booming stereo system, fully loaded refrigerator, washer and dryer, and bedroom. Not yet dressed for the Grammys himself, Tucker peeps Dave Chappelle's pinstripe suit from head to toe, circles him like a tailor assessing a client, squints his eyes to gain the correct focus, cocks his head the way they do in his native Georgia, then exclaims, with that whiny megaphone of a voice of his, "Man, Chappelle, you look like a preacher who done lost his congregation!"

There is a comfort level that Chappelle feels on this bus with Chris Tucker. It is a safe space before the rush of his evening to come. As Earth, Wind & Fire's "Fantasy" wafts from the stereo system, Tucker and Chappelle engage in the sort of easy, carefree banter reminiscent of childhood pals. Chappelle does not have to explain to Tucker what cross he is bearing, because Tucker understands instinctively. They met in the early 1990s, a period that witnessed a renaissance in American comedy and Black American humor, thanks to what Eddie Murphy had wrought

throughout the 1980s: the comedian as rock star. And if you were a Black stand-up comic, you automatically had that infrared light trained on your forehead, targeting you as the next Eddie Murphy. Chris Rock had it. So did Martin Lawrence, so did Cedric the Entertainer, Bernie Mac, Damon Wayans, Chris Tucker, and, yes, Dave Chappelle. Tucker had his mind-boggling explosion first, becoming a box-office smash and multimillion-dollar star in the process. And today Chappelle is there, or somewhere near there, and it has been a tremendously complex adjustment. As he would say on another day: "It's like someone saying, 'You're the CEO of a $50 million company—good luck!' And then kinda leaving you to your own devices. I've been a comedian since I was fourteen. But I've never really been a CEO."

Tucker and Chappelle disappear to the back of the bus to converse in solemn, hushed tones. It would become a pattern throughout Grammy night, of Chappelle huddling with the likes of Chuck D, Jamie Foxx, Stevie Wonder. You get the impression that Chappelle is both fighting and finding himself amid all the impromptu discussions. Then the Tucker bus barrels into the parking lot of the Staples Center. When it is made known that Chris Tucker and Dave Chappelle are on board, the atmosphere becomes electric. The two old buddies say their goodbyes for the moment (Tucker has to don a suit) and pledge to cross paths at Prince's annual post-Grammy bash in a few hours. In one breath he is relaxed and hysterical with Tucker on the bus, and in the next breath Chappelle, as his loping strides stamp the pavement, is suddenly taut, and in dire need of another cigarette. He fumbles inside his jacket and pants pockets. Light. Drag. Eyes flicker open and shut. Exhale. Sigh. Okay, he is ready for that close-up.

Passing through the celebrity entrance, Chappelle is taken aback by the instantaneous and hearty adulation he receives from parking attendants, security personnel, greeters, laborers, sound technicians, and stagehands. Inside, as he snakes his way through the hordes offstage, there are pounds on the back, firm

handshakes and hugs, and several cries of "Welcome back!" "Are you okay?" and "We missed you!" There is Madonna with an entourage of what seems like fifty. "I think she gave me a dirty look," Chappelle says impishly, although I don't see Madonna see Chappelle as her cloud of bodies whisks her by the *ooohs* and *aaahs*. There is Carlos Santana and Paul McCartney. There is Sting and Jay-Z. There is Green Day, led by frontman Billie Joe Armstrong, running like unabashed groupies up to Chappelle for a picture, testifying to him how much they admire his work. There are the youth, Black, White, it does not matter, here with parents or whomever, screaming—*screaming*—as Chappelle saunters by, begging for autographs and photos, chanting Chappelle catchphrases that have become a part of the American vocab—"I'm Rick James, bitch!" Chappelle is at once tickled and embarrassed by this ruckus, stops for every single person, famous or not, who says his name, then finally makes a beeline to the rostrum to do his Sly Stone bit. There is lengthy applause and an appreciative air. Chappelle basks in it for a brief second, then says, "The only thing harder than leaving show business is coming back." One minute is a lifetime in the entertainment industry, and Chappelle, done and satisfied, swiftly retires to the sound-equipment loading zone, grabs a squat on a golf cart, and lights up a Camel as he digests this Grammy affair—his triumphant return, on his terms—with his publicist.

As he sits there pulling on his cigarette, I rewind to the Dave Chappelle I met in 1993 in New York City via my then girlfriend, an actress who'd attended Washington's illustrious Duke Ellington School of the Arts with him. Then fast-forward to the last time I saw Dave in person, Saturday, September 18, 2004, when he staged and filmed *Dave Chappelle's Block Party* in the very nook of Brooklyn where late rapper the Notorious B.I.G. had grown up. On that rainy September day, Dave Chappelle was, so I thought, at the apex of his personal joy around his successful show, and very much at ease with his spanking-new

notoriety. Dave swam through the crowd, soaking in its love for him, reaching for people as they were grabbing at him. He chastised employees who were taking too long to permit fans through the barricades to see this free concert featuring him, Kanye West, Erykah Badu, and other personalities; and Chappelle made it a point to bring residents on buses, at his own expense, from his Yellow Springs community in Ohio to Brooklyn for this Woodstock-meets-Wattstax gathering. Indeed, Chappelle had financed much of the day, including the film crew, from his own bank account. It was surreal, truthfully, to view Dave Chappelle in this light, because it had been a long time coming.

I remember being at the Boston Comedy Club in Greenwich Village and watching this tall, bone-thin young man with the contagious, toothy smile, the deep-socket, saucer-like eyes, and the perfectly oval head atop a twig of a neck wreck the mic, the stage, and the room like an old-school rapper. Only nineteen at the time, Chappelle was nicknamed by Whoopi Goldberg "the Kid." Even then there was a razor-sharp racial consciousness to Chappelle's material—he had a keen eye for that gray area between social satire and pop culture—and on that occasion I was lucky to witness something very special. Here was the classic working-class intellect of Charlie Chaplin's conniving tramp, the jazzy, in-your-face audacity of Lenny Bruce's birth-of-cool bebopper, and the gut-bucket, bluesy aches and pains of Richard Pryor's dead-on mimes, all in one. There are comedians who have to work at being funny, but Chappelle seemed born to it.

Back at the Grammys, Chappelle discards another cigarette (I've lost count at this point), the show is over, and we head out of the Staples Center to Prince's party. As the rented black SUV nudges its way around West Hollywood, Chappelle is relieved. "I didn't know what to expect, even though I swear Madonna gave me a dirty look." Laughter pops inside the SUV as we arrive at Prince's mansion. And what a mansion it is. Tall iron gates. Beige granite with the numbers of the address deliberately jumbled. A

swarm of chiseled, no-neck security men. Parking valets zigzagging from vehicle to vehicle. A gothic doorman with black eyeliner, black fingernail polish, and a black tongue ring, standing there with a guest list on a clipboard. "Is this a club or Prince's home?" Chappelle asks no one in particular. Dave Chappelle is not on the sheet, but he's admitted after Prince himself is told who is waiting outside the iron gate. A shuttle van is sent down to ride us up the hill to Prince's palace. It is a thirteen-second excursion we could have done by foot.

If Dave Chappelle is hyped to be here, he does not show it, and as we go by two hostesses at the colossal threshold to Prince's home, one of them says to Chappelle wryly, "You need to thank Prince for letting you in." No reaction from Chappelle, but he does make it a point to spot Prince, promptly, and walks right over to thank him for his hospitality. Although Chappelle stands nearly six feet and is long and wiry, it is the elfin Prince, in natty outfit—a blue blazer, white slacks, white shoes—who is the Goliath in this instance. Dig if you will this picture: Chappelle's a kid all of a sudden, the pubescent Dave who worshipped Prince in the 1980s. His gaunt face is tight and nervous, and his gleaming eyes bounce like ping-pong balls from the Purple One's face to the hardwood floor. But ain't Dave Chappelle famous too? And for sure, dues-paying members of the fame club are omnipresent and accounted for at this joint: Mariah Carey, Alicia Keys, Jeremy Piven from HBO's *Entourage*, and Morris Day and the Time, the headliners for the evening.

But rather than indulge in the festivities, Chappelle retreats outdoors to the patio area, to a double-back chair positioned against a back wall next to one of four bars operating this evening. Swirling around him are servers feverishly rotating finger foods, music royalty like Carey, Jermaine Dupri, and Common powwowing near the kitchen, industry check writers making deals over cocktails, industry wannabes swapping business cards and phony pleasantries, party crashers whispering, pointing, and

stargazing, and Morris Day and his sidekick, Jerome, working the crowd into a sweaty frenzy as the band whips through its classic songs like "777-9311." But Dave Chappelle sits, and sits, and sits, from round midnight to after four a.m., methodically smoking his cigarettes, sipping on spring water, eating the cupcakes floating on the server trays, and engaging anyone who sits down next to him. He looks uncomfortable in this scene. Indeed, slouching low in the chair, his spine curved into a tight knot, Dave Chappelle looks as if he is hiding: hiding from his peers, hiding from the attention, hiding from that part of himself that is a major star.

After all, Dave Chappelle is really just a simple Midwestern homeboy, with uncomplicated, wholesome Midwestern values, who happens to have a bottomless well of talent.

Through the course of the evening, from Raffles L'Ermitage to the Grammy Awards to his cushiony seat as a spectator at Prince's party, Chappelle seems to be having an out-of-body experience. It is him, but then again it is not him at all. Or, rather, as he says to me during one of the many hours we are there with Prince and company, "Man, I don't drink, I don't dance, I don't party—this ain't really my thing." Problem is that when you become an icon, as Dave Chappelle has become, it does not matter what you want. The people want *you*. And so Dave Chappelle is trying to understand how to give the universe what it demands of someone with his calling while keeping some version of himself for himself. And that is why he refuses to do a Hollywood shuffle, ever. What is evident, here at Prince's mansion, as his bottom remains pasted to that chair, is that he is not going to budge, not now, not for just anyone.

At the close of the night, Chappelle finally leaps from his seat when he eyeballs music impresario Quincy Jones. Like a little boy, he shyly introduces himself, but of course Jones knows who he is. When Chappelle was a student at Duke Ellington, Jones came to screen the documentary film *Listen Up*, brought

copies for the school, and books of the same title for the entire student body. Chappelle tells me that Jones came into the auditorium while he was onstage doing comedy, and that goose bumps covered his body. "You never really stop looking at these people as how you saw them as a child, as a kid," Chappelle says in reference to Prince, to Quincy Jones, to Eddie Murphy, his boyhood idol. "I mean, man, I *love* them."

And they love Dave Chappelle, but Chappelle truly believes, in his heart, he is not part of the club. "Look at where I live, man. I don't have that kind of connection with me being famous. Fame for me is like a place, a country I'm taking a tour through. You just don't walk around feeling like, *I'm a goddamn star.* You walk around feeling like *you*."

Chappelle, as it turns out, stays too long in Los Angeles. He is moving in too many directions, is too unsure of himself in that environment, too cryptic about those phone calls he is retrieving from lawyers, colleagues, whomever, which leave him one minute elated and the next very obviously on the edge of dismay and anger. And when he ultimately has enough of the sun, the shades, the posturing, Dave Chappelle decides he is going back to Ohio, to be with his family, to detach himself, for a few days at any rate, from the showbiz machine.

Yellow Springs is a sleepy outpost in southwest Ohio, population hovering near four thousand, and address of the ultraliberal Antioch College, where Dave Chappelle's late father was once a professor. Everyone seems to know everyone, everyone speaks, nods a head, or proffers a wink, a peace sign, or a thumbs-up. The Underground Railroad, that gateway to liberation for escaped slaves from the South, ran through some of Yellow Springs' older dwellings, with secret hideouts still intact. And it is in this mostly White community of artists, intellectuals, and activists that you can get a supersized cup of espresso or herbal tea at Dino's Cappuccinos, a vegetarian meal at the Sunrise Cafe, and

be Dave Chappelle, regular American citizen. Practically from the hour he hits the pavement on Xenia Avenue, the hub of this remote village, Chappelle is rejuvenated.

There he is borrowing a random kid's skateboard and darting skillfully between moving and parked cars. There he is chasing one of his two teeny sons, like a giant monster, into his family-pack Toyota SUV. There he is teasing and making faces at his lovely wife, a petite Filipina from Brooklyn. And there he is, in a montage of scenes, with his brother, home for a spell from his postgraduate religious studies in California; with his sister, clad, like Chappelle's brother, in full Muslim garb; and with his mother, a prominent African American Studies scholar and the first Black woman in this country to be named, in 1981, a Unitarian Universalist minister. And his mother, too, is a Muslim.

For Dave Chappelle, there is a tranquility about this town, where no one probes his or his family's faith or personal lives; where no one asks for an autograph or photo but once during the five days I am here with him; where an employee at Yellow Springs' lone movie theater shrugs her shoulders indifferently when told, by Chappelle himself, that *Dave Chappelle's Block Party* will be coming soon; where he, in spite of the change in environment, blazes cigarette after cigarette like a fireplace burning log after log. Except here in Yellow Springs, his lips do not clamp down as hard on the cigarette, and the sucking in of nicotine is not as resolute as it was in Los Angeles.

But Dave Chappelle is still not entirely at peace. And he is finding himself incapable of pausing to talk. *I don't think I can do this*, he says. In a way, he still seems to be fleeing whatever he was fleeing when he left for Africa. He is in constant motion, pacing up and down Xenia Avenue on the cell phone and thumbing, as usual, through the BlackBerry. And each time we settle into Dino's or the Sunrise to talk, it is not long before he is up again, his mind and soul so tormented, it appears, that he is not

even sure enough of who he is at this very moment to talk about himself. It is not until I am here for two days that we climb into Chappelle's Toyota and begin driving in circles around Yellow Springs, during sunlight and late at night for hours, for three straight days, and he begins to speak.

It comes in a swirl, impressionistic and crackling funny, and Chappelle's reticence is swept away in a cascade of words and turns of the steering wheel. "I got crib memories. I can remember people looking down at me when I was in the crib. I have a *loooong* memory. Perfect for holding grudges! . . . In the last year, I started getting perspective on how my machine works—my joke machine, or my creative process. Which is at odds with how this business works to some degree, 'cause I'm a complainer by nature, which is just part of my machine . . . I left in pre-crack Washington and came back in post-crack Washington, so I got the before-and-after picture. It was literally jolting, like, *What the fuck happened?* My freshman year of high school, over five hundred kids my age were murdered . . . Miles Davis said it was his fantasy to choke a White man, but he made some of the best music he ever made with Gil Evans. It's like artists can transcend race like nobody can . . . I finished my first show and the crowd went fuckin' nuts. All the comics were in a lounge, and they go, 'How old are you?' And I said, 'I'm fourteen.' And they said, 'Goddamn' . . . Years later I was pulling up to a hotel in DC—I had a nice car at the time—and I get out and this old White man is the valet, with a red sweater on. And I hand him the keys, he hands me a ticket, and he goes, 'That's not my car.' He goes, 'I wish it was my car.' And I go, 'Oh, yeah, that's nice, thanks.' So then, finally I realized—I'm thinking he's the valet, and he's thinking I'm the valet. But I said, 'Well, at least I was thinking that 'cause you have on black slacks and a red sweater.' He was thinking that 'cause I have Black skin [*laughs*], 'cause nothing about me was lookin' like a valet . . . I'm the first person in my family that wasn't a slave, that didn't go to college.

My great-grandparents were slaves and still went to college . . . Suffering and humans go hand in hand. Look at comedy. It's dominated by Black people and Jewish people. That is American comedy. And if Blacks and Jews didn't do comedy, we'd be relying on the Irish. 'Cause they were the next-funniest thing . . . The only movie they kept offering me over and over was fuckin' *Soul Plane*. They kept giving me the script and I'd say, 'I passed on this script.' And it would just keep coming back. 'No, I don't want to do *Soul Plane*!' . . . Maybe the pendulum is swinging back and people want entertainment that has a little more substance. Dude, the number-one song on the radio is 'Shake That Laffy Taffy.' There's a group of people out there that rebel against that. Like, *This is the shit you're cramming down my throat? 'Shake That Laffy Taffy'?* . . . Genius is such a grandiose term. I didn't do it all by myself. Sometimes I get credit for things I don't really deserve. And other times I *don't* get credit for things that I *do* think I deserve . . . This phrase kept coming up: *It's not personal, it's just business.* If you ever hear a White man say that, even if you are White, run for your motherfucking life. When a person tells you something's not personal, it's just business, that means some ice-cold shit might be about . . . I want to, like, play Sambo, but I want to give those characters some depth. No, just kidding. No, I'm just kidding, man . . . You know, nowadays it ain't easy to be *any*goddamnbody."

And Dave Chappelle flows so freely now, on and on, his Toyota SUV seemingly a safe space, a therapist's couch. Round and round Yellow Springs until I have the town memorized and we're mainlining the coffee. Until, on one particular side street, Chappelle presses the brakes and prods the vehicle along and mutters somberly, "That is where my father is buried." It is a quaint, one-story stucco home. His dad's grave is in the backyard, and his widow, Chappelle's stepmother, a White woman, is home right now. We drive on, and I think back to when I first met Chappelle, how he'd introduced me to a young White man

whom he described as "my brother." Today it makes sense. It was his stepmother's son.

It is this sort of double consciousness into which Dave Chappelle was born in Washington, DC, on August 24, 1973, in the shimmering shadow of Watergate and Vietnam, amid civil rights–era residue, a precocious boy who, by his own account, had a very happy childhood. His father, "a hippie," held down a corporate job for years as a statistician but was really a lover of music, of art, of books, a man with an IQ of 185. His mother, the more overtly rebellious of his parents, once worked for the revolutionary Patrice Lumumba in the Congo and was an independent thinker and dedicated intellectual, constantly reinventing herself in the pursuit of a better grasp of life. Though together only for the initial brushstrokes of Dave Chappelle's life, the two shared duties in shaping the mind of their youngest child. "Growing up, I knew kids who lived with both their parents that didn't have as close a relationship with their parents.

"I grew up in Silver Spring, Maryland. We were like the broke Huxtables. There were books around the house, everybody was educated to a college level. We used to have a picture of Malcolm X in Ghana. Last Poets records. We were poor but we were cultured."

And there was the home education money could never buy: little Chappelle sitting among adults as they watched and debated *To Kill a Mockingbird*. Organizational meetings to abolish racism. Regular visits by people as diverse as folk singer Pete Seeger and jazz balladeer Johnny Hartman, the only singer ever to record with the legendary John Coltrane. In fact, on one visit it was Hartman, noticing that the seven- or eight-year-old Chappelle had a knack for humor, who first planted the seed of his being a comedian.

"I was the funny dude. I was real comfortable with adults. I was cutting up in front of Hartman and he was like, 'Man, you're a funny kid.' And he says to me, 'You're gonna be a co-

median.' And I was like, 'What's a comedian?' And he's like, 'It's a guy who tells funny stories for a living, like Richard Pryor or Redd Foxx.' I said, 'I want to be a doctor.' And he was like, 'Eh—'"

And why not? African Americans of Chappelle's generation, carried along in the wake of the Civil Rights Movement, could be anything, they were told. For they were the first generation of Blacks to be raised in an integrated America, to attend multiracial schools, to have friends of many backgrounds. "I use to hang out with the Jewish kids, Black kids, and Vietnamese immigrants," says Chappelle. The truth is, many African American parents like Chappelle's struggled and sacrificed so that their children would not have to, so that they could attend a different kind of school, live in a different kind of neighborhood, dream a different kind of world. What they conceived, ultimately, was the first wave of African Americans who were what the writer Trey Ellis once described as "cultural mulattoes." Born to two progressive Black parents, one a we-are-the-world bohemian, the other firmly rooted in Black nationalism in Washington, DC ("Chocolate City," as dubbed by Parliament Funkadelic), Chappelle followed his father, during his middle-school years, to Yellow Springs, where his friends and his new family were suddenly, well, White, which created this unique capacity to stand out and blend in, to cross boundaries and set up roadblocks, to make fast friends and quick foes. Or, as the Black sage Dr. W.E.B. Du Bois wrote, "One ever feels his two-ness—an American, a Negro; two souls, two thoughts, two unreconciled strivings; two warring ideals in one dark body, whose dogged strength alone keeps it from being torn asunder."

On my last night in Yellow Springs, Chappelle takes a path foreign to me. When I ask him if this is the sixty-five-acre farm, his "anti-Hollywood estate," as one journalist coined it, Chappelle smiles mischievously and says, "Uh, this is one of my houses.

I'm going to smash a rock over your head and take those tapes. You'll never know which house I'm living in." Because it is pitch black, save some strategically arranged lighting sprinkled about the property, all that can be said about Chappelle's real estate is that it is expansive.

Back on the familiar route, Chappelle noses the SUV through and around the empty streets of Yellow Springs with much on his mind. His face, creased with a smile just a second before, droops. He is a man with monumental decisions to make. The Comedy Central haze is so damn thick that Dave Chappelle wants to say, *Fuck the world! All of it,* but he knows that he cannot. It is evident now that there is pressure from all sides for him to return to the show, to pay off former associates (or deal with the legal consequences); that he is saddened by the wedge that has been driven between him and others, most notably Neal Brennan, his former longtime friend and writing partner on *Chappelle's Show.* This is the crux of why Dave Chappelle left the show, why he went to Africa to breathe amid his stunning success, why he prefers life in Ohio. He doesn't like to feel, as an artist, as a comedian, as a Black man in America, like he is being controlled, told what he should and should not be doing—ever. This is why, at the close of each episode of *Chappelle's Show,* there is that image of a shirtless Chappelle with slave shackles on his wrists. This is why Chappelle prefers live stand-up to television, and especially to Hollywood films. And this is why, throughout the course of these final few hours together, Chappelle repeatedly brings up David Mamet's recent *Harper's* essay, "Bambi v. Godzilla: Why Art Loses in Hollywood," as well as Spike Lee's hotly debated flick *Bamboozled.*

Then, out of the blue, he begins talking candidly, for the first time, about his conflicts with Comedy Central, his voice lower than before, his words coming a little more slowly.

"I don't want people to think that I feel completely victimized. Like, I always try to make a point of trying to acknowledge

the fact that I made mistakes in this process. But believe me, I wasn't making 'em by myself. As a matter of fact, I had an enormous amount of help making mistakes. More help than I get when I'm doing the right thing.

"So basically the renegotiation during the show's second season was what it was. I felt like I was really pressured to settle for something that I didn't necessarily feel like I wanted. The DVD comes out, it's a whole 'nother ball game. Everyone's asking me, 'When you coming back, when you coming back? You'd do it for x number of dollars, wouldn't you?' Like, real specific questions, and it was like, *I don't know*. You know, I just got real tight-lipped about shit, because the same questions kept coming up over and over, you know, so when that happens, you stop assuming that these are idle questions. You start assuming that somebody wants to know something, and they're asking you via a bunch of different people. And if I would divulge that information, and I did want to come back, it would give me a very weak negotiating position if they knew what I would do something for. Common sense. 'Nigger, be careful' is what they say on the streets, right?"

Chappelle asks me to turn off the tape recorder. Should he vent, should he be careful? He sparks a cigarette and continues.

Between the first and second seasons, Comedy Central was sold. "There was a lot of new faces. Viacom had acquired the entire asset of Comedy Central. Certain things happened that were strange at the time." Chappelle straightens his back and mimics the voice of an older White executive: "'Dave, we're having a symposium on the n-word, and we wanted you to speak about your use of it. It's just for our information.' And I did it, but afterward I was like, *That was real stupid of me*. Why the fuck would I explain to a room full of White people why I say the word *nigga*? Why on earth would I put myself in a position like that? So you got me on a panel, me and all of these, like, Harvard-educated, you know, upper-echelon authors, me, and a rapper. So here I am explaining, and I was real defensive 'cause

of what was going on at the show at the time—we had just shot the Niggar Family sketch, and I was at a symposium on the word *nigger*. So I'm feeling like I'm fighting censorship. They say, 'We just want to know how far we should go with something like that.' And the subtext of it is, *Do you want to know, or do you want to tell me something?*

"You have all these Harvard-educated people saying, 'I think the word is reprehensible,' and talking about the destructive nature of blah, blah, blah . . . You know, pontificating."

Silence. A sigh.

"But the bottom line was, White people own everything, and where can a Black person go and be himself or say something that's familiar to him and not have to explain or apologize? Why don't I just take the show to BET—oh, wait a minute, you own that too, don't you? Same thing happened with the Rick James episode. They gave us the notes and there were like forty-six or some insane number of bleeps that we would've had to put over it. 'Well, Dave, then why don't you go in and explain to them yourself.' So now I'm sitting in a room, again, with some White people, explaining why they say the n-word, and it's a sketch about Rick James, and I don't want to air a sketch with that many bleeps over it; it will render it completely ineffective. Give me another week and I'll just come up with something else. Run a rerun. 'No, we can't run a rerun, we've got ad buy-ins and blah, blah, blah.' Okay, well then, fine, I don't want to do it then. And so then there was a compromise. It was the only episode that aired with a disclaimer. But again, it was a position where I was explaining to White people why the n-word. It's an awful, awful position to put yourself in.

"I'm just saying it's a dilemma. It's something that is unique to us. White people, White artists, are allowed to be individuals. But we always have this greater struggle that we at least have to keep in mind somewhere." Particularly if you, like Dave Chappelle, hail from a family of intellectuals and if you, like him,

have been studying history since you were a child, are attuned to the world in a particular way, have a great-grandfather who is remembered in the Smithsonian Institution, and believe, in your heart, that you are a bridge builder between different cultures. That you can have close friends, like Neal Brennan, who are White, a wife who is Asian. That you have the right (and the bruises) to use the word *nigga* any way you choose. But at the same time, you feel that you also have a specific responsibility to Black America, that you have to think about the sights and sounds you put out there on television because you are not interested in being merely a source of enjoyment for White America at the expense of Black America. This is what occurs when Black art goes pop, and that Black artist happens to have a functioning soul. *One ever feels his two-ness—*

For sure, it is Chappelle's birthright to talk, provocatively, in his art, about race in America. Yet somewhere in that process of journeying from a grossly underestimated comic to the funniest man in America, Dave Chappelle began to feel trapped by the reactions from the suits, from the fans, from the media, from the scholars, from that voice inside his head. *These jokes are dangerous in the wrong hands,* he would say. That pressure, from all sides, from himself, would lead you, if you were living inside Dave Chappelle's head, to make a mad dash away from the money, real and projected, the fame, the pressures to do season three, of being labeled a brand, an icon, a genius. Just to think—

He drives on, through the dark Ohio night. "I'm in a much better place than I was when I went to Africa. And now things are starting to make more sense, like a fog that's lifting. But there's a part of me personally that's still like a work in progress. It's like the blood's rushing back into me. I feel more optimistic, more hopeful. But I still don't have the definitive course. People are thinking that I'm out here to avoid fame, and that's not it. What I'm trying to avoid is corruption."

And what of the relationship with Neal Brennan, who worked

the door at the Boston Comedy Club as Chappelle first began to make a name for himself? When Chappelle was in Africa, Brennan told *Time* of an exchange he'd had with Chappelle, in which he said he had told the comic, "You're not well." Now parking on Xenia Avenue, the lone vehicle on the strip, Dave Chappelle pushes a sigh up from his chest, rolls his window up and down to blow out cigarette smoke, and weighs in on the question.

"I think Neal is a brilliant dude. We were close, man. These situations are intense. I'm sad. I'm not going to say I am angry. I *was* angry. The thing about show business is that, in a way, it forces dysfunctional relationships in people."

Chappelle falls dead silent one final time, not wanting to say too much about his former partner. Lights another cigarette. Blows. Talks again, becoming nostalgic as he fans the smoke and the subject away from Brennan.

"I have to say, it was by far the best experience I ever had working in television. When you hear me say, like, 'I quit,' and all this stuff, I mean, that was literally just like the tension and the dramatic situation of creating something. And the network executives have their responsibilities and I have *my* responsibilities, so this is a natural tension of these relationships. By far, it was better than any situation I ever had in corporate television. It was like taking somebody on a tour through a young Black man's subconscious, and I don't think America has been there. So in a way it was kind of like reality TV, right?"

As he steers his Toyota home, I ask him, if not *Chappelle's Show*, then what is it that he wants to do next? Beaming with that mischievous grin again, Dave Chappelle tilts his head against the driver's seat, shoots smoke out of his mouth like an erupting volcano, then says, deadpan, "Spit hot fire."

He laughs. "I want to tell my jokes. I want to have time with my children. I want to entertain people. And at one point, I'll walk away from show business. But I don't want to walk away empty-handed."

September 11 (excerpt)

Originally published in *Someday We'll All Be Free*
September 2006

But what is terrorism? We have been bombarded with the term so much since September 11 that I made it my mission to search for as concise an explanation as possible. One thing is evident from my painstaking research: there is *no* universal definition and, oftentimes, how terrorism is interpreted depends on who is doing the interpreting. But, for the sake of this essay, here is a make-it-plain reading of the word terrorism:

> *The systematic use of violence to create a climate of fear in a person, group, or population to bring about a particular (political) objective.*

What might those folks have felt that innocent morning, inside the World Trade Center towers, when one then a second plane torpedoed their lives? What might those folks have felt as they bellowed for help, phoned loved ones, stuck out their chests, and shook hands with death? Terror: a sensation no human being who has *ever* lived life on the chapped bottom lip of the earth's mouth could possibly fathom. Death. A sudden, nerve-racking, premeditated death, planned by someone, somebody, some institution or organization or network or government. Death. No regard for human life, for the brutal pain of your heart galloping into your throat, washed back down to the pit of your gut by mucus and the gloomy resignation that your

flesh, your bone, your breath, will be no more. Death. Your soul standing butt-naked, battle-scarred and bloodied, before God . . . And the preacher shouted and the church choir sang, once more, of terrorism—

The systematic use of violence to create a climate of fear in a person, group, or population to bring about a particular (political) objective.

Given this definition, these words we sing, might it possibly be that September 11 was not the first day that we human beings witnessed what could be defined as terrorism? Violence, yes, the foundation of terrorism. Physical force, yes, for the purpose of violating, damaging, destroying. Emotional and spiritual violence too, for the purpose of violating, damaging, destroying. *Why do they hate us?* The speed of the violence, of the terrorism, can be quick and decisive—as what occurred on 9/11. Or it can be methodical, planned, measured, like a slow homicide. Yes, slow terrorism. Quick-fast, slow, does it matter, really? It is still that evil word, that evil deed.

Terrorism, as in those quote-unquote brave hearts of the mythologized European explorers' movement—best symbolized by Christopher Columbus—who made their way to this part of the world, christened it the New World, christened it the Americas, the West Indies, the Caribbean. Terrorism, as in how they erased nations of millions we know as Indians, person by person, original dweller by original dweller, with tactics and values which resulted in nothing less than wholesale genocide. How many tens of millions were held captive? How many generations were destroyed? How many lives are still affected today because of the peculiar appetites of those explorers, those settlers, and their financial backers? *Why do they hate us?*

* * *

Terrorism, as in what slave traders and slave owners did to Africans, hunting them like animals in their native land, capturing and kidnapping them, incarcerating them like exotic specimens, torturing them, beating them, screwing them—literally and figuratively—tossing them overboard, leaving them little else to do but to toss *themselves* overboard, leaving them little else to do but to commit infanticide, dragging them to some strange scene to make them work for free, because the god who ordained slavery said so, and that god said it was mad cool to disrobe a people of everything they knew, make them hate themselves and love everything about the master and his way of life. How many tens of millions were held captive? How many generations were destroyed? How many lives are still affected today because of that peculiar institution? And why haven't the ancestors of these slaves been given one shiny brown Abe Lincoln penny in reparations? *Why do they hate us?*

Terrorism, as in what the British did to the Chinese from the 1830s through about 1860. The major drug-trafficking organization in the world during that time, the British government, grew opium in India through its East India Company, then shipped tons of it into China in exchange for manufactured goods and tea. But was it a righteous trade? It produced a nation of opium addicts, pre-crackheads, if you will, with opium parlors everywhere. How dare the Chinese, under the leadership of Lin Tsehsü, rebel finally in 1839, against this purposeful assault on its shores? The Brits—bad, bold, and brazen—had the gall to have anti-opium laws on the books for its people in England, but saw nothing wrong with dumping the stuff on other countries. *Resist resist resist* the poet Sonia Sanchez is fond of chanting, and the Chinese tried. The Opium Wars, for the next twenty-one years, were on and poppin', as we say. The British military muscle prevailed. When the dust had settled, opium was legalized in China; an indiscriminate export of Chinese nationals by the British to

their colonies in the Caribbean (and to America—fundamentally forced, cheap labor); and families, communities, generations, suffered through the effects of this legalized drug hustle. *Why do they hate us?*

Terrorism, as in what occurred on Saturday, March 25, 1911, at the Triangle Shirtwaist Factory, a ten-story structure in the Greenwich Village neighborhood of New York City. Approximately five hundred employees, by and large young Italian and Jewish immigrant girls (some as young as fourteen or fifteen years of age), were rushing to meet their quotas for the day. These girls and young women were kin to the swarms of destitute Europeans who fled the wintry wretchedness of the old country from the mid-1800s to the early 1900s, to land on Ellis Island with only cardboard suitcases and the clothes on their backs, and then marked, stamped, and pushed into slums, tenements, and sweatshops; into a working-class dungeon; into a prison for the bottom half of society. An imprisonment that incorporated disease, famine, substandard wages and working conditions—and no rights whatsoever. So these women slogged and slogged until four forty-five p.m., a mere fifteen minutes before the end of the workday. Someone, it has been suggested time and again, dropped a match or a cigarette on the floor. Fabric or tissue paper burst into flames and the fire spread rapidly. These women were working on the eighth, ninth, and tenth floors. While some were able to escape via elevator, many did not. Specific doors were locked by the employers to keep union organizers out, particularly since these workers had struck a year before, a strike which called, as fate would have it, for better safety precautions and more sanitary conditions. The factory floors became an incinerator. Panicked, terrified of the fire, these girls and young women began to jump from the windows, plummeting to the streets. The hard thud of a speeding body was unbearable to watch. *Thud.* One, then another. *Thud. Thud.* And

another. *Thud.* Suddenly a heap of dead bodies. *Thud. Thud. Thud.* The odor of hot boiling blood, everywhere. Flattened, contorted bones jutting from purple-veined skin, everywhere. And inside the burning building were the bodies jammed against doors, unable to escape. Charred bodies, burned to a crisp, and some found bent over sewing machines. Bodies gone but souls still at work. The final tally: 146 dead, with some of the bodies completely unrecognizable. This towering inferno roared and extinguished in less than thirty minutes. And the owners, the employers, two men, suffered no hardship, no conviction, and were permitted to resume business, in another location, within two weeks of this tragedy. *Why do they hate us?*

Terrorism, as in the Third Reich, Hitler, Nazi Germany. Terrorism, as in the very deliberate and diabolical mission to scapegoat the Jews, to disenfranchise them, to wipe them and the Jewish faith from the face of the earth. Millions of bodies purged, forever. Remember their names, and we say Kristallnacht. Remember their names, and we say Auschwitz. Remember their names, and we say Dachau. The world was watching God as the Devil built concentration camps, orchestrated death marches, engineered mobile killing squads, and used the gas chambers as both courtroom and extermination camp. Splintered families like scattered tree branches chucked, aimlessly, into a faceless well. Orphaned children like miniature fingers axed off, detached, removed, one by one, from two puffy, rubbery hands and tossed, carelessly, into a simmering trash bin. Dingy, striped garb like the melancholy outer coating of a blue-toothed mutt whose rusty brown mouth drips the foam of noiseless disillusion. Body markings like blowtorched hieroglyphics on the head, hand, chest, and back; coded language for the refugees who have buried themselves, alive, inside their own meatless feces. Scraped bald heads like distant, dying light bulbs that bleed, from metallic, matted eyes. *Help. Help. Help.* The sharpened, razor-blade promise of a

rock-hard death as assured as one's final rickety pulse. *Why do they hate us?*

Terrorism, as in the horrific ritual of female genital mutilation. Imagine the terrific fear of a young African girl, eight, nine, ten years old, taken from her home with the consent of her family to a river, where she is blindfolded, peeled naked, forced to lie on her back, as two people hold her legs, another sits on her chest, and a fourth person stuffs a piece of cloth into her mouth to short-circuit the shrieks of agony. Then the vaginal area is meticulously shaved. Then a pause. Silence. Then the operation begins. Cut. Rip. Cut. No anesthesia. Trauma, shock, damage to the organs surrounding the clitoris are likely. So is serious infection. And, my God, the pain that little African girl must bear. Cut. Rip. Cut. Cannot walk without pain. Cannot urinate without pain. Cannot, eventually, engage in sexual intercourse without pain—that is, if that girl makes it to adulthood. So many have died from this mutilation. *Why do they hate us?*

Terrorism, as in the young schoolboy in Anywhere USA who is repeatedly dissed at home by his nice suburban parents; repeatedly dissed at school by his nice suburban classmates. His only outlets are video games and the Internet. In these alternative spaces he fashions an alternative identity, one bent on being the opposite of his candy-coated existence. One set on revenge, on murder, because he has been taught time and again that the solution for any conflict is more conflict, is violence. He will get even with everyone who ever violated him, made him feel useless, empty, like an outsider, different, strange, weird, crazy, a loner, an introvert. How easily he secured a gun. And how easily he strolled into school one morning, first to the principal's office. *Bam.* Then to homeroom. *Bam. Bam. Bam. Bam. Bam. Bam.* Then to the library. *Bam. Bam. Bam. Bam.* Then to a bathroom. *Bam.* A springtime procession of dead bodies, including

his, swimming in tears, screams, and blood. This girl, shot in the face and now blind. That boy, shot in the back and now a paraplegic. This teacher, shot in the head and now on life support, forever. *Why do they hate us?*

Terrorism, as in the morning of April 19, 1995, when Timothy McVeigh, a decorated veteran of the Persian Gulf War, parked a rented Ryder truck with explosives in front of the Alfred P. Murrah Federal Building, in downtown Oklahoma City within sight of the day-care center on the second floor. McVeigh lit a fuse leading to two tons of ammonium nitrate fertilizer and racing fuel. At 9:02 a.m., an enormous explosion erupted which sheared the entire north side of the building, killing 168 and injuring something like 500. First America focused its fury on unknown international terrorists, mainly Arab Muslims. But all too soon it became apparent that these terrorists were homegrown. McVeigh was arrested less than ninety minutes after the blast, only seventy-five miles away, during a routine traffic stop. He became the prime suspect almost immediately. Through the address in Decker, Michigan, which McVeigh customarily used on forms and applications, the FBI zeroed in on Terry Nichols within two days of the bombing. Nichols, who met McVeigh in the army in 1988, had long drifted through a life of disappointments, few lasting relationships, and no secure livelihood. Nichols and McVeigh quickly discovered that they shared a distrust of the federal government: Nichols didn't keep his money in a bank, didn't pay taxes, and he once tried to renounce his American citizenship. Two days after the bombing, Nichols—toting his then-toddler, Nichole—turned himself in at the Herington, Kansas, police station, asking the local authorities why his name was in the national media in association with the crime. Nichols never went home again, as he was first held as a material witness and eventually charged as a coconspirator. *Why do they hate us?*

* * *

Terrorism, as in the repulsive form of police brutality which claimed the life of African immigrant Amadou Diallo in the Bronx on February 4, 1999. Born in Liberia, West Africa, to parents from the West African nation of Guinea, Diallo was an easygoing and erudite young man. He was an exceptional student from his boyhood on, attending some of the finest schools in the world, such as the French International School, Cambridge University, the British Consulate College in Thailand, and the Asian Institute of Microsoft. It was Diallo's dream to one day enroll in college in the United States. In 1996, three years before his untimely death, Diallo moved to New York City to form a business with a relative. Soon thereafter, the hard-nosed survival games of this great metropolis kicked in, and Diallo found himself working six days a week, twelve hours a day, peddling gloves, socks, and videotapes in Manhattan, on the hectic thoroughfare of West 14th Street. But he never lost his passion for education. It was this hunger for knowledge that energized Diallo's interest in various religions. A deeply spiritual human being, he embraced Islam at age eighteen, and Diallo often highlighted passages in the Qu'ran that featured dialogues between Christians and Muslims. On that night of February 4, 1999, Amadou Diallo would come to the end, abruptly, of his life journey. It was after midnight and he was already at home from a long day. But Diallo decided to go back out to get something to eat. As he returned to his apartment, he was approached by four White New York City police officers, each a member of the controversial Street Crime Unit. (Controversial because the Street Crime Unit had a history of shaking down and roughing up, unnecessarily some said, young Black and Latino men.) The police would later say they thought Diallo matched the description of a rapist on the loose in the area. What happened next and what words were exchanged between Diallo and the four police officers remain murky to this day, but we do know that Diallo pulled out a wallet and it was at that point that the officers unleashed a

fusillade of forty-one bullets right outside Diallo's Bronx apartment building. In those split seconds the officers had become judge, jury, and hangmen. Nineteen of those bullets shredded Amadou Diallo's puny frame. He had come to this country looking for his own slice of the American pie. But, alas, he and his aspirations were no more. Diallo was twenty-two and had no criminal record. Months later the rape suspect in question was apprehended. And after a media barrage, massive protests, and the downward spiral of Mayor Rudy Giuliani's approval ratings as he stubbornly supported these police officers despite evidence to the contrary, each of the four police officers was acquitted of each and every criminal charge. The trial had been moved out of New York City, to the upstate capital of Albany, and the not-guilty verdicts were rendered by a jury composed of individuals generally detached from the stark realism of the often contentious police-community relations in the city of New York, particularly between White police officers and communities of color. *Why do they hate us?*

Terrorism, as in the vile murder of Shani Baraka and her partner Rayshon Holmes in the summer of 2003. Shani, the daughter of eminent African American poets Amiri and Amina Baraka, was living part-time with her oldest sister Wanda. Wanda was married to a man who was mad abusive, foul, vicious, dangerous. I should add that this man was Black, a Muslim, and a community activist. Wanda tried, on a number of occasions, to get away from this man by calling the police on him several times, seeking protection via a restraining order, to no avail. Even after Wanda's estranged husband had finally moved out, and after a restraining order was in place, he came back twice to terrorize her, his wife. Once, he threatened to kill her. Another time he tried to demolish the pool in the backyard, and Wanda's car. The Baraka parents feared the worst. Their oldest daughter was the victim of perpetual domestic violence, and their youngest

daughter, Shani, a teacher, a basketball coach, a role model for scores of inner-city youth, was residing there. Shani was warned several times to get her belongings, to get away from that situation. Finally, one sweltering August day in 2003, Shani and her partner Rayshon went to retrieve the remainder of Shani's possessions. Wanda was out of town. It remains unclear, even today, if the estranged husband had already forced his way into his former home or if he arrived after Shani and Rayshon. No matter. He hated Wanda and he hated Shani for being Wanda's sister, and he hated Shani and Rayshon for being two women in love, for being lesbians. His revolver blew Shani away immediately. Next, it appears there was a struggle between Rayshon and this man. Rayshon was battered and bruised, then blown away as well. Gone. Just like that. Dead. Two tiny women. In two tiny caskets. The saddest funeral I have ever attended in my life. And because I have known the Baraka family for years, this double murder was very difficult to handle. I howled so hard and long that I doubled over in pain in the church pew. I howled so hard and long that I nearly fell to the floor, beneath the pew in front of me. And then the preacher shouted, and the choir sang, *Why, dear God, do they hate us?*

A Psalm for New Orleans, Verse 5

Originally published in *Someday We'll All Be Free*
September 6, 2006

On Monday, August 29, 2005, when Hurricane Katrina hit the Gulf Coast of the United States, I was in the middle of a bout with depression and I had deliberately allowed my satellite television service to lapse for lack of payment. I was having a grueling year financially, and I had decided to spend the final warm weeks of the summer in quiet contemplation, without the distraction of outside stimuli. I did know it was hurricane season, and I had been hearing—from where, I cannot recall—that residents were fleeing cities like New Orleans. But I thought none of that unusual, since every year around August storms pummel that part of America. As I chatted with friends and colleagues on the phone, and as I made my way around Brooklyn and New York City, it became clear that something awful was occurring. The levees broke. The levees have been breached. Which levees? Who did it? Where? Why? What I remember, unmistakably, was the look and sound of horror emanating from the faces and mouths of people I knew, especially Black people, in New York City. A super-catastrophe was unfolding on American television and I, without my satellite service, was missing it. But I didn't feel I was missing it. I could have paid the bill and gotten the signal turned on. I chose not to. It was excruciating enough to hear and see so many individuals crying and complaining about what the government was not

doing, about how these poor people, these mostly Black poor people, were dying, literally, before our very eyes. *Why do they hate us?* shot through my brain many times. What had these poor people, these Black poor people, done to deserve such mistreatment from the city of New Orleans, from the state of Louisiana, from the Bush administration in Washington, DC? I saw, as I walked through my Fort Greene neighborhood in Brooklyn, clusters of individuals conversing on this tragedy in the making. I heard some proclaim, loudly, that the response to this catastrophe was *so different* from the response to September 11. Was racism at work? they asked unflinchingly, the bulging shape and tone of the question pregnant with a ready reply. There were bold newspaper headlines with captions like "Shame of a Nation." There were numerous calls and emails I received from random parties, some I knew, some I did not, asking what I was going to do, if anything, to help. The inquiries were not unusual, since people who know me know that I am an activist, that I care about human beings, *all* human beings, that public service is, without question, one of my great life callings. But for some reason I was frozen for days and days, waiting like everyone else for local, state, and federal authorities to rescue these tax-paying and steadfastly loyal American citizens. But there was not much happening other than finger-pointing and bewilderment by the folks in authority positions. Finger-pointing and bewilderment as death and destruction pounded the door of New Orleans and the Gulf Coast.

Over the next several days we heard the stories of elderly people locked in their homes dead or near death. We heard theories on how the levees were purposely destroyed, how the locals heard a loud blast right before the floodwaters came. We heard the tales of people expiring on the highways, on the ramps of the interstate, on the roofs. I wondered what Black leadership, our so-called national Black leadership and national Black organizations—Jesse

Jackson, Al Sharpton, Louis Farrakhan, Kwesi Mfume, Marc Morial, the NAACP, the National Urban League, the Southern Christian Leadership Conference, the Black Leadership Forum, the Congressional Black Caucus, the Black fraternities and the Black sororities, all of them and more—were going to do in the face of what was undeniably a stupefying governmental indifference to the greatest natural disaster in American history. Finally, I felt compelled to do something myself. I phoned April Silver, my dear friend and fellow activist, and suggested we promptly organize a benefit here in New York City. I determined that right after the benefit I would hop on a plane and journey to the affected region, because I needed to see this atrocity—the one I had not seen myself on television—with my own eyes.

On Thursday, September 8, we held an event called "A Benefit for New Orleans" at the chic venue Canal Room in the Tribeca section of Manhattan. We created no flyers, we did very little media, and relied instead on the Internet to spread the word. We scrambled to pay for a fifty-three-foot tractor trailer, quite difficult since so many Katrina sympathizers were renting trucks to ship supplies to the devastated Gulf region. It was a party with a purpose. When I showed up a bit late, I was awestruck by the piles of donations already on the sidewalk and street in front of Canal Room. I was likewise mesmerized by the way attendees, led by the superb event producer Leslie Wade, had organized themselves into help units, transferring bags of clothes, toiletries, and the like, from hand to hand. It was mostly young people, mainly Black, although I was delighted to see White and Latino and Asian faces present as well. For Hurricane Katrina was not merely a Black tragedy. It was an American tragedy, a human tragedy. What was just as extraordinary was the fact that a number of folks—perhaps the lion's share of attendees—hung outside and worked even as there were many inside partying hard. Partygoers operated in shifts. One crew would come

in and the other would exit and bond with those packing the truck. Three hours into the benefit, at approximately ten p.m., the truck was completely full and on its way to the Gulf as a joyous applause cascaded through the night air.

Problem was, we still had a mountain of items blocking half of the West Broadway strip where the club was situated and no money left for another truck. April had brilliantly rallied the mothers of rap stars Kanye West, Mos Def, Talib Kweli, and Common to get their sons to flip the bill for the first truck. But what would we do now? I announced this new development from the stage. At what would turn out to be the most loving and spiritual *party* I have ever experienced in my life, people not only offered suggestions for trucks and school buses (all to no avail, regrettably, as the hour sped to eleven p.m.), but also dug into their wallets and purses to contribute funds for a second truck. Kamilah Forbes, one of the producers of HBO's *Def Poetry Jam*, handed me her cell phone at one point and on the line was writer and visual artist Danny Simmons, brother of music mogul Russell Simmons. Danny put in a few hundred dollars. And so did the actor Michael Rapaport, who happened to be strolling by as I was pacing nervously outside, befuddled as to how we were going to secure a second vehicle. Michael abruptly thrust somewhere between two and three hundred dollars into my hand and told me not to tell anyone. I must, in this space, because Michael was so genuine with his concern.

And in the most fantastic twist of fate of the entire evening, a young Black man who heard of "A Benefit for New Orleans" on one of the few radio shows we did leading up to the event, showed up with his girlfriend at around eleven p.m. to make a drop-off. Noticing the commotion outside (I don't think I've seen so many people on cellies at the same time, in such a crowded place, making the same sort of calls), the gentleman asked how he could help. He was a truck driver who happened to have his own fifty-three-foot tractor trailer parked in his backyard in

Brooklyn. Call it divine intervention. Call it the magic of human possibility when people unite behind a common cause. Whatever it was, we were saved. One hour later, the man was back and the few dozen or so attendees left loaded the remainder of the stuff well past two a.m. He was on his way to the Gulf as some folks fought back tears. All he wanted was food, gas, and toll money—nothing more. That gentleman must have been an angel.

One of the more curious moments of that long night came when two White men, a couple of self-proclaimed rock and rollers, stopped in front of Canal Room because they were deeply touched by the show of support for the victims of Hurricane Katrina. As he surveyed the volunteers, one of the men asked me, without any shame, "How come no Whites are helping you?" I was initially perplexed. Of course, a number of White sisters and brothers had dropped off donations and supplied their labor throughout the evening. But this man was correct in asking the question, for the overwhelming majority of volunteers were Black. From what I'd heard, the overriding image displayed on television news programs were that of Black faces and Black bodies. I heard Black people, American ones, West Indian ones, and African ones throughout New York City and throughout that evening at Canal Room say how severely traumatized they were by seeing us suffer like that in the Gulf Coast.

I'm not suggesting Whites or other people were not also moved. Nevertheless, there was something about the Katrina imagery that punctured the collective Black psyche, the collective Black pain, and, truth be told, the collective Black rage. My God, after what we've been through in America, after what we have withstood, after what we've given to this country in blood, sweat, tears, and our lives, why does it feel that we are strangers in a house we helped to build? *How come no Whites are helping you?* echoed in my head a few more times that night, although I tried to put it out of my mind. There were some well-meaning

Whites there, a few who came, who helped, who stayed until the very end. But not many. And it was generally "liberal" or "progressive" White sisters and brothers, the ones with a dose of social consciousness in their veins, who came. But unlike the regular, non-activist Blacks who showed up in droves for this benefit, because they were moved to do something, nearly all the Whites who came were either activists or social justice advocates.

Four hours later and with no sleep whatsoever, filmmaker Nicole "Cynical" Smith, a singer my company represented at the time named Shannone Holt, and I were on our way to Baton Rouge, Louisiana. To be mad frank, Cynical and Shannone were simply the first two individuals I asked to accompany me: Shannone, an artist with an activist spirit, had the guts to want to do it, and Cynical, equally fearless, had the camera to document everything. Obviously, flying directly into New Orleans was not an option. Renee Lapeyrolerie met us at the Baton Rouge airport— she was a New Orleans–based publicist who I'd worked with previously during the *Essence* Music Festival. Like much of the New Orleans population, Renee had fled the city by Friday, September 9. I was extremely happy to see her, to know she was okay, but I realized that Renee, like most New Orleanians, was not okay emotionally. How could she be after living through a harrowing episode like Hurricane Katrina? But here was Renee, willing not only to pick us up from the airport, but also to drive us into New Orleans so we could see the destruction for ourselves. It was Renee's first trip back since fleeing the city.

We stopped first at a Baton Rouge mall for lunch. Everything appeared calm among the mostly White patrons. "Strange," Shannone said, "like nothing ever happened in New Orleans." Strange, to be sure, and creepy too. As a Black person, you do not want to believe that what went down in New Orleans did not matter on a very personal and spiritual level to these good

White folks in Baton Rouge. But I had to wonder. *How come no Whites are helping you?* My nerves were so frayed I wanted to walk up to a White sister or brother, a White family, and say, *Hey, don't you get that Hurricane Katrina is as much of a tragedy, if not more so, than September 11? Don't you get that any human misfortune is* your *human misfortune, regardless of the race or group of people?* But, sadly, this journey was already feeling like a Black thing, not a human thing. I shrugged the shoulders of my mind, and we were off to New Orleans.

I rode shotgun while Renee drove, and Shannone, Cynical, and former New Orleans mayor Marc Morial's younger brother Jacque sat in the backseat. Jacque, a true bohemian and the complete opposite of his corporate-styled older sibling, was not going into New Orleans. He simply wanted a ride to the outskirts. When we dropped him off at his car, near a restaurant on the highway, Jacque said to us, emphatically, "Be very careful." From that point on, if we were going to get through the swarm of state troopers and military personnel blocking all routes into New Orleans, we had to be mad cagey. And we were. I will not say exactly what we did, but let's just say we were waved through every single checkpoint right into the city, as if we were on official business.

Renee wanted to check on the status of her house, while Shannone, Cynical, and I wanted to document, report, and help, if we could, in some small way. Yet nothing could prepare me for the wreckage to the city of New Orleans. Nothing. The mangled power lines. The enormous trees snapped in two like tiny sticks. The light poles ripped from the earth and dumped, dead center, through the roof of a house. The debris, the smashed glass everywhere. I have never experienced a war in person, but New Orleans looked like it had been targeted and bombed by a merciless enemy. And we were not in a majority-Black neighborhood, like the Lower Ninth Ward where floodwater was ev-

erywhere. We were in one of the more upwardly mobile and predominantly White areas. Before we arrived at the Lower Ninth Ward, we drove through this affluent neighborhood and through the business district of New Orleans. There was the Superdome, the same Superdome where I'd seen Aretha Franklin and Teena Marie perform two short months before. The same Superdome by which each night of the *Essence* Music Festival I marched, along with throngs of Black people, Black people from New Orleans, Black people from God knows where, to hear music, our music. It was mind-boggling to see the Superdome in its new, dilapidated state. Mind-boggling, too, to think of the recent inhabitants, folks for whom the Superdome, once a place that entertained them, had now become a place where some died, some starved, some suffered through thirst and hunger, and, to our collective shame, some were raped, molested, or otherwise physically assaulted. These are the narratives I would hear over the next seventy-two hours.

The business district of New Orleans was a ghost town, except for the random police officers here, the National Guard on foot patrol there, and media crews with their RVs doubling as temporary homes and remote studios. When we arrived at Renee's house, she was overcome with relief that Hurricane Katrina had not inundated it. Her home is in the Sixth Ward, not far from the French Quarter. It has a dazzling yellow exterior, and a nice and simple decor inside. As Renee was grabbing odds and ends to take back with her to Baton Rouge, Cynical meandered down the street. I began to follow until I saw a battalion of National Guard troops, their guns cocked and ready, and I froze dead in my tracks. Fear gripped me while I thought of the numerous stories I'd read before flying down south, of Black males being shot on the spot due to suspicion of looting. I had no media credentials, only a New York State driver's license—and my word. Then I saw a tall, slender Black man standing just beyond the

National Guard squad, speaking in an animated manner into a cell phone. I decided to walk right on by these armed soldiers. I nodded, they nodded, and as I turned the corner I saw Cynical filming a group of Black males with red, black, green, and gold hats (the colors of solidarity for Black people worldwide—red for the blood, black for the people, green for the land, and gold for the natural resources of the earth—and, truth be told, also symbolic of natural resources taken as Africans were being enslaved or colonized). I saw two young White women and a young Black woman interacting with these men, who I would learn referred to themselves as the "Soul Patrol." During the height of the calamity, this group, led by an elderly woman named Momma D. (she was not present when we stumbled upon them), had taken it upon themselves to assist community members in reaching safety. According to Brother Earl, a member of the Soul Patrol, they shepherded boats or whatever they had at their disposal to rescue dozens and dozens of New Orleans residents, and not just Black people. "We did not discriminate. Lot of poor Whites here too, ya know?" Brother Earl said.

But what of the lives they did not save? The Soul Patrol tied those bodies to trees or poles, thinking, hoping, the authorities would pick the bloated, insect-bitten bodies up. No, I did not see any dead bodies during that day in New Orleans. Honestly, I did not want to. The smell of death lurking everywhere was enough, as was the *feel* of death about us. I'm sorry to say I have seen dead bodies prior to this trip. Such is life in Black America. But it is quite another matter entirely to smell the flesh of dead bodies, to feel as if you are walking atop that flesh, your Timberland boots crushing fingers, toes, eyes, noses, teeth, guts. My heart throbbed furiously as I listened to the Soul Patrol vent, preach, protest, and plan for their own exit from New Orleans. They were some of the last residents in the city except for, according to Brother Earl, a plethora of senior citizens barricaded in their homes, praying that no one—as in the police or the military—

would come to remove them from their homes, from their city.

I realize this may sound strange to some, but you must understand that people on the margins of society, any society, have very little they can hold on to, very few possessions, so their homes, whether they own them or not, are often all they have. Not even a hurricane will detach some from what they are most familiar with, from that which their identity, their being, their memory, is inextricably tied. And if it is meant for them to die there, in that home, well, so be it. I heard the story of an old Black woman who, fearing the worst, climbed into her bed and waited for the floodwater—and death—to come and get her. The water did in fact rush into her dwelling, but rather than ending her life, it floated the woman, atop her mattress, out of the house, into the streets, where she, too, was rescued.

After saying goodbye to the Soul Patrol, we drove to the French Quarter, to a sector where a number of national television crews were set up for satellite feeds. While waiting to do a quick interview with Black Entertainment Television, I stood a good distance from Cynical and Shannone, alone, not really thinking about where I was for several minutes. It was that heavy, to be there in that heat and humidity, imagining what it must have been like at the Superdome, in the Convention Center, on a highway, on a roof, on top of a car or van, screaming, crying, begging for help. Or dying a slow death. Just then, a Black Hawk helicopter began hovering overhead. At first I paid it no mind because military tanks had been rolling down this main street during the several minutes I waited for the BET interview to commence. But then I noticed the Black Hawk spotting me, lowering itself as if someone in it was watching me, identifying me, targeting me. I don't want to sound mad paranoid but, again, I was a Black man standing in the middle of New Orleans after residents had been told to evacuate. Someone, clearly, was trying to figure out who I was. I imagined myself getting shot at

if I, as a means of testing these military heads, started running in the opposite direction of my traveling companions and the television crews. Unbowed but not about to do anything dumb either, I did the interview and joked about the Black Hawk eye-balling me with Shannone, Cynical, and Renee. We left for the Lower Ninth Ward, perhaps the most devastated corner of New Orleans in the aftermath of Hurricane Katrina.

Anyone who has ever lived in or spent considerable time in an American ghetto knows that on a good day the ghetto resembles a war zone. Everywhere you go you encounter urban blight, garbage, scampering rats and roaches, cryptic graffiti on walls, the stench of urine and feces, and the very sense that death is but a door knock away. Combine what I just detailed with the savage assault of Hurricane Katrina and busted levees, and you have an idea of the gruesome state of the wet and contaminated Lower Ninth Ward of New Orleans. What really got to me were the remnants of human struggle everywhere: a shoe here, a torn shirt there, a discarded gas container, a half-eaten biscuit, an un-opened bag of potato chips, empty Coke and Pepsi bottles, un-identifiable food stored in aluminum foil or plastic containers. People's lives shattered and strewn across grass and concrete. Cars, SUVs, and minivans submerged in grimy brown water. Stray dogs and cats—many of them obviously starving, for I could see their bones jutting through their skin—foaming at the mouth, picking through litter for scraps of food. An indescrib-able agony ripped through my heart and I pushed air from my lungs. I thought of the ignorant people back in New York City, who asked in a condescending way why people remained in New Orleans when they knew a hurricane was coming. Clearly, some people have no idea what it is like to be poor, what it is like not to have a car, a driver's license, what it is like to be completely dependent, as my mother and I were completely dependent, on public transportation.

I thought of this as we drove up and down a number of streets in the Lower Ninth Ward. I wondered who was responsible for the eight or nine city buses just sitting there in the middle of the street like dinosaurs. Did anyone think to use those buses to help residents escape, to save their lives, their very Black lives? You don't want to believe that some people in power are that callous, that removed from the people, that removed from God, that they, by their inactions or very slow actions, decided these poor folks were not worthy of being rescued. Is this where the eagle has landed in America? Could a Black mayor and a White governor and a White president watch this human drama unfold from their seats of privilege and do little more than blame each other or their subordinates? In a fit of anger, Mayor Ray Nagin told the folks in Washington, DC, to get off their behinds and do something. When it became clear that the catastrophe was larger than a natural disaster, President Bush flew on Air Force One over—*over*—the region and kept it moving back to the White House. Governor Blanco led what quickly went from a search-and-rescue campaign to a law-and-order campaign in the city, locking up scores of individuals for "looting." I ask any fair-minded American reading this: what would you have done if you, your wife, your family, were stuck on a roof for two, three, four days, in blistering heat, with no evidence that help was on the way? Would you have allowed *your* family to starve knowing there was a grocery store right on the corner of your block? I do not condone stealing, but I also do not condone the reckless and abusive neglect displayed toward the people of New Orleans. I do not want to see any people hurt, not Black people, not White people, not Latino people, not Asian people. But because New Orleans at the time was 70 percent Black, because much of that Black population lived below the poverty line, and because that poorer part of the Black population was most defenseless against a hurricane and the breaching of those levees, we have to ask a very critical question: does any-

one care about poor Black people in America, or are they, we, merely that expendable?

Night was quickly encroaching on New Orleans, so Renee suggested we jet before things became dramatic in that city, given the concentrated military and police presence including, I noted, New York City police officers. As we drove through and out of New Orleans, I looked around and back a number of times, trying to retain every detail of the devastation, wondering what the city would be like once it was rebuilt. The next day, in Baton Rouge, Shannone, Cynical, and I went to visit a family of eight living temporarily at the local Nation of Islam mosque. Minister Andrew, head of the mosque, was kind enough to introduce us to the clan: a husband, a wife, the wife's sixty-nine-year-old mother, and five children. It was heartbreaking to see a proud husband, a proud wife, a dignified and quiet elderly woman, and five beautiful and innocent children sleeping in one room, on the floor, their lives reduced to the clothes on their backs, the change in their pockets, the bits and pieces of identification they managed to grab before their entire home was flooded. You have heard their tale before: no, they did not leave because they did not feel things would get this bad. They, like other citizens of New Orleans, had survived previous hurricane seasons. Who was to know that this family, like many families, would be forced to their roof for a day, two days, three days, four days and counting, waving, screaming, crying for help, only to see rescue teams fly past them and offer a thumbs-up; a thumbs-up, the father said to me, that was roughly equivalent to the middle finger as far as he was concerned. *Why do they hate us?* The father's right hand was sliced in half from his wrist to the base of his index finger because, in order to get his family to the roof, in order to preserve his family's life, he had to punch iron bars and glass.

I looked at the man's hand, his big, puffy hand, and I thought

of the men, Black men over the years, who had used their hands to work, to fight, to break free of whatever it was that was condemning them to an unavoidable and certain death. The husband and wife would take turns talking, as the grandmother and the children sat stoically, their eyes and souls drifting. I imagined what was going through the grandmother's mind. She lived through Hurricane Betsy back in the 1960s; she lived through Jim Crow and segregation; she lived through the miracle of the Civil Rights Movement and the promises of freedom, and equality; she lived through being called nigger, colored, Negro, Black, Afro American, and African American; she lived through the first Black mayor in New Orleans, through the rise of a powerful Black middle class; she lived through the explosion of a Black underclass in New Orleans, through a kind of Black-on-Black violence she could not have predicted in her own youth; and here she was now, living through Hurricane Katrina. This sixty-nine-year-old Black woman had seen so much, lived through so much, that as the waters gushed from the streets into their house, she told her daughter and her son-in-law to leave her, to let her die, that she would be fine in the by-and-by. I choked back tears as I listened to the wife and husband talk of this older woman, of their children. I choked back tears as the children—three girls and two boys—finally spoke, saying they did not understand why the government hated them. *Why do they hate us?* I choked back tears as the husband asked these questions to no one in particular: *Ain't I a man? How they gonna try to split our family up, Grandmomma over there, the children over here, leaving me and my wife by ourselves? Is this slavery? Is we in jail?* I choked back tears as the wife bit her upper lip and asked, rhetorically, *How can the government go help people overseas but it cannot help its own people in America?*

I talked with and listened to this family for nearly three hours, before excusing myself from everyone and stepping into the oven-like Louisiana sun. I walked several feet away, to the

edge of the parking lot, and I vomited. It was as if I had vomited what I had seen, what I had heard thus far, what I felt about the neglect of this family, and about each and every New Orleans family left to fend for themselves. I got the vomit out of my system, and I cried. I felt powerless. I wanted to give this family money, but no amount of money could begin to remove the daggers dug into their minds and souls. I wanted to hug this family, but no amount of sympathy could prepare them for the months and years and lifetimes it was going to take to heal the hurt they were now carrying around like a birthright. An emotional wreck, I went back into the mosque, thanked the family for their time, said goodbye, told them I would pray for them, and drove with Shannone and Cynical to Houston's Astrodome. Renee, the Soul Patrol, New Orleans, Minister Andrew, that family of eight, and Baton Rouge were all in the rearview mirror of our minds.

Part III

Kerry Washington: Woman on Top

Originally published in *Ebony*
May 9, 2013

I see Kerry Washington standing, back slightly turned, at the appointed place for our interview, Glow Bio juice bar on Melrose Avenue in Los Angeles. Jet-black hair sleek and straight, shiny black blouse, tightly fitted blue jeans, and black pumps with monster heels. She possesses a beauty and sexiness that electrifies arteries in the heart. She is honey-brown skin, delicately painted by God. She is that ancestor's gaze through almond-shaped eyes rooted in her Black American-Jamaican-British-Scottish bloodlines.

She suddenly swings around and greets me: "Hi, I'm Kerry." There's no entourage, no assistant, no attitude, even though she's starring on a must-see TV drama that has spawned a cult following since its debut last April. It's just the actress, at the location she chose because she is extremely health-conscious and because her nutritionist happens to own Glow Bio. As I would learn while spending time with her at the restaurant, at this magazine's photo shoot, and on the set of *Scandal*, this falls in line with who Kerry Washington is at her core: unbelievably supportive of friends, strangers, castmates, production assistants, or anyone within reach of her kindness. She is someone whose gratitude and humility comes through with every "thank you" she goes out of her way to extend for any kindness shown her.

* * *

"I'm an only child. That's why I pretend all the time," the actress, thirty-six, offers in response to my query about what growing up Kerry was like, before laughing mischievously and purposely slurping her protein drink. "I have a very strong imagination and spent a lot of time daydreaming."

She then gets lost in just such a daydream about herself, starring little Kerry. Dig if you will the picture: like the hip-hop culture also born in the Bronx, Kerry is a product of her environment. "I grew up in Jamie Towers, sort of working middle class. We weren't in the projects, but we were across the street from the projects and on the other side were single- and double-family homes. Same Castle Hill neighborhood where Jennifer Lopez grew up."

Chris Rock, who starred with Kerry in the film *I Think I Love My Wife*, shares this: "All you have to do is meet Kerry's parents and witness her relationship with them and you'll realize why she's not your typical psycho actress." Her dad's family has roots in South Carolina and Brooklyn; her mother's, in Jamaica and Manhattan's Lower East Side. And one of her grandmothers worked as a maid (or "the help," as Kerry often says) for years on Park Avenue. But it's the influence of her mother on Kerry that may be the most profound. "I was really lucky to be raised by a woman who taught me that what was inside was much more important than what was outside." So the energy, athleticism, creativity, and artistic cravings that raged beneath the surface of the admittedly precocious young Kerry were carefully nurtured and funneled through positive outlets.

Ask, and you shall receive remembrances from the girl who excelled at acting, dancing, and singing. You'll learn about the young lady who grew up discussing big issues with her parents while digesting the news and PBS. "My mom saw this very active, imaginative, talkative child and just tried to find ways to channel that energy, whether it was the children's theater company or ballet class or trips to the library. Whatever it was, she

was supportive of my brain activity," the actress says. Tap deeper into her roots and you get the girl shipped from her hood to attend the elite all-girls Spence School on Manhattan's tony Upper East Side. While there, the seeds of Kerry Washington the actress and advocate took root; she fell in love with "pretending" and being a cultural bridge builder. But a glimpse of her then would have borne little resemblance to the fashionista she's become. She admits of her high school days, "I wore, like, pajamas to school every day. I was not that girl."

Fast-forward a few years, and you get the George Washington University Phi Beta Kappa graduate who chose to pursue a degree in liberal arts rather than study acting in a conservatory program. "I have always felt like if my job as an actor is to tell the stories about the human experience, then I was going to be better off studying history, anthropology, psychology, and sociology, so I would be able to understand the human experience."

Years of community and grassroots theater training followed. And there were the eight months spent in India after college; stints as a substitute teacher, a yoga instructor, and an East Village vegan restaurant hostess; an engagement to actor David Moscow that was broken after two years, all the while fine-tuning her acting. Suddenly, her name came to be interchangeable with her roles, such as Chenille (*Save the Last Dance*), Della Bea (*Ray*), Kay (*The Last King of Scotland*), Nikki (*I Think I Love My Wife*), and Susan in David Mamet's Broadway play *Race*. And now, there's Olivia on *Scandal*.

> *Kerry was selected to be Olivia Pope because her talent spoke for itself. She read for the role and she just WAS Olivia Pope. Kerry brings a lot of intelligence and specificity to the character. She and I have these intense discussions and every time I come away in awe of her thought process and her at-*

tention to detail and her passion for getting every moment right. I'm lucky to get to write for her.
—Shonda Rhimes, creator of Scandal

I remember eyeballing the first ads for *Scandal*, making a mental note that Kerry Washington was the star, then shoving it out of my mind because, though a fan of her work, I had thought of her only as a film actress. But a curious thing began to happen: everywhere I went, people were calling themselves "gladiators" (as the main characters do on the show).

Kerry, the first Black woman to star in a major network American TV drama since Teresa Graves in 1974's *Get Christie Love!*, has the kind of power we have never seen in the hands of a Black female character on television. But still, she is very clear that Olivia Pope has, uh, issues.

"One of the things that challenges me most and that I love most about playing her is how flawed she is," she says. "In her professional life, she is so powerful and is this self-made woman. She is the answer to Broomhilda's prayers," she adds, referring to her role in *Django Unchained*, Quentin Tarantino's controversial blockbuster about slavery, race, and revenge.

She goes on to tell me how humbling it is to be able to have a career in which the lives of two powerful women from opposite ends of history—Broomhilda, a slave, and Olivia, a powerbroker—can overlap. "I'm grateful that these two women on opposite ends of history, on opposite ends of their experience, both strong women but in such different ways, can exist at the same time," Kerry says, smiling broadly. "But in [Olivia's] personal life, she is a mess! And I kind of love that. I love that I get to embody all of that complexity because I also think it takes a certain level of progress for us to have a Black woman that powerful be an emotional mess on television. She's post–Clair Huxtable."

Although the thespian is quite forthcoming when dissecting her television character, she's a steel trap when it comes to her

private life. When I try to pose a question about her off-screen life, she stops me cold: "I don't talk about my personal life in the press."

During one of my *Scandal* set visits, I am struck by how funny Kerry is, whether sticking one finger in her nose or trying mightily to open a bottle of wine during a take—and failing miserably. "I do not drink and have no idea how to do this," she admits between scenes. It is wild to see the morphing of Kerry Washington into Olivia Pope: Kerry is always smiling and even engages in back-and-forth hood jokes with costar Columbus Short while playfully shooting video of this writer with her iPhone and answering to "K-Dub." But once the director yells, "Action!" Olivia consumes Kerry's body: her facial features become tense, and the free spirit is replaced by a calculating woman who rarely smiles as she goes about her business as a fixer.

So just who is Kerry Washington, considering she does not discuss her personal life and routinely gets lost in these characters she plays? It is a bit of mystery—but who doesn't like a mystery? Yup, there is something about this woman, and part of it has to do with the fact that she has not only made it in Hollywood, but she is also doing so on her own terms. She is a Black person who is a game changer in a game she did not create. Although Kerry is certainly someone who does not want to ever be limited by her race, she is clear that race still matters, even when it comes to *Scandal*. When first approached about the role, the actress says she was excited about the show but, as a big supporter of President Obama, did not want to do anything that would undermine his administration. "I was a little concerned because [the character has] a scandalous relationship with the [occupant of the] White House," she confesses. "I thought, *If the president on the show is Black, I will not do the show.* Because to me, it was too important a moment. I didn't want to do anything that compromised my relationship with the [president] or

that made it seem like I had an insider view on the Obama presidency. I thought that would be so disrespectful and so against all the work that I had done," she says.

But after meeting with Rhimes and being told the president on the show would be a White Republican, "I'm in!" was her enthusiastic response.

Frequently in the fairy tale that is her true story, Kerry Washington has been more "in" than "out" with various projects and causes. To wit, she spoke at the 2012 Democratic National Convention; she is a proud feminist who champions the causes of women and girls; she is a Movado spokesmodel; and she is one of President Barack Obama's appointees to his Committee on the Arts and Humanities.

So what's next?

Kerry isn't certain where she'll go from here. Her next film, *We the Peeples* (a Black version of *Meet the Parents* that allows the actress to show her "goofball" side"), will be released in May. She says she knows she needs to write more. Other aspirations include starring in and producing a biopic on the life of 1970s political activist Angela Davis and to one day be the head the National Endowment for the Arts. That day, it was easy to envision her becoming an actress/director on a project, just like Barbra Streisand, one of her childhood sheroes. Asking her about power after watching her wield it comfortably on the *Scandal* set, it is one of the few times she hesitates before very thoughtfully replying, "Power to me has always been about choices. So I never thought of myself as not having power because I've always [exercised] my right to say no." She continues by acknowledging that in Hollywood, however, true power can come in the ability to say yes, as in approving and moving forward with projects, despite what others might think. "Having the power to green-light something for the sake of green-lighting something is not what I'm interested in. But if I can be of service in this town by adding to the voices of diversity—diversity of thought, diversity

of experience, being a woman, being a person of color—then I want to be of service in that way."

Kerry Washington has moved far beyond the point of just being of service to Hollywood. She's now on the fast track to joining such megastar Black actresses as Dorothy Dandridge, Diahann Carroll, Cicely Tyson, and Halle Berry. The little girl from the Bronx with the big imagination is now officially in a position of power—on her own terms.

Why Is Baltimore Burning?

Originally published in *HuffPost*
April 28, 2015

I am from the ghetto. The first thirteen years of my life I grew up in the worst slums of Jersey City, New Jersey. If you came of age in one of America's poor inner cities like I did, then you know that we are good, decent people: in spite of no money, no resources, little to no services, run-down schools, landpersons who only came around to collect rent, and madness and mayhem everywhere, among each other—from abusive police officers, and from corrupt politicians and crooked preachers—we still made a way out of no way. We worked hard, we partied hard, we laughed hard, we barbecued hard, we drank hard, we smoked hard, and we praised God, hard.

And we were segregated, hard, by a local power structure that did not want the ghetto to be seen nor heard from, and certainly not to bring its struggles out in plain sight for the world to see.

Indeed, my entire world was the block I lived on and maybe five or six blocks north, south, east, west. A long-distance trip was going to downtown Jersey City on the first of each month so our mothers—our Black and Latina mothers—could cash their welfare checks, buy groceries with their food stamps, and if we were lucky, we got to eat at Kentucky Fried Chicken or some other fast-food restaurant on that special day.

When I was about fifteen, I was badly beaten by a White police officer after me and a Puerto Rican kid had a typical boy fight on the bus. No guns, no knives—just our fists. The Puerto Rican kid, who had White skin to my Black skin, was escorted

off the bus gingerly. I was thrown off the bus. Outraged, I said some things to the cop as I sat handcuffed in the backseat of a police car. He proceeded to smash me in the face with the full weight of his fist. Bloodied, terrified, broken in that moment, I would never again view most police officers as we had been taught as children: "Officer Friendly"—

Being poor meant I only was able to go to college because of a full financial-aid package to Rutgers University. I did not get on a plane until I was twenty-four years old because of that poverty, and also because I did not know that that was something I could do. These many years later, I have visited every single state in America, nearly every city big and small, and almost every ghetto community you can name. They all look the same.

Abandoned, burned-out buildings. Countless churches, funeral parlors, barbershops, beauty salons, check-cashing places, furniture-rental stores, fried-chicken spots, and Chinese restaurants. Schools that look and feel more like prison holding cells for our youth than centers of learning. Playgrounds littered with broken glass, used condoms, and drug paraphernalia. Liquor stores here, there, everywhere. Corner stores that sell nothing but candy, cupcakes, potato chips, soda, every kind of beer you can name, loose cigarettes, rolling paper for marijuana, lottery tickets, and gum—lots and lots of gum.

Then there are also the local organizations that claim to serve the people, Black and Latino people. Some mean well, and are doing their best with meager resources. Others only come around when it is time to raise money, to generate some votes for one political candidate or another, or if the police have tragically killed someone.

Like Rekia Boyd in Chicago. Like Miriam Carey in Washington, DC. Like Tanisha Anderson in Cleveland. Like Yvette Smith in Texas. Like Aiyana Stanley-Jones in Detroit. Like Eric Garner in New York City. Like Oscar Grant in Oakland. Like Walter Scott in South Carolina. Like Freddie Gray in Baltimore . . .

Yes, we have the first Black president in the White House, but it feels like open season on Black folks in America once more. One hundred years ago this year, the Hollywood image machine was given a huge boost by a racist and evil film called *Birth of a Nation*, a movie so calculating in the way it depicted Black people that it set the tone, quite literally, for how we were portrayed and treated in every form of media for decades to come. One hundred years ago, it was common to see photos of African Americans, males especially, lynched, hanged from trees, as the local good White folks visibly enjoyed their entertainment of playing hangman.

One hundred years later, *Birth of a Nation* has been replaced by a twenty-four-hour news media cycle still obsessed with race, racism, racial strife, racial violence, but no solutions and no action steps whatsoever, just pure sensationalism and entertainment. One hundred years later, the lynching photos have been replaced by cell phones capturing video of Walter Scott running away from a police officer, like a slow-footed character in a video game, only to be shot in the back—*pop! pop! pop! pop! pop! pop! pop! pop!*

Except all of this is mad real. Black people in America—the self-proclaimed greatest democracy on earth—are being shot here, there, everywhere, by the police, in broad daylight, with witnesses, sometimes on video. And with very few exceptions, nothing is happening to the cops who pulled the triggers. No indictments. No convictions. No prison time.

And every single time one of these scenarios occurs, we are handed the same movie script: Person of color is shot and killed by local police. Local police immediately try to explain what happened, while placing most of the blame, without a full investigation, on the person shot. The police officer or officers who fired shots are placed on paid "administrative leave." Media finds any and everything they can to denigrate the character of the dead person, to somehow justify why she or he is dead.

Marches, protests, rallies, speeches. Local police show up in military-styled "riot gear." Tensions escalate. Folks are arrested, people are agitated or provoked; all hell breaks loose. The attention has shifted from the police killing an innocent person to the violence of "thugs," "gangstas," "looters." The community is told to be nonviolent and peaceful, but no one ever tells the police they should also be nonviolent and peaceful. Whites in power and "respectable Black voices" call for calm, but these are the same folks who never talk about the horrific conditions in America's ghettos that make any hood a time bomb just waiting for a match to ignite the fury born of oppression, marginalization, containment, and invisibility. These are the same people who've spent little to no time with the poor.

If you aren't from the ghetto, if you have not spent significant time in the ghetto, then you would not understand the ghetto . . .

No matter. Big-time civil rights organizations, big-time civil rights spokespersons, and big-time church leaders are brought in to redirect, control, and contain the energy from the people at the bottom. Started from the bottom, now we here . . . But they really cannot, because the people have seen this movie a million times before. They know it is madness to be told to let justice take its course. They know it is madness to wait out a legal system that rarely if ever indicts and convicts these police officers who've shot and killed members of their community. They know it is madness to be told to stay cool, to be cool, when they have no healthy outlets for their trauma, their pain, their rage. They know it is madness to hear pundits and talking heads of every stripe on television and radio and via blogs analyze who they are, without actually knowing who they are. They know it is madness when middle-class or professional Black folks speak the language of the power structure and condemn the people in the streets instead of the system that created the conditions for why the people are in the streets. They know it is madness

that so-called progressive, liberal, human-rights, or social-justice people of any race or culture have remained mightily silent as these police shootings have been going down coast to coast. And they know it is madness that most of these big-time leaders and big-time media only come around when there is a social explosion.

So they do explode, inside of themselves, and inside their communities. They would love to reach areas outside their hoods, but the local power structure blocks that from happening. So they destroy their own communities. I understand why. I am they and they are me. Any people with nothing to lose will destroy anything in their way. Like *anything*. Any people who feel as if their lives are not valued, like they are second-class citizens at best, will not be stopped until they've made their point. They, we, do not care if our communities have not rebounded from the last major American rebellions of the 1960s. We care that we have to live in squalor and misery and can be shot at any given moment by each other, or by the police, and no one seems to care. A rebellion, a riot, are pleas for help, for a plan, for a vision, for solutions, for action steps, for justice, for God, someone, anyone, to see our humanity, to do something.

Condemning them is condemning ourselves. Labeling the Baltimore situation a "riot" because it is mostly people of color is racist, given we do not call White folks behaving violently after major sporting events "rioters" or "thugs" or "gangstas," and Lord knows some White folks have destroyed much property in America too. It ain't a democracy if White people can wild out and it is all good; but let people of color wild out and it becomes a state of emergency with the National Guard dropping in, armed and ready.

Black lives matter, all lives matter, equally. I believe that, I believe deeply in peace and love and nonviolence. I believe in my heart that we've got to be human and compassionate and civil toward one another, as sisters and brothers, as one human

race, as one human family. I believe that our communities and police forces everywhere have to sit down and talk and listen as equals, not as enemies, to figure out a way toward life and love, not toward death and hate; a way toward a shared community where we all feel safe and welcomed and human.

Yes, I love people, all people. But I also believe in justice, for all people. And I know that what has been happening in America these past few years is not remotely close to any form of justice or equality. Imagine, if you will, White folks being shot and murdered by the police like this, what the reactions would be.

Imagine if George Zimmerman had gone vigilante on a White youth with a hoodie in that gated Florida complex. Imagine White parents having to teach their children how to conduct themselves if ever confronted by the police. Imagine that Aiyana Stanley-Jones was a little seven-year-old White girl instead of a little seven-year-old Black girl, shot by the police as she slept on a sofa with her grandmother, in a botched raid. It would be a national outrage.

Baltimore is burning because America is burning with racism, with hate, with violence. Baltimore is burning because far too many of us are on the sidelines doing nothing to affect change, or have become numb as the abnormal has become normal. Baltimore is burning because very few of us are committed to real leadership, to a real agenda with consistent and real political, economic, and cultural strategies for those American communities most under siege, most vulnerable. Policing them to death is not the solution. Putting them in prison is not the solution. And, clearly, ignoring them is not the solution.

Finding My Father

Originally published in *The Education of Kevin Powell*
October 2015

sunset nails the lip of a building:
a shadow eyes
* an ashy windowpane.*
an old man sits on his cane
regurgitating cups of lenox
and the savoy:
I drink his face it burps
southern clay and city welts

My first trip to Africa made me think a lot about my father.

One day, a woman from Seattle by the name of Minty LongEarth sent me a private message on Facebook saying she admired my work, and that she helped people find their family roots, and would be glad to help me if I ever wanted to do a search. I could not believe her generosity of spirit, and gladly took her up on the offer. I couldn't give Minty much to go on. My mother and I did not know my dad's birth-place, his birth date, or even if he was still alive. Every now and again Minty hit me with a lead via Facebook but they all turned out to be dead ends.

I had resigned myself to the fact that I would never find my father. Then nearly a year after my Africa visit, in October 2013, I was randomly surfing on the Internet and stumbled across a different spelling of what could be my father's name—Elish, in-

stead of Elize Cunningham. This was all it took—with that new spelling, Minty was able to find my father. I was excited and relieved.

Elish Cunningham was born and raised in a town called Laurens, in Laurens County, Greenville, South Carolina, on March 11, 1932. But then Minty broke my heart: my father had died on February 19, 2002, eleven years before our discovery. I cried tears for a man I had met only three or four times when I was a boy, until he cut off my mother and me when I was eight. I cried because I would never get to speak with him again in person, to ask him how he met my mother, how he felt toward her, why he did not marry her after promising to do so, and why he disappeared from our lives.

Nevertheless, the more Minty told me about my father, about his family, going back into the late 1800s, the more curious I became. I wanted to visit his hometown, to see for myself what had made him who he was.

But before I went to Laurens County, I spent Thanksgiving Day, 2013, with my mother. As we always did, she and I ate mostly in silence. Now retired, after twenty-five years of laboring as a home health-care worker for the elderly, my mother had suddenly been thrust into being an elder herself, and I was all she had other than her senior-citizen apartment and some meager savings. She walks with a limp now, her body worn down from years of work, since those early days, at age eight, of picking cotton in South Carolina. Ma was rushed to the hospital a few years ago, her first visit to one since she birthed me, when her high blood pressure made her so dizzy she could not stand or function. I cried profusely on that day at the hospital because the one constant in my life has been my mother. It was surreal for me to see her lying there strapped to the bed, resignation in her eyes. I am thankful she recovered and is better.

At some point during our Thanksgiving meal I told my mother I was going to go to South Carolina to see where my

father was born and raised. As forever happened when I brought up my father, her blood boiled. She screamed at me, telling me how betrayed she felt. I told her that my father, dead or alive, would never replace her in my life, that she would forever be both my mother and my father, but that I must take this journey for my own peace of mind, to find at last the other half of myself. When I added that my father was dead, I sensed, for a moment, that my mother softened, and I saw a distant look in her eyes, as if she'd traveled back to the 1960s, back to the time before I was born, back to that day, whenever it was, that they met.

I headed south with my longtime friend Cynical, the film-maker who'd traveled to the Gulf Coast with me to do relief work after Hurricane Katrina. When we arrived in Laurens County, we went straight to the cemetery where Minty had told me my father was buried, next to a church where generations of his family worshipped. I struggled through the grass and weeds to find my father's tombstone and grew frustrated as I saw his last name again and again, but no sign of him. I moved farther and farther back through the cemetery, until finally I found him. I screamed with relief and sorrow and dropped to my knees in front of the tombstone. I spoke to my father, telling him that I was happy I'd found him at long last. I told him about my life, about how much he'd hurt my mother and me, about my many days of wishing for a father, of the great trials and confusions of my life, of how I was a man now in my forties. And I told my father that I forgave him, that I held no grudges against him or his family, and that I only wished that I had spoken with him one time before he died. Then I walked away.

After the visit to the graveyard, Cynical and I went to my father's last known address, but nobody answered when we knocked on the door. We had better luck at the next house. We banged several times because we heard children playing loudly. Still no answer. We nearly gave up, until an old woman finally opened the door. I asked her name, and when she told me, sure

enough, it was one of my father's sisters. When I told her who I was, the woman stood in disbelief, and then promptly bear-hugged me. I experienced an overwhelming sense of joy—for the first time since the 1970s I had met someone related to my father.

A three-day whirlwind of meetings ensued, with cousins, aunts, sisters, and brothers I either did not know existed previously, or only knew of faintly. I learned that my father had married only once in his life and had children born in the 1950s, 1960s, 1970s, and 1980s. Papa truly was a rolling stone, and no one was quite sure how many children, in total, my father had. He himself was one of eight children—four girls and four boys. I learned that my paternal grandfather was not Black, but half-White and half–Native American, and had been the product of a White man raping an Indian woman there in South Carolina. I also learned that my father's father had had a violent temper and a severe drinking problem, both of which he passed down to my father. My father had moved north, to New Jersey, in the 1950s. He always worked hard, always had money in his pocket, and always had an eye for women. His ex-wife told me that he was foul and disrespectful toward women. She cursed my father and his soul like my mother did any time I mentioned his name. I learned that he accepted paternity for some children and was suspected of fathering others. I learned that my father asked for me several times toward the end of his life, reminding family that he had a son up north. Because my father referred to me as "Cel-vin" with his slow Southern drawl, the entire family thought that was my name, and no one had a clue how to find me when he died. This was the reason that I was not included in the obituary list of his children, which saddened me.

Best of all, I learned that his family—my father's family— loved me. They welcomed me into their homes, into the family church, and into the entire community. My brother Michael Cunningham, whose photo my father had given to my mother

back in the 1990s, had a brother who was killed tragically when they were children. Michael told me how happy he was to have a brother again.

But so much happened so fast over the course of three short days that I knew it would take time for me to process my feelings about these strangers, even though they told me that they loved me as if I had lived there all along. I could not quite understand how to return the love my father's family gave to me. I knew my mother's family tree—the Burrisons—their names, their faces, fragments of their life stories, because of the oral histories that had been handed around from kinfolk to kinfolk and generation to generation since I could talk and understand words. I could not discern how to return the love my father's family gave to me. I've had to be my own father my entire life; I've had to figure out how to be the man I so badly wanted my father to be.

When Michael's SUV led the rental car Cynical and I were driving to the entrance of the highway home, I returned his "I love you," but wondered if I would ever see him or any of them again, or if I even wanted to. The choice was mine.

As Cynical and I headed north through the dark roads of North Carolina and Virginia and DC and Maryland and Delaware, to the morning dusk of New Jersey, I thought back to the many years I had traveled this same route on a Greyhound bus with my mother and Aunt Cathy and my cousin Anthony, our lives packed into those cheap suitcases, with aluminum foil filled with fried chicken and hot sauce on Wonder Bread. I had come so far, yet I remained so close to the little boy with his face pressed against the expansive window of the Greyhound bus. I thought of my Aunt Pearlie Mae—my mother's oldest sibling and the first to die in 2010—and how at the funeral my mother, my Uncle Lloyd, my Aunt Birdie, and my Aunt Cathy had each carefully selected the plot where they would be buried when their time came. I thought of my journey through life—through

the ghetto, poverty, violence, abuse, Rutgers University, MTV, *Vibe*, hip-hop, Tupac Shakur, September 11, Hurricane Katrina, my campaigns for Congress, and my first ever pilgrimage to Africa. As a speaker, as an activist, as a writer, I have been to five of the earth's seven continents, me the little boy once so terribly frightened of the world. I have witnessed people come and go and I've seen people live and die. I thought I would not make it to fifteen, to eighteen, to twenty-one, to twenty-five, to thirty, but here I stand, someone who challenges racism, sexism, classism, homophobia, religious hate of any kind, and the reckless disregard for the disabled.

As a young boy, I never thought that I would live to see a Barack Obama elected as president. Nor did I imagine that in the twenty-first century in our America, I would be in the middle of protests and organizing around the racial-profiling murder of Trayvon Martin, or kneel on the front lines of Ferguson, Missouri, at the very spot where Michael Brown, a Black youth, was shot and killed by Darren Wilson, a White police officer. Or that so many women I know—of every race and of every age—would be the victims of some form of sexual violence in their lifetimes. Definitions of manhood, mine or any other male's, should not be based on the domination and exploitation of women and girls, ever, nor on the domination and exploitation of each other as men. With this awareness earned from hard-core rites of passage I would wish on no one, I no longer take my life for granted, nor do I take the lives of others for granted. I am thankful for life, for my life, and I have found the strength, because of years and years of therapy, to forgive my father and my mother, and to also forgive myself. I've been damaged, I've been broken, I've been 'buked, I've been scorned, I've been unready for manhood, unready for my humanity. I've made so many mistakes in my life, hurt so many people, and hurt myself on far too many occasions. Out of that pain and trauma, I've found the will to live in a way that I did not think possible. Today and for the rest of

my life, I believe in peace, I believe in love, I believe in therapy, I believe in healing, I believe in self-care, I believe in myself. And I humbly ask and pray that those I've disrespected or wounded in some way in my past forgive me, please.

I cannot say what the future holds for me, but I know that I want to live in a world in which life offers incredible opportunities to every human being. I want a world in which we treat every person with dignity, with grace, with class. I want a world where people who do have privilege and power and great wealth also have great humanity; that they come to understand that privilege, power, and wealth are spiritually and morally empty without empathy and compassion for those who are not them. I want a world in which my story does not continue and multiply, from generation to generation, tragically. I see clearly that I am one of the lucky survivors—that I should have died several times, long ago. Today my life means nothing if I do not live it in service to others, if I do not help others, through my words, through my actions. I wake every morning without fear and I face the world anew. I no longer live with crippling self-hatred and low self-esteem. I value myself and what I have to contribute to this world.

I cannot control how long I will live and I do not want to. But I can control *how* I live, what I do, what I say, what I write, how I treat people, and how I treat myself. This is why after years of alcohol abuse and neglect I am a vegan these days and will never drink liquor again. This is why I practice yoga and meditation; why I run marathons and hike mountains and why I marvel at every new day; and this is why I treat myself as a temple, not as the garbage can I once did. I truly believe that God—she—created us all to be equals, to be one human race, to be loved, honored, and respected, in spite of where and how we were born. She would have it no other way, and I hear her, louder and clearer than ever.

I know that my life, regardless of the troubles I have seen,

has not been in vain. I can breathe now, and I know now that my life matters. If we can withstand our many falls and mistakes and efforts to sabotage and destroy our own lives, if we can withstand oppression, discrimination, hatred, and abuse from others, from those who have power but no love for people, all people, then maybe, just maybe, we can come out of the harshness and magic of our life experiences as better human beings. I am doing my best now, more than ever, to be better. My mother raised me to be a man; time and again she has told me to do the right thing. Finally, I can say to my mother: *You were right, Ma. I know what the right thing is, I am doing it, Ma, I am doing it.*

Will Racism Ever End?
Will I Ever Stop
Being a Nigger?

Originally published in the *Utne Reader*
March 2016

The Lord is my shepherd, I shall not want.
—Psalm 23

What happens to a dream deferred?
—Langston Hughes

What brush do you bend when dusting
your shoulders from being offended?
What kind of den did they put you in
when the lions start hissing?
—Kendrick Lamar

I am not a nigger, or a nigga, or a nigguh. I am not your nigger or anyone else's nigger, either. Nor do I belong to some specialized society that contains within its boundaries niggers, or niggas, or niggaz4life. No—
I am a man, a Black man, a human being, and I am your equal. After this piece goes live, I am never again going to utter that word *nigger* to describe myself, to describe Black people, to paint a picture of a certain type of mentality born of racial oppression, self-hatred, confusion, of ignorance; not publicly, not privately. No—
Yet when I look at race and racism in America in the twenty-

first century, how could I not help but feel like I am nothing but that loaded and disgusting word? I often wonder if it actually matters that I came up from the ghetto; me, the product of a single mother who escaped, barely, the color-line insanity of the Jim Crow South only to confront a different kind of race and class insanity in Northern slums; me, the son of an absent father who completely and permanently abandoned my mom and me when I was eight because he was a broken Black man and did not know it; me, a Black boy who has known poverty, violence, abuse, fear, hopelessness, depression; me, who made it to college on a financial aid package, never got my degree, but still made a name for myself, against all odds; me, who has published twelve books and who has visited all fifty American states—as a writer, as a political activist, as a speaker; me, the kid who did not get on an airplane until I was age twenty-four, but who has since been to five of the seven continents, and who is interviewed virtually each week on television and radio and elsewhere for media outlets from every corner of the world.

What does it matter that I, as my mother has said with her grits-and-butter South Carolina dialect, "speaks well," that I have the ability to converse with equal comfort on college campuses and on concrete street corners, that I can easily flow from exchanges on presidential campaigns and gender politics to basketball and pop culture? What does it matter, indeed, if I have produced a body of work, my writings, my speeches, my humanitarian and philanthropic efforts, in service to people, all people, and that I really do see you, me, us, as sisters and brothers, no matter who you are or what you look like, as part of the human race, the human family, if you, in the smoked-out buildings that are your mind's eyes, refuse to see me, or refuse to see me as a whole human being, or, worse, simply see me as that word? Or what if you see me as an animal, a monster, some *thing* to be dissed, avoided, detested, labeled as angry or a thug or difficult or arrogant or a problem or a burden?

Yes, a nigger, that creature and creation born of a vicious racism seemingly as long as the nightmares of my African ancestors shocked and awed as they were bamboozled and kidnapped from the motherland centuries back; their sweaty raw bodies the infrastructure for the first global economy in this world—slavery, the transatlantic slave trade. That slave trade built and enriched Europe, built and enriched America, and turned places as different as New York City and the American South and the West Indies and Latin America and the United Kingdom into real and metaphorical castles for powerful and privileged White people. Meanwhile, the bodies of my beautiful ancestors were brutalized by a diabolical scheme to bend and bomb any memory of their names, their identities, their very beings, until they became that which they were told: niggers . . .

So there is simply no way to have what my Alpha Phi Alpha fraternity brother David Young dubs "courageous conversations" about race and racism in America if you refuse to hear me, if you refuse to read this essay to the very end, if you refuse to acknowledge that my history is your history too. We are chained together like those slaves were chained together on those ships and those auction blocks.

I can hear my White sisters and brothers say now, as many often declare to me when this uncomfortable dialogue occurs, "But I did not own slaves, I had nothing to do with that," or, "My relatives did not do that." It does not matter if you or your long-gone relatives were directly involved or not, or if you believe "that is in the past." The past, tragically, is the present, because we've been too terrified to confront our whole history and our whole selves as Americans.

Furthermore, what matters is that a system was put in place, rooted in slavery, based on White-skin privilege and White skin color, that revolved around power, land, property, status, shared values born of oppression and discrimination and marginalization, and that has never changed in America. Never. That system

and its values have been passed generation to generation as effortlessly as we pass plates at the family dinner table. So it does not matter if you never openly refer to a Black person as a nigger or not. It does not matter if your college fraternity puts on Blackface and mocks Black culture on Halloween or not. It does not matter if you are a practicing racist or not. It does not matter if you call yourself a Democrat or a Republican or an Independent. It does not matter if you call yourself a progressive or liberal or a centrist or conservative. It does not matter if you have Black friends or a Black wife or Black husband or Black partner or Black relatives or Black or biracial children (biologically or adopted). It does not matter if you love hip-hop or other Black music and Black art, or that you grew up in or around a Black community, or spend much time there now as an adult. It does not matter if one or a tiny handful of Black writers, or Black artists, or Black public intellectuals, or Black spokespersons, or Black entertainers and athletes, or Black media personalities, or Black anything are given major platforms and fame and awards and tons of money and status to prove racism is not what it was, or, equally tripped out, to tell you about your racism. That nutty game of the "special" Black person, handpicked to represent the rest of us, is as old and tired as racism itself. We are all your equals and all equally valuable—from the hood to Hollywood, from Harlem to Harvard—not just the select few anointed and celebrated by White American tastemakers.

So what ultimately matters is what you are willing to give up, to sacrifice, in every aspect of your life, to speak out and push back against that which has taught you that you are superior and that I am inferior, that you are always right and I am always wrong, pretty much in every space imaginable, both consciously and subconsciously. Silence is unacceptable in the face of injustice, and being neutral is being a coward and an accomplice to the evil sides of our history.

Thus, to be mad blunt, in our America racism is race plus

power and privilege; who has the favorable race or skin color, who has the power and privilege, and who does not. Yes, Black folks and other people of color sure can be prejudiced, bigoted, hateful, and mean toward our White sisters and brothers. I certainly have been in past chapters of my life, but I am no longer and never will be again. I believe in love of self, love of us all. But be that as it may, I am also clear that we Black folks do not control or own the majority of politics and the government, education, the mass media culture, social media and technology, Hollywood, corporate America, sports teams, music and other entertainment, the arts, the book industry, police departments, anything that shapes the thinking of every single American citizen and resident during our waking hours. Not even close. We do not set the standards for what is considered beautiful or attractive, what is considered courageous or intelligent, nor do we dictate what becomes popular, visible, viable. And we certainly do not say what matters in history, what does not, what stories should be told, and which ones are irrelevant, not for the multitudes—not even close.

Our stories, our versions of America, of our history, are marginalized, put to the side, specialized, ghettoized. This is why a brutally violent "explorer" like Christopher Columbus is mythologized as a hero, why Thanksgiving celebrants are in denial about the horrors done to Native Americans, why things like slavery and the Civil Rights Movement are essentially skimmed over, if taught at all, to any of us, in public schools or private schools, be we wealthy or working class. Racism in America means being so immune from it that you do not even think about being White. You just are. Does this mean that I believe every single White person in the United States is racist? No, not hardly, because I have encountered far too many brilliant, honest, big-hearted, and integrity-filled White sisters and brothers who are willing to challenge their power and their privilege, even at their own material, physical, and spiritual ex-

pense. I have far too many White sisters and brothers in my life who are dear friends, allies, supporters, confidantes, mentors, and sheroes and heroes of mine. But what I do believe, because I have lived it and because I inhale it habitually, is that racism is a toxic and deadly cancer; no one is immune from it, and even the good and well-meaning among us have been profoundly contaminated with it, simply by virtue of your not wanting to have this conversation, or because you are having a hard time reading my words this very moment.

Yes, I do see very clearly that we are all connected, and I truly love and acknowledge every race, every ethnic group, every identity, and every culture that exists in America, on this earth. But I, we, would be lying if we did not also admit that the longest-running drama and the single most dysfunctional racial relationship in American history is between White people and Black people. That as long as that dynamic dysfunction exists, there is no way we will ever do right by Native Americans who were the victims of genocide, or ever look at Latinx immigrants as anything other than cheap labor and outlaws, or ever view Asians as anything other than the stereotypically quiet and often invisible "model minority." And definitely no way we will ever come to know and understand and feel the humanity of people who are Arab, Middle Eastern, Muslim, while the Black-White conundrum continues, excruciatingly, uninterrupted. Stated the way they did in "the old country"—down south—when I was a child, my momma and them said, religiously, that a liar is a thief. Well, it is way past time we stop lying to ourselves, fellow Americans, and stop stealing away the solutions that are in our very hands, and have always been there—

We've had at least three major opportunities in American history to confront and end systematic racism directly, but we merely toyed around with the notion, then backed away.

The first was when the colonies were warring with the mother

country, England, for independence. How incredible it would have been if "founding fathers" like George Washington and Thomas Jefferson had seriously and instantly freed their own slaves while declaring in their promissory note that "all men are created equal." How incredible if Native Americans were treated with dignity and grace, and a part of the vision, instead of as mortal enemies. How incredible if poor Whites and women of all hues, too, were included in the concept of freedom, justice, and equality. And, my God, how incredible would it have been for those Black slaves, my ancestors, to become free women and free men and free children, to participate, from the very beginning, in the building of what we claim to be a democracy?

The second chance was during the Civil War and its aftermath known as Reconstruction. We who truly know American history know that President Abraham Lincoln was not the great emancipator he is hailed to be. Sometimes he was for slavery and sometimes he was against slavery. And unambiguously his releasing Blacks from bondage in selected states gave the North more men to fight and win the war. You think not? Then Google one of Dr. King's last speeches where he referred to Lincoln as the "great vacillator." But, regardless, Lincoln's Emancipation Proclamation was put forth; he was assassinated, yet still there was a flickering hope of a better day as colored folks marched from plantations to liberty. But that long walk to freedom turned out to be fool's gold. Reconstruction lasted only a dozen years, until the Compromise of 1877 put Rutherford B. Hayes into the presidency, troops protecting the basic rights of Black folks were removed from the South, and an insidious White domestic terrorism—physical, mental, spiritual—exploded across America for nearly a century.

Blame Black folks for every moral issue in our fair land. Make Black men and Black women the poster children for every bad behavior or crime or social misstep in America. Tell Black folks that voting is a ticket to a better society, and then deny it

from them every chance you get, with poll taxes, with voter ID laws. Create a perpetual atmosphere of intimidation and fear where Black folks never know if they will be tarred, feathered, hanged from trees, lynched, bombed, shot, racially profiled, or choke-holded to death . . . simply for being Black . . .

It is a minor miracle of the gods and heavens that in the midst of that post–Civil War America Blacks were able, under harsh segregation laws, to build homes, own land, create schools of every variety, set up businesses that met each of their basic needs, and have whole communities, largely separate from White America—because they had no other choice. A minor miracle, too, that as racism reared its dreadful head and destroyed people's lives and neighborhoods, there were not more race rebellions, each and every year, across America during the Jim Crow era.

Look what happened to my great-grandfather, Benjamin Powell, who was murdered amid this racist hysteria in the early 1900s. He had the audacity to own four hundred acres of land in the Low Country of South Carolina, right near Savannah, Georgia. He had the nerve to be an entrepreneur, a cook, and a man who did things his way on his own terms. The good White men of that community did not take too kindly to a Black man with that brand of swagger, who thought and knew he was their equal. They pressured my great-grandfather to sell the land. When he did not, one day his wife got a knock on the door and was told my great-grandfather had choked on his own food and was found dead in nearby water. No, they had killed him. My great-grandmother was forced to sell 397 acres of that land to the White men for one penny each, and scores of my relatives on the Powell side fled for their lives to other states, never to be heard from again. Years later, when my mother was an eight-year-old girl, she would pick cotton on that very same Powell property, her life reduced to being the help for the good White people, the same good White people whose relatives had a hand in killing my great-grandfather—

We got one more opportunity to correct the racial wrongs in the last century. It was called the Civil Rights Movement. We who know history know there had been energy and agitation for decades around voting and civil rights, but the height of that effort occurred roughly between 1954 and 1968—the years of the *Brown v. Board of Education* Supreme Court decision and the ruthless murder of fourteen-year-old Emmett Till in Mississippi, and Martin Luther King's assassination on April 4, 1968.

What a majestic movement it was. People, Black people of all backgrounds, and some loyal White allies too, peaceful, largely nonviolent, but courageous in the face of job firings, shootings, bombings, water hoses, attack dogs, not letting anyone turn them around. African Americans were not asking for much. *Can we vote? Can we be full-fledged citizens? Can we move about without fear of being murdered simply for who we are?*

The movement was powerful, it was diverse, it had voices as different as Fannie Lou Hamer, Ella Baker, Dr. King, Malcolm X, and the Black Panther Party. It desegregated public spaces, it appealed for voting and basic citizenship rights; it challenged police brutality and poverty and economic injustice. There were many big and small victories, and I owe the fact that I am a first-generation college student to these many unsung warriors of the civil rights era. But then it was over—

As soon as Dr. King's blood was scrubbed and washed from that Memphis motel balcony, America, our America, under the guise of taking the country back, began an all-out assault on those very minimal triumphs that occurred during the civil rights era. We have witnessed Nixon, the Reagan Revolution, the crack epidemic, the HIV/AIDS pandemic, mass incarceration and the prison-industrial complex; we have seen record numbers of poor Black folks thrown off welfare and locked in jails during the era of President Bill Clinton and First Lady Hillary Clinton; we survived the administration of George W. Bush, his infamous

wars and his failed "no child left behind," and that hideous stain on America's face called Hurricane Katrina. We stand idly by as gentrification, under the pretense of urban development, destroys longstanding Black and Latino communities, from Brooklyn to Oakland, from the Bronx to Seattle, from Detroit to Atlanta, leaving the very poor people Dr. King urged us not to forget largely alone to fend for their lives, isolated and alienated by the triple evils of racism and classism and indifference. Public schools and an overemphasis on testing and zero-tolerance discipline in these poor communities are a disaster; there are few to no jobs; there is constant fear of the police and of each other; there is endless violence born of self-hatred and despair; there is little to no hope; there are racist and classist stereotypes they confront every single day of their lives; there is the looming threat of prison or an early death that has swallowed their peers and family members.

If this is what integration was supposed to be coming out of the Civil Rights Movement, then it has been a complete and monumental failure for poor Black people in America. Black communities are not what they were; the multifaceted and thriving Black "businesses" of yesteryear have been reduced to barbershops and beauty salons, churches and funeral parlors, and the mom-and-pop soul food restaurants. The class divide between poor and middle-class African Americans is larger than ever, and there is a convenient and perpetual need to blame poor Black folks for everything that ails Black America—like guns and violence, like drugs—when we know, factually, that White folks—rich ones and poor ones—shoot guns, are violent, and take drugs too. But people lie and make up convenient truths to suit their agendas, and we know that when racism and intra-racism are the order of the day, it's very easy to blame the ghetto, the hood, or so-called niggers.

And it is within that context, now, that we also bear witness to the meanness and venom manifested during the Obama years

with a president elected by a rainbow coalition that made some believe, naively, that the United States was at its best: full of empathy and compassion and magically postracial. Instead, during his term, Barack Obama has received more death threats than any other commander in chief in American history; he has been thoroughly disrespected by congressional members and other elected officials, sometimes to his face; and the "they" we Black folks like to talk about still question Obama's nationality and ethnic origins, his religion, his loyalty to the country. It is a Fox News Channel mentality that thrives on fear, hatred, violence, and intimidation. It is a Republican Party where even Lincoln's flip-flopping politics would be welcome given the fire-breathing inhumanity spewed from its leadership in these times.

It has been in this climate that there seems to be an explosion of racial-profiling cases throughout America. Say their names and you hear Trayvon Martin, Sandra Bland, Michael Brown, Rekia Boyd, Oscar Grant, Aiyana Stanley-Jones, Eric Garner, Renisha McBride, Tamir Rice . . . so many dead Black bodies that I have lost count. Some killed by police, some killed by civilian White folks, some Black adults and some Black children, some where it was clear cut and captured on video, some where the circumstances are murky, the alleged causes feeling like the lies they told my great-grandmother after her husband was found dead in that water.

But let's be clear. These racial murders did not end with the Civil Rights Movement. They never ended. I have been an activist since I was a teenager, since the 1980s. I have worked on so many racial-profiling cases that I have come to expect, weekly, news of yet another Black woman or Black man killed. What has changed is that we have, in these times, cell phones and social media to record and share these tragedies. I do not know if that is a good thing or a bad thing. For every single time a Black person has died at the hands of a police officer, or White person, usually a White male, in their car, in their church, in their hood,

my soul grows taut and my heart aches because I know but for the grace of the God I believe in, that can be me.

That is because to be Black in America is to live a sort of death every single day of your life. It makes for a stressful, paranoid, and schizophrenic existence: am I an American, or am I not? You do not know how you will be assaulted, so you brace yourself for the worst and hope for the best. For me that means I am forever thinking about things my White sisters and brothers do not have to think about. Like if I carry my black iPhone in my hand, will it be mistaken for a gun, and will I consequently get shot by a cop? Like if I, a marathon runner, jog my miles through certain neighborhoods at certain times of the day or night, will someone call the police on me, or, worse yet, will they morph into George Zimmerman to my Trayvon Martin and be judge and jury and executioner of my life? Like if I dare to show an emotion like outward confidence, will I be deemed a menace to society, a threat to the status quo, an uppity nigger or "boy" who needs to know my place, the way some in America have been offended by Super Bowl quarterback Cam Newton, his smile, his smirk, his proclamations that he is Superman, his doing the dab dance whenever he makes a big play?

Like if I dare to challenge or question a White woman, a White man, as I have many times—the White female journalist on the New York public radio podcast, the White male editor of that national men's magazine, the White women and men who like to come on my social media pages to criticize and challenge, randomly and disrespectfully, my posts—will I be penalized, ostracized, deemed a problem child simply because I use the mind my God gave me?

Like if I dare to express, aloud, pride in my heritage, my culture, my people, and to acknowledge, through my art, as Beyoncé does with her song "Formation," will I be told that I am offensive and unacceptable to Middle America because I also reference the revolutionary elements of my history like the Black Panther Party?

Like if I dare to convey any anger, as I did when I was in my twenties as a cast member on the MTV reality show *The Real World*, will I be branded as such for the rest of my life, to the point where, two decades later, I have absolutely outraged White people coming on my Twitter or Facebook pages, cursing me out, telling me they did not like me then and they do not like me now? Or like every single time I am on Fox News Channel, or some other network, talking about issues like violence, guns, abortion, race, gender, whatever it may be, and I inevitably get tweets, emails, you name it, threatening my life, calls for me to go back to Africa, to kill myself, to be killed, just because I happen to be a Black man in America with a voice and an opinion—

This is what the cancer of racism does to me, to people like me. We die and have to resurrect ourselves day to day. We laugh and party and praise God hard to keep from crying and dying inside, from committing slow suicide. We cry and battle low self-esteem and debilitating angst and sadness simply because we wonder, aloud, what did we do to be so Black and blue? We swallow the racism until it becomes as natural to us as our heartbeats, and that internalized racism becomes Black self-hatred, Black abuse, Black-on-Black violence physically, spiritually, mentally; it becomes the Black elite, the Black gatekeepers, the so-called Black leaders and thinkers, the ones who have no real plan, no real vision, no real imagination when it comes down to the real challenges facing Black America, yet are quick to pimp or put down Black America, particularly poor Black America, every chance they get, but have nothing to say about American racism and its devastating effects, like ever; it becomes the Black woman writer who recently attacked me so nastily on social media because she did not like my private, off-the-record feedback on her work or her approach to Black issues; or it becomes the Black male airport worker who loudly disrespected me at the security checkpoint because his false sense of power told him I was nothing but a nigger to be bossed around and controlled;

or the many times in my own life where I, too, have been so wounded by this system of oppression that I lashed out at any and all Black folks because in doing so, I was trying to smash the mirror that was myself once and for all. We are pained, we are hurt, we are distressed, we are bewildered, many of us do whatever we must to dull the awful sensations of racism—with drink, with cigarettes, with drugs, with sex, with video games, with sports, with music, with violence, with mistreatment to self and to others—a very vicious cycle, a treadmill we can never seem to escape—

No one—*no one*—should have to live like this, think this, or be like this. No one should have to teach their children how to react if stopped by the police. No one should have to tell their loved ones to "be safe" or "be careful" when they leave home, not knowing if they will ever return, not in the twenty-first century, not after all this nation has been through, not after all the many lives lost. No one, including me, should wake in the mornings wondering if this will be my last day on earth, if I will die at the hands of a police officer, or a White racist, or a deeply disturbed human being who is Black like me . . .

Yeah, it is utterly exhausting to have to navigate daily the macro and micro slings and arrows that are American racism. It is doubly exhausting to have to do so and also explain to good, well-meaning White people over and over again what racism is, what they can and should do and why, and then, in some cases, be expected to hold their hands emotionally. Black folks in America are sick and tired of being the emotional and spir- itual help for White Americans who want to get it but do not. We are also sick and tired of being the historical mammy figure, or the postmodern nanny, forever catering to your needs while our needs get woefully neglected. You want to end racism in America and on this planet, my White sisters and brothers, now, and once and for all? You have got to do the work yourselves,

in your communities, with people who are White like you. I can and will be your ally, your friend, will work in coalitions with you. But just like when I was first challenged, by women, to think about sexism and gender oppression as a man in a different way back in the early 1990s, I could not just expect women to do my work for me. I had to do it. Nor could I expect women to hold my hand. And I had to do this work with men and boys, not women and girls, primarily. Because I needed to go to the source of the power and privilege, not to the victims of that power and privilege.

This is not easy work, challenging systems of oppression. But the choice of doing nothing or remaining inactive means a continued death of the American soul, of the American psyche, and an acceptance of the sickness that is within all of us. To be ignorant to what I am saying is a sickness. To think I am lying or exaggerating is a sickness. To think you are somehow immune from all of this is a sickness. And to twist things around, to believe that you are somehow the victim, in sheer opposition to history and modern-day facts, is a sickness, a sort of mental and spiritual escapism devoid of truth and devoid of a desire for real healing and real reconciliation in America.

The above said, this is so much bigger than #OscarsSoWhite or #BlackLivesMatter, although both are symptoms of the bigger problem. The Academy Awards are so White because America still believes it is so White, that White stories matter and that the stories of people of color do not, except on rare occasions, and with the same basic types of characters and plots. Rarely are we permitted to be complex, multilayered, thoughtful humans on film or television, except for the masterful producing work of, say, a Shonda Rhimes, that rare Black person shining in Hollywood. This is why I say Black lives do not really matter; because if they did, we would not need to say it over and over again. Who, precisely, are we trying to convince of this fact?

This is also so much bigger than how we perceive a Peyton Manning or a Tom Brady versus how we perceive a Cam Newton or a LeBron James; although we know White men can be angry, confident, sullen, rude, sore losers—no backlash for Peyton Manning after his Super Bowl XLIV loss and demeanor versus nonstop backlash for Cam Newton after his Super Bowl 50 loss and demeanor; we know White men can be fathers of children without being married to the mother and never accused of making babies out of wedlock, even if they did—Exhibit A is Tom Brady's first child versus Cam Newton's first child; same scenario but a different public reaction. And it is not mad cool when a famous or nonfamous Black woman or man shows a range of emotions, including anger and confidence: she or he becomes a pariah, a thing to be marked, labeled, hated, condemned, and watched by false angels with dirty faces. Think of Serena Williams, think of Nina Simone, think of Sandra Bland when she was pulled over by that Texas cop. That said, we know a certain segment of the American tastemaking machine likes its heroes to be heterosexual White men. So if you are, say, a heterosexual Black male hero, you must be the apolitical and socially detached Michael Jordan type. You cannot be Muhammad Ali, or someone like Ali in his prime like, say, Cam Newton. Nah. You cannot desire to be in control of your own career, your own life, and your own destiny, like LeBron. Nah. You must be obedient, you must be grateful, you must be an employee only, one who does not think or know your own value; you must be neutral, and you must castrate yourself and your dignity, by any means necessary—

And so, you see, that is why this is also so much bigger than a Donald Trump, although we know that Trump represents everything that is wrong with America, not just because he is an angry, foul-mouthed, disrespectful, opportunistic, racist, sexist, and classist heterosexual White male, but because he knows he has power and privilege, and uses it to injure others, without any

remorse whatsoever. Trump's racism is the same racism of Barry Goldwater, of Nixon, of Reagan, of George W., of Paul Ryan, of Rudy Giuliani, of Chris Christie, of certain kinds of straight White men of means and access, who couldn't care less about middle-class and working-class White Americans, but who have conveniently created and spread a lie, in thinly veiled racial tones, that the enemy of these White folks in Middle America, in the American South, is the Black folks and other people of color who threaten their freedoms, their jobs, their security, and their rights. Whether Trump really means what he is saying or if he is simply being highly opportunistic is inconsequential. Fact is, he is saying those things, people feel and believe him, and he continues a story line that has brought great harm to America for centuries now. Because the greatest trick of a racist is getting folks to believe that racism doesn't exist in the first place, or that the people with no power and no privilege are the real racists, the real oppressors.

But in spite of the questions in the title of this essay, and in spite of all I have written here, I really do have limitless hope for humanity, for America. It is in my spirit, it is in my bones, and it is in my DNA. I have no other choice. I do not want to say the clichéd thing about racism not ending in my lifetime, because I will continue to do everything I can to help it end, before I die. And as I crisscross America weekly, yes, I do hear the sad and sordid tales of racism on college campuses, of Black student leaders and Black student athletes protesting one insult after another. And yes, I do see, in innumerable communities, people fighting the good fight against racism, against hate. But I also see, as I speak at and facilitate public conversations in places as different as Perrysburg, Ohio, and Minneapolis, Minnesota, a genuine fatigue with the racism, with the hatred, with the fear and ignorance and violence and division, with people not talking with and listening to each other, especially when it is not comfortable

to do so. Yes, I have hope because of young people, the diverse groups of youthful Americans I encounter everywhere I go, who at least have a willingness to hear, to learn, to share. It is their fearlessness, their idealism, their openness that keeps me going, that makes me believe we can change history and change this world.

Finally, we have heard for years, at least going back to the presidency of Bill Clinton, this call for a national conversation on race. What I have come to realize is that this is a political football for certain kinds of political leaders to toss about when there is yet another racially motivated tragedy in our America. That if there truly is to be a conversation, a raw and real dialogue, it must come from the bottom up, from we the people. I've said all I can say about America, about American history, about what racism has done to me, to my family. I am drained and near tears, to be downright honest, from writing this piece, because it has forced me to revisit both new and old traumas, to revisit new and old wars with myself, with others, wars that I really do not want to fight. I want to heal; I want us all to heal. This healing work must happen with White sisters and brothers and it must happen with Black sisters and brothers, and sisters and brothers of every racial and cultural upbringing in America. Protests, rallies, marches should continue to happen as long as racism exists, as long as there is inequality, injustice, and the absence of opportunities for all people. They must. But we also must be conscious of how this racism cancer eats at us, how it destroys us from the inside out, how we must learn the difference between proactive anger and reactionary anger. Proactive anger builds bridges, possibilities, alliances, movements, and, ultimately, love. Reactive anger destroys bridges, breeds dysfunction, and spreads more madness and confusion. Yes, passion is necessary, and we should be angry because of what I have described in this essay, for it is a natural human emotion. But that anger must not become the very hate we say we are against.

For White Americans, this means you've got to reinvent yourselves if you are serious about ridding our society of racism. You've got to ask yourself, *Who and what was I before I became White? What does it mean to me to be human, to be a human being, and what, again, am I willing to do, willing to sacrifice, and willing to give up to be a part of this necessary healing process?* You must learn to listen to the voices of Black people and other people of color, you must not feel the need, through arrogance or insecurity, to tell us who we are, what we should be thinking or feeling or doing, and you must, with love and respect, understand when we may be hypersensitive to race, to racism, given the history and present-day realities of our America. Shutting us down or ignoring us or unfriending us says you do not truly want a conversation, as equals, especially if that conversation makes you uncomfortable.

As for me, I just want to be at peace, I just want to see love in the world; I just want to love and honor myself, who I am, without it being considered an affront or danger to someone else, because of racism, because of hate and ignorance and fear. I do not want to be, forever, that exasperation and anguish in Sandra Bland's voice on that video where the Texas cop pulled her over, my life the heavy drag on the cigarette she smoked, not knowing that just a few days later she would be found hanging in a Texas jail cell. I do not want to pick up a gun and commit suicide at the door of the Ohio statehouse because my demons got the best of me like twenty-three-year-old #BlackLivesMatter activist MarShawn M. McCarrel II. I do not want my life to end prematurely, at your hands or at mine, and I do not want my life to be in vain, because of what I am. I do not want my work for freedom, justice, and equality for all people to kill me, is what I am saying, to destroy me, to render me mute and useless, to myself, to others. That means I just want to be a whole human being, a free human being, and respected as such. And I just want to live in an America, and on a planet, where I can dream, for-

ever, instead of being tired, irritated, uncomfortable, and scared, forever, that my life will somehow wind up as a nightmare—

The Day Our Prince Died

Originally published in *HuffPost*
April 25, 2016

I finally shed massive tears for Prince a few days after he left us. Was not sure if I knew how to do so given the hole-in-the-heart sorrow I feel. I am sleepless, numb, and terribly sad that Prince is dead, gone from us forever. I have not been able to eat properly, or to think straight for extended periods; I just watch and listen to one Prince video clip or song after another. This is like the death of a family member, a close friend, someone you could not imagine life without—

I only met Prince once. It was back in 2006 and I was writing a cover story on comedian Dave Chappelle for *Esquire*. Chappelle presented at the Grammys and then got a personal call from Prince to come to his Los Angeles–area home for an after-party. At some point Chappelle and I separated and as I stood alone marveling at the purplish-ness of Prince's mansion, there he was to my left, sizing me up. "You're the writer, right?" I was stunned Prince knew me. I muttered, "Yes," but could not look at him. When I finally gathered nerve to face him, he had disappeared. I never saw him again that evening. A year or so later Prince's lawyer asked if I might be interested in helping the legend pen his autobiography. I was going through serious life struggles, so nothing ever came of it. I've always wondered what if.

You see, I am more than a fan; I am an admirer of Prince for the musical, social, fashion, and artistic revolutionary he has been for five decades. From disco and the birth of hip-hop and punk, to Kendrick Lamar and Katy Perry, there has been Prince,

visible, in the shadows, somewhere. He has been a multigenerational global superstar when there have been few others in world music history, save the Beatles, Michael Jackson, Madonna, Bob Marley, Stevie Wonder, Nina Simone, Bob Dylan, Diana Ross; and maybe one day folks like Beyoncé, Ed Sheeran, Bruno Mars, and Adele.

I cannot say that I understood Prince at first. It confused me, as a ghetto youth, his very raw and public utterances in his lyrics about his racial and sexual orientation, the way he dressed, so very different than the average Black boy in the hood. But I paid attention because there was something behind the shiny permed hair, the thick mascara and makeup, the bikini underwear and androgynous clothes, the super-high heels, and those big and round and hyper-animated brown eyes. Michael Jackson may have been more my superhero then, but Prince was the rebel, the troubled youth, the out-of-box brown-skinned Mozart only folks on the ragged edges of our own families and communities could truly appreciate. Prince represented for the nerdy kids, the weird kids, the bad kids, for the Black kids like me who were told we were "acting White" if we spoke a certain way or liked certain kinds of music. Nah, he was not acting White. He was being every part of himself, his whole self.

Prince was post–civil rights America. He was that child integrating that public school, those kids sitting in at the lunch counters, the young freedom riders crossing state lines on a bus—Black students and White students, dreaming a world where a shining Black prince, named Prince Rogers Nelson, could be whatever the heck he wanted to be. Even if that meant being the sort of man, the sort of Black man, who refused to kowtow to someone else's definition of what a man was, or was supposed to be. Prince talked sex, he talked love, he questioned God, he questioned himself, he weighed in on social issues like AIDS and violence, and he had the balls, quite literally, to pose butt-naked, as a matter of fact, on the cover of one of his al-

bums. So Prince was, in a word, free, and it was electrifying and shocking to behold—

When *Purple Rain*, the movie and the soundtrack, fell like a piano from a skyscraper window in the summer of 1984, it was also in that radioactive season that I began college. "When Doves Cry," the lead single, was everywhere. The sound was so distinctive, so hypnotic. Was not until many years later that I learned Prince intentionally dropped the bass from the track at the last minute. And yo, those lyrics, that song, pretty much every song he ever made, thirty-nine albums worth in his lifetime—

What I am saying is Prince was a prophetic poet and a holy-water preacher baptized by his ancestors' Louisiana gumbo and the good fortune to have a momma and a daddy who were both jazz artists. You think Prince, you think African griots chanting peace-and-love psalms in their village; you think Black slaves making melodies with the methodical movements of their perspiring bodies as they picked cotton from sunup till sundown; and you think Prince, you think Jelly Roll Morton on piano, Chuck Berry on guitar, and Ella Fitzgerald and Jackie Wilson borrowing the dopest sections of God's song-and-dance dream team to make the supernatural from scats of a migration jazz song: Louisiana swamps and second lines begat Minnesota frost and unfiltered funk.

Prince was, in a phrase, unapologetic Blackness like a molasses-tongued Mississippi Delta bluesman; yet Prince was also Dr. King's mountaintop vision of the beloved community too, a humanitarian for the human race, the flower-child hippie who might've also been down with the Black Panther Party, ya dig? That meant Prince was an Afroed soul brother who did not want to be locked and loaded as merely a Black musician, but still, he was very much straight outta Black mavericks like Little Richard, James Brown, the Isley Brothers, and Sly Stone.

Yes, Prince was a bridge-builder, a mash-up of pop royalty pasts and pop royalty futures, a crosser and eraser of race, gen-

der, class, and sexual identity boundaries, an imaginative and curious student of America, our America, from his Midwest stoop where the blatant racial hang-ups may not have been as hardcore in his hometown of Minneapolis as, say, the South or even New York City. That is why he told an exec from Warner Bros. Records, as a teenager, that not only was he going to produce his first album, but not to make him Black. Only a pint-size Black male secure in his swagger would dare say something like that to a multinational record label, to White men with power. As in, *Do not tell me, Prince, that my music can only be one thing.* Not when you are a prodigy, as Prince was; and not when he would be a one-man version of the Beatles, evolving from teen idol to serious adult arranger of his varied musical taste buds—taste buds that would come to fist-bump Joni Mitchell, Miles Davis, David Bowie, Jimi Hendrix, Laura Nyro, and even the rap music he avoided at the tip-off of his magical mystery tour—

This is why it is so hard to write this piece. I am writing about a very private dead man who may have been addicted to prescription drugs during the sunset of his life, a sunset none of us were prepared for mentally. It stabs and it cuts like a sharpened machete to say Prince is dead. Because I am writing about someone who, in spite of the worldwide adulation, and in spite of the revolving door of individuals who labored with him through the decades, may have been a very lonely man, emotionally, spiritually, still seeking answers, his Jehovah's Witness faith notwithstanding. "Nobody loves a genius child," Langston Hughes once wrote in a poem. I also think we've called folks like Prince a genius so much that we make them loners and tormented and reclusive by default. We expect them to perform, to create, and make art, to entertain and mesmerize us, regardless if they are always able to or not. I wonder how Prince managed to get through his last live shows in Atlanta; I wonder about the alleged drug overdose on that private jet after the Atlanta shows; I wonder what years and years of leaps and splits and

spins and dips, in high heels no less, had done to his puny body. Broken down, perhaps, the way an aging athlete plays and plays until the body just gives up and things fall apart.

No matter. What we should say now is that Prince was a man, very much his own man. That man twice married and twice also lost children—one right after birth, one a miscarriage. That man withstood torrential public disses and humiliations because he chose to write *SLAVE* on his face and challenged his original record label, Warner Bros. Records, for what he felt was an unfair contract for artists. That man who I saw perform live so many times I lost count, who hypnotized me speechless each and every concert, in large arenas, in small intimate spaces, because he looked and felt and smelled like music, like his very flesh was a polyester quilt of searing falsettos and space-shuttle guitar riffs—

So I want to remember Prince as the greatest live performer I ever saw; for the good fights he fought to the very end; how he wrote that song for Baltimore after the city exploded in racial turmoil in 2015. How he continued to the very end to be a loud and present voice for the rights and power of artists to own and control their own destinies. How he mentored and supported so many younger artists, so many organizations and institutions, most of it very privately. How he acknowledged, loudly, the Black Lives Matter movement. And how he, Prince, remained true to himself in the nightfall of his days, as his heart and his breath stopped in that dusty elevator at his Paisley Park compound in the Minnesota he never abandoned, even as an entire planet bathed and washed him, time and again, with the very purple rain he had mind-sprayed on us.

That is because Prince, once an epileptic boy in a plastic bubble with a guitar and a dream, became in his fifty-seven years of a wonderful life, very much the kind of man, the kind of human being, who will never ever need to write the word *SLAVE* on his face where he is now—

My Mother. Barack Obama. Donald Trump. And the Last Stand of the Angry White Man. Part 1

Originally published in *My Mother. Barack Obama. Donald Trump. And the Last Stand of the Angry White Man.*

2018

Nobody knows my name, nobody knows what I've done.
—Bessie Smith

This is what it sounds like
When doves cry.
—Prince

My mother is sick, and she has been in much pain for nearly two years now. There is no easy way to say this other than to say it directly. She is distressed, and I am distressed, extremely, by this situation. I cannot say that it was not expected, my mother becoming ill, but nevertheless, I cry regularly—merely by thinking about it. My mother's illness began in November of 2016, the same month Donald Trump defeated Hillary Clinton to become the forty-fifth president of the United States. My ma, forever a very proud and very self-sufficient woman, has mostly kept things to herself throughout my life. For example, I still do not know the uncut version of how my mother and father met, how he courted her, under what conditions she became pregnant with

me, or why, completely, my father was not there when I was born, or why I only saw him two or three times the first eight years of my life, before he told her he was done, that she had lied to him, that I was not his son. Nor do I know, wholly, the back-story of my mother's childhood in the racist, segregated America of the 1940s and 1950s and early 1960s of which she was born, and raised, and socialized to be who she has been ever since. Oh yes, she has given me plenty of unsolicited testimonies, several of those tales I have heard repeatedly, but when your mother is sick and your heart feels like it is going to fracture the way the earth does, abruptly, during an earthquake, you, an only child, cannot imagine your existence without the one person who has been there for you constantly, from the moment you drew your first breath; and you begin to hear and see and feel your mother's stories in a radically different way.

My mother has long had diabetes and high blood pressure and acute arthritis, has long taken prescription drugs for these ailments. And when my mother dutifully retired, at age sixty-two, after twenty-five years as a home health-care worker to senior citizens, just as she was becoming a senior citizen herself, I noticed in that very moment her walking with a dramatic limp, that she was wobbling instead of moving upright, and wobbling with tremendous discomfort. It was as if her mind had texted a message to her body that the backbreaking work begun when she was a little girl, picking cotton in the sun-fried fields of the American South, was over, at long last, and that her short, plump frame was instantly to pay the price for it: the years of twisting and bending and stretching and lifting and carrying; the years of being the help to others, to their families, while also raising her own child, alone; the years of walking and bussing it to work, through rain and high winds, through snow and dangerous ice, through the humbling heat of summer and the callous cold of winter; up the stairs she walked and down the stairs she walked, those twenty-five years of caring for the elderly, of washing and

bathing those not able to wash and bathe themselves; those twenty-five years of picking up those aging bodies that sagged in her arms like a heavy load, including the ones who died as she was nurturing them in some way; everything had finally taken its ugly toll on my mother. In those first years of her retirement I only half-heartedly and guiltily tried to get my ma to seek real medical attention, not more prescription drugs. Her response to me, each time I tried, is what she has been saying to me endlessly: "Boy, you don't know nothin'. I'm an independent woman. I'ma be all right."

But my ma is not all right, this much is clear to me now. When she finally broke down and told me, on that November day, that she had been having awful dizzy spells, that her hands and ankles were badly swollen, that she could barely use her fingers, that she felt electrified whips of torture, on the regular, shoot across her back, her arms, her legs, I knew that my mother was in a terrible place. It made me think back to maybe a half decade before when she called me in a panic and told me she needed to go to the hospital immediately. I was in Brooklyn, where I have lived for over half my life at this point, and my mother was there in my hometown of Jersey City. I frantically phoned an old high school friend, Leonardo, to get to her since I knew it would take me awhile to make it across the Brooklyn Bridge and through the Holland Tunnel. He did, and when I reached the hospital there was my mother lying belly-up on a metal table, in a hospital gown, with multiple tubes protruding from her body. I was shocked to see how much weight my mother had gained, how much her stomach had ballooned since her retirement. It was almost as if I had been so consumed with my own life, with my work of being a writer and an activist and a public speaker, with, truthfully, my own trials and tribulations, that I did not know my mother, did not know the troubles she had seen. In that hospital room, I sat with my ma as a battery of tests were run, and during one especially somber lull I stood up

with my back to her and sobbed uncontrollably, with my hand muffling my mouth, at the dreadful thought of losing her. *No, Ma, not now, please . . .*

The hospital doctor was blunt. My mother had to lose weight, she had to lessen her sugar intake, she had to stop cooking and eating the over-the-edge cholesterol-loaded stuff. My mother agreed to do what was told to her, to stay the course with her prescription drugs too, but she straightaway returned to the diet given to her at birth, the only diet she knew, one that filled her up, that gave her great satisfaction and joy: soul food. So, I became the ever-convenient punching bag for her feelings of being dispossessed of her identity: my mother mocked me whenever I broached the idea of changing her diet, ridiculed me for being a vegan, and maintained that I was the one who was going to get sick because I "only eat lettuce." She did not understand that part of the reason I had become a vegan was because I had watched her and other family members, and many folks around me, get preventable diseases because of what they ate and drank. I just did not want to knowingly go down that path. I especially thought of this when my mother told me, from that metal table, that she had not been a patient at a hospital since she'd given birth to me in the late 1960s. A stunning revelation that my mother, like so many of our self-sacrificing mothers, had gone her entire life ignoring one symptom after another until it halted her in her wobbly footsteps. It was then and there that I could see the stark-naked fear in my mother's eyes, but she dared not express it to me aloud. She did not want to talk about anything other than my getting her away from that hospital as fast as possible.

But this second health scare has been different. It was almost as if in the years between that hospital visit and November of 2016 my mother's body just kept going in a downward spiral on the inside, until her hands and arms and back and legs and feet decided to give up and become one huge and debilitating tor-

ment. I will be honest and say I did not know what to do at first, how to best support or help my mother. I'd heard stories from friends who had become their parent's or parents' caretaker. I had seen social media posts through the years of a parent falling gravely ill, then slowly dying, and the devastation it brought to the child or children. I had people in my life, close friends, who had been through a similar rite of passage, where the child suddenly becomes the parent and the parent suddenly becomes the child. But nothing—*nothing*—prepares you for this role, this responsibility, when it is automatically and ruthlessly you who is that person taking care of that parent. You sit and listen to your mother download what she is feeling in the various parts of her body. You hear her even as you are scanning the redness of her tired eyes, the budding wrinkles you never saw before across the smooth chocolate plane of her face, the layers of loose flesh that dangle, like mushy wet clay, about her chin and neck. Your ears digest her words as your eyes make their way across her shoulders, down her back, to her arms and hands, where you see, clearly, that they have swollen as if someone has blown air into each of her fingers and the palms of her hands. You jump-cut to her ankles and feet and, yes, someone has air-pumped those too. Your mother speaks of the years of soreness, of the many falls while working, that she has hidden from you until now. You seek help, ask advice, because as that only child you have no sister or brother to turn to, this is all on you—

I know my mother's eating habits are atrocious. I know my mother, especially since her retirement, has neither walked much nor exercised in any form, that she spends uncounted time in her favorite living room chair, a recliner, inhaling hours upon hours of television—the news, the talk shows of personalities like Steve Harvey and Ellen, anything, I imagine, that makes her feel good. After consulting with a wide range of people online and offline, one bit of advice stuck with me: just be there for her. How, I did not know at first, because my mother is not very

sociable, does not like to go out much, except to church and the grocery store and errands to pay her utility bills. My mother, who I love dearly, can be mean, rude, perpetually enraged, if I am going to be transparent about it all. That alone built the sky-high mental wall that separated us since I was a little boy. And I am so clear that if not for two-plus decades of therapy, nearly a decade of yoga practice, and having my art, writing, as an outlet since I was a teenager, there is really no way I could stay long in my mother's presence. I know far too many who have absorbed equally abusive behavior from their parent or parents—verbally, physically, emotionally, all of the above—who keep great distance from them and, in some cases, have cut them off and out entirely. I simply cannot do that to my ma, because, well, I love her, because I would not be who I am without her, and because I know what she has survived. It ain't been no crystal stair. So here she is, in her seventies now, in the golden years of her life, just trying to be happy and comfortable. My mother rises early in the mornings and goes to sleep early at night, oftentimes falling asleep while watching television right on that recliner. So, in the first moments of those November 2016 days, I decided to ask my mother, rather than tell her, how I could be of service. Her response: "Take me grocery shopping every week, so I do not have to walk there."

And that is exactly what I began to do. Grocery shopping with my mother. Something I had not done since I was a kid. There in Jersey City, a community I had escaped at age eighteen for college, that had both shaped and wounded me in unthinkable ways, to the point that it has left a permanent scar on my mind, a love-hate relationship that I am certain I will take with me to my grave. But I had to help my mother, which meant I had to suck up any lingering negative feelings I had about her, about my hometown, about being there physically, more than I'd been in years. And there I have been, week after week and month after month, with my mother, at her local market, the

one she prefers, outside picking out the shopping cart for her to make sure the wheels move exactly right. There inside, always grabbing five or six plastic bags for her fruits and vegetables. In the first weeks of grocery shopping I challenged her on her food selections, especially after we had visited my holistic doctor in Brooklyn. I should have known better. The moment we left my doctor's office my mother said to me, point blank, "I do not give a fuck what he said. Fuck that motherfucker. Ain't nobody gonna tell me what to do!" And these were some of the nicer words spoken by this Christian woman who is so verbally fluid she can pivot from random Bible scriptures to the crudest foul language so spontaneously that even Dave Chappelle or Chris Rock would blush. But I took to heart what my holistic doctor said to my mother: that far too many medical professionals only try to control the sickness, very few ever talk about healing. Thus, I pray to myself daily, as my doctor's words ring in my head whenever I grocery shop with my ma, that she will soften her stance, that she will heed his words in spite of her intense resistance, and come to understand the gravity of what my doctor said to her, of what she must do: change her diet over time, begin to do some kind of exercise, slowly wean herself off prescription drugs, and stop seeing sugar and fast foods as her two best friends. Yet as we go up and down aisle after aisle in this grocery store, my mother grabs the worst possible things to eat, and I am deflated, defeated, and find myself arguing with her about her food choices, and her arguing back with me, cursing me, and matter-of-factly saying to me, on several of these trips, "You are trying to take away what makes me happy!"

It was on one of those occasions when my mother said that to me, after a few months of these weekly grocery trips, that I let it go. I stopped questioning her food choices aloud, and just did what she told me to do: to push the cart for her when it became too heavy; to "notice my pocketbook" whenever she quick-stepped away from the store shopping cart to grab one

item or another; to quietly move her cart out of the way given her habit of always halting abruptly in the middle of one aisle or another and leaving it there to block others; to learn exactly when to offer assistance in the store, when to reach for an item she needed, when and how to unpack and put away her groceries once home, and where, precisely, to put her personal shopping cart every week in her bedroom, by her mirrored dresser. It has been because of these trips, over time, and as I have withstood with my mother all kinds of weather, all kinds of obstacles to my work schedule to be there for her, and all kinds of insults and toxic words and put-downs from my ma, that I finally began to see the whole woman that she is, and how she came to be, in ways I had never fully grasped before . . .

How she was born and raised in the Low Country of South Carolina; Ridgeland, South Carolina, Jasper County, in a two-room wooden shack; how she shared that cramped shack with her mother and father—the only grandparents I have ever known—and three sisters and a brother. How they were so poor that they would sometimes only have syrup to pass around in bowls as their meals. How they were so poor that modern conveniences like a bathroom with a working toilet or electricity, even, was not an option. There was a lightless and dingy outhouse in the yard that they had to enter to go to the bathroom. There were kerosene lamps to see in the pitch-black night. Yes, they were so poor that the girls sometimes had to take turns going to school because there was only one decent dress to wear, and thank goodness the four of them were relatively close in age. They were so poor that my mother began picking cotton at age eight in the fields owned by local White folks—my mother out there as a little girl with people old enough to be her parents or grandparents, each of them trying to make a way out of no way. There were also stories of what America was like during those days. My mother would say to me often, when I was a boy, that I had no idea what they experienced in the American South, that

we were poor, yes, but that I could not imagine how poor they had been. What I gathered, as a child, as a man listening to my mother today, is that poverty is economic violence against human beings and it is a nonstop assault on your mind, on your soul, on your body, and it damages you permanently, even if you are able to escape it, and that it was passed by my mother's parents to her to me as if we were earnestly passing a collection plate in one of our churches.

And then there was the very serious divide between Black people and White people, that it seemed like White folks hated Black folks mainly for being Black, but it would not be until many years later, when I was in college and began to study American and African American history, in a very serious and critical way, that I finally comprehended, fully, the breadth of what my mother and her family and families like theirs endured in that old country, in that old America. I mean, imagine your life, if you are my mother, a very beautiful and intelligent little Black girl, with very dark skin, being told practically from the time you could understand words and images that you were ugly, that you were not equal to Whites, that your life was doomed to be the servant, in some form, for White America, but never completely a life for yourself. I have wondered, as I have made my way up and down the aisles of that grocery store with my mother, what she might have wanted to be when she grew up, or if she even had any dreams at all. On a few of those grocery trips I tried to ask my ma but got rebuffed each time. Because, I have learned, Black people in America, with a few exceptions, often do not want to talk in detail about the past, not the dangerous parts of it anyhow, not the parts they miraculously survived. We just keep going, as my mother keeps going, wobbling from aisle to aisle in that grocery store, pushing her cart with a deep sense of focus and determination, as she pushed her life, as she has pushed me my entire life.

Yet I have also wondered about her explosive anger, her fire-

hot temper, the one that was passed to me, like how the super-rich pass family inheritances, where she might have gotten it from, what made her so terribly full of rage as a little girl. So uncontrollably angry, my Aunt Birdie once told me, that the tip of my mother's nose would become pockmarked with beads of sweat. I think of my mother's father, Pearly Powell, a very short and thickly built jet-Black man, who, I heard from the time I was a kid, had an equally volcanic temper, how my mother and her three sisters and brother and his wife, my grandmother, lived in day-to-day terror of his outbursts. He who wore blue overalls as Southern Black folks did in those days. He who hated White people, because of how much they hated him, because of how they treated Black men like him; and also, quite frankly, because of how some of the White men had savagely murdered his father, and then stole the majority of my great-grandfather's land from my great-grandmother. Yes, my grandfather was a mean man who knew how to fish and hunt and raise vegetables and fruits, who knew how to toil in the earth, and to steer, effortlessly, the mule-led wagon that got him around, because there was no money for a car. Yes, my grandfather was a mean old man who was taught, by the White world, by America, by his family, that violence was the solution for all problems, and, without hesitation or shame, did to my mother and her siblings and his wife what my mother did to me as a child: beat them ferociously. Beat them the way Black slaves were beaten ferociously by White masters and White overseers on those plantations. Beat them ferociously the way Indians were beaten by those who lusted for this American land at all costs. Beat them ferociously the way women have been beaten by men since the beginning of time. Beat them ferociously the way people of all backgrounds have beaten each other bloody in that thing we call war. Beat them down, ferociously, the way the severe poverty beat down my grandfather and grandmother and my mother and her sisters and brother, to the point where they

were painfully frightened of people, of the world, I have been told by other relatives.

And beat them down the way my grandfather and grandmother were beaten down by Whites of all ages, who called them "Uncle" and "Aunt" instead of Mr. and Mrs. Powell, because there was basically no respect for Black people, not even if you were a White youth or child. "Uncle" like "Uncle Ben" and "Aunt" like "Aunt Jemima," names given to Black people in America to sideline us, to marginalize us, to make us feel like, yes, we are still slaves, forever the mammies and nannies and sharecroppers to that part of White America that refuses to call us by our rightful names, refuses to see us as whole and complex human beings. The way, my mother told me, the White kids would call the Black kids where she grew up "nigger" and "coon" and "spear chucker" and "darkie" and "spade" and "jungle bunny" and "jigaboo" and every other name one can think of, names that made their way into American popular entertainment and lasted over a century, from the 1800s to the 1900s, via minstrel shows and minstrel songs, entertainment that, yeah, amused and drew much laughter from Whites in America while simultaneously making Black girls like my mother feel like they were worthless, unattractive, nothing, with no possibility whatsoever of any sort of a future, unless they worked for it until their bodies fell apart, quite literally. And even that would never be enough.

And, yes, I think of what my ancestors must have felt when, while there in Africa, European invaders came with guns and the Bible, co-opting and manipulating local Africans to assist them in kidnapping and enslaving people Black like me, to bring them, forcibly, to haunted ships that would cross the Atlantic Ocean; how they made their way—those that did not die or commit suicide—to places like New York City, like Charleston, South Carolina, like various parts of Latin America and the Caribbean, to become, as captured human beings, the first global economy in this new world. A world they did not create, a world

that transformed them into something—some *thing*—new, different, foreign, completely, from who they had been. African people turned into human property. The mental and physical and spiritual terrorism of that experience, for a couple of centuries, stripped of their names, their spiritual belief systems, their goddesses and gods, their music, their culture, their identities, their very beings. Made to do what the slave masters and those plantation overseers told them they had to do. Told, perpetually, that they were inferior, stupid, not worthy of being treated as human beings. Made to work the fields, to work in the big house, to be baby makers and baby breeders, to be the master's mistress by the only word that fits: rape. To be property sold at will, on a whim, whenever the mood struck. Families here today but torn asunder tomorrow: a family member liable to be sold at any given moment. Marriages not honored and respected consistently. Children ripped away from parents. Mental and physical violence as an everyday reality, torture and brutality as an everyday reality, who cared if their hands were up, defenseless, who cared if they said they could not breathe? The utter insanity of it all, enough to make a people wonder what they had done, indeed, to be so Black and blue. Yet in the midst of that they still created music—field hollers, spirituals, what would become the blues, jazz, rock and roll, soul, reggae, calypso, merengue, salsa, and, yes, hip-hop. You can slice or chop out their tongues, you can emasculate them, you can tar and feather and burn them and then hang them from trees, you can kill them and steal their land as you did to my great-grandfather Benjamin Powell, but you cannot stop them from singing, you cannot stop them from pushing, you cannot stop them from dreaming.

That is why I am so very clear that the dreamers of my immediate family were my mother and her two sisters, Catherine and Birdie, who dared to see another world outside of the backwoods Southern village they had been born into. These three sisters, led by my Aunt Birdie and my mother, plotted their escape,

first to Miami, to work in the homes of wealthy White folks, to save enough money to then move north, to Jersey City, where a cousin they were close to had settled. After less than a year in Miami, my mother and Aunt Birdie scooped up the youngest girl, Catherine, back home in South Carolina, and brought her "up the road" with them. When they landed in Jersey City, they first shared a bed, the three of them, in a one-room rental, but no matter, as they were determined not to return to the old country they had fled. There was no therapy, there was no yoga, there were no healing spaces or sister circles or meditation groups or #MeToo and #TimesUp for my mother and her two sisters. There has been no path to ever resolve the decades-long arguments between my mother and Aunt Birdie. There has been no exit for my Aunt Cathy to bolt from the decades-long bullying of my mother, her closest relative. They simply have had each other, they simply have had whatever they brought with them from the South to the North, and they simply have had to figure out, for themselves, how to win, how not to die or commit slow suicide in this foreign place, in this new land.

We talk much about America being built by immigrants, but that is only partially true. No, America was a sacred ground that Indians occupied first, and that the ancestors of people like my mother built, for free. It is also a place where people like my mother have been assaulted and molested and abused and injured, by systems of oppression, systems of discrimination, systems of hate, their entire lives. Women like my mother do not know a world where the triple evils of racism and sexism and classism have not done a war dance on their psyches, a half step forward, dozens of steps backward, just to make it to tomorrow. For those reasons, I can only imagine the ecstasy my mother must have felt when, as a young woman, she met my father, she in her early twenties, he in his early thirties. I do believe that my mother fell in love with my father, fell in love with the idea of being swept off her feet, as has been depicted forever in Ameri-

can movies. And I do believe that my father, equally as damaged and broken as my mother, did what he had been socialized to do, as a man: he stole her virginity, he stole her heart, he got her pregnant with me, he left my mother to travel to that hospital, alone, to give birth to me, and he abandoned my mother to raise me by herself, on welfare, food stamps, government cheese, and the sort of poverty and desperation and hopelessness I would not wish on anyone.

As I have journeyed with my mother through her illness, through the aisles of that grocery store, in those quiet moments in her apartment when we just sit and stare at the television, I have wondered often if my mother ever allowed a man to touch her again. I have wondered often why my mother spoke for years, when I was a child, of getting married, to my father, to anyone, then at some point just stopped saying it, giving up completely on the possibilities of love for herself. I have wondered often if anyone ever hugged or kissed my mother, if anyone ever told her that they loved her, that she was loved, that she *is* love.

I thought of this one day in my mother's living room when she slipped off the plastic-covered recliner and landed on the floor, unable to get up. Frightened, I leaped to the floor to help her, but my mother's weight is more than mine, so I struggled tremendously at first. As I held her in my arms, I looked into her eyes and I saw the little Black girl who was never told that she was beautiful, who was never told that she could be somebody, at any point in her life. I saw the little Black girl who, like the Black woman she would become, had to put on the protective armor of anger, of defiance, of single-minded determination, merely to exist and survive in an American ghetto. I saw the Black woman who would come to challenge crooked landlords and stingy employers and no-good men and supremely judgmental school officials who would try, on several occasions, to either kick her bad-tempered child from school or put him in special education. I tugged and lifted my mother up, as she had

done with her patients as a home health-care worker for many years, both smiling and crying as I did so, because I was embarrassed to be so close to her, the closest, physically, we had been since I was a little boy in her arms, holding tightly to her for love and protection.

Back in her recliner, my mother sighed heavily, and I sat on the sofa, dabbing the dripping sweat from my forehead. Ours has been an incredibly rough relationship. I have carried resentments against my mother since I was a child. As a boy, I blamed her for our poverty, for my father's abandonment, for everything. I hated her, then, every single time she called me "dummy" or "stupid" or a "mental case," a term she had picked up somewhere, God only knows where. I was absolutely terrified of my mother, the violence and abuse she heaped upon me as a child, the times she asked me, "Are you gonna be good?" as she beat me with a belt or a thin, stinging tree branch, or her bare hands, leaving welts every single occasion on my arms and legs; the times she confused me so, in one breath saying, "Do not be like your father!" yet in another, "You are just like that no-good father of yours!" I have hungered with outstretched hands, sobbing like a baby, as a boy, as a teenager, as a man, through the fogs and clouds and storms of my life, to be told by my mother that she loved me, for her to hug and kiss me, but those things simply never happened.

So, as I held my mother in my arms for what felt like my entire lifetime, I prayed with my eyes wide open and I said to myself, *I forgive you, Ma. I forgive you for the mean words. I forgive you for the violence, for the beatings. I forgive you for hiding major parts of your life story from me, I forgive you for it all.* I really have no other choice. I do not want to be that child, like some of my friends, who, even though their parent is dead and gone, still resent or hate that parent, as if they are mentally chained to that trauma and that hurt no matter what. I do not want to be that person, I do not want to be trapped, I want to be

free, and I know that in forgiving my mother, as I have come to be her caretaker, I am also forgiving myself too, at last.

Then I looked around my mother's apartment as I always did, and saw what had always been there with fresh eyes: the certificate from her former labor union about her years of service; the photo of a Black preacher I did not know holding a Bible with his head cocked just so; the ghostly image of the White Jesus at the Last Supper; the clock to tell my mother time, as she has always wanted to be on time, even in retirement; and above the sofa, above my head, a framed picture of Barack Obama, his wife Michelle, and their two daughters, Sasha and Malia. When I was a youth, I remember going to the homes of many Black people, relatives and nonrelatives both, and how virtually every single apartment or house had the photos of Martin Luther King Jr. and John Kennedy and Bobby Kennedy together. Back then I was perplexed as to why, but I gathered they meant something to Black folks in America, these three men who were all killed when they were young.

Years later I would come to understand that in a nation where people who are not White and privileged are treated as outsiders, as undesirables, as interlopers, we look for sheroes and heroes we can connect to, who speak to us, who speak for us, who can be and are what we will never be in our own lifetimes. We need and look for what they call in the Black Pentecostal church "supernatural miracles." Except for one Black preacher or another, my mother had never had images of Black people on her walls before, not even Dr. King. But in Barack and Michelle, I am sure, my mother saw the supernatural miracle of their marriage and a love she will never have for herself, and she saw a Black man as president through the eyes of that little Black girl in South Carolina who could have never imagined such a reality, not in her lifetime, not in a million lifetimes.

Michael B. Jordan on *Black Panther*: "We're giving Black people power"

Originally published in *British GQ*
February 26, 2018

I t took half a century for the Civil Rights Movement to deliver an African American to the White House. But in a nation where police disproportionately target and kill young Black men, where opportunities for Black voices are still narrow and prescribed, and where counterprotesters feel emboldened to say Black lives don't matter, the fight is far from finished. Now, Michael B. Jordan, star of Marvel's $200 million blockbuster *Black Panther*, is picking up the baton.

The first time I truly noticed Michael B. Jordan was in the 2013 low-budget indie film *Fruitvale Station*. Yes, I knew his journeyman standing from TV shows such as HBO's *The Wire* and the soap opera *All My Children*, but nothing prepared me for his spirit-chilling depiction of police shooting victim Oscar Grant. In this extraordinary performance as the young Black man shot and killed by a police officer in Oakland, California, in 2009, Jordan simultaneously morphed himself into a major actor and a living, breathing symbol of what most Black men fear: being killed simply because we are Black.

In *Fruitvale Station*, Jordan was a poetic embodiment of the issues Grant and many men like him face in life and death. It was an ancestral dance about Black lives mattering that brought

to mind Viola Davis and Denzel Washington. It was social realism: Michael B. Jordan was Oscar Grant and Oscar Grant was him. That the events of the film would end in the city where the Black Panther Party was born, at the height of the Civil Rights Movement in the autumn of 1966, was not lost on me. Nor the fact that Grant was gunned down a mere three weeks before Barack Obama was inaugurated as the US's first Black president. Jarring, all of it, and hypnotic and prophetic too.

Afterward, as the credits rolled, I sat in the theater, crying unashamedly at my country's sordid love affair with racism. And I said to myself, *This young man is going to be somebody . . .*

And being young, gifted, and Black, as Nina Simone once crooned, for Jordan, meant being handed the *Rocky* franchise by Sylvester Stallone, in the form of the blockbuster movie *Creed*. It also meant costarring in the new Marvel juggernaut *Black Panther*. Created, coincidentally, by comic book innovators Stan Lee and Jack Kirby just months before Huey Newton and Bobby Seale founded the political organization of the same name, *Black Panther* was the first superhero of African descent in mainstream US comics. It has been a long time coming for this franchise to make the transition to cinema, but here it is, at long last.

With such a large budget and a predominantly Black cast, there has never been an otherworldly warrior treatment like *Black Panther*. Indeed, it comes at a time of great change and turmoil in the United States, from the wildly unpredictable presidency of Donald Trump to endless racial violence and divisions to nervous conversations about diversity and inclusion. Directed by Ryan Coogler, the film marks the third time, after *Fruitvale Station* and *Creed*, that he and Jordan have collaborated, very much in the tradition of the classic partnership between Martin Scorsese and Robert De Niro. All of this is unprecedented, especially the fact that it is two young Black men staking claim to a Hollywood that would not have been open to them in this way when Spike Lee first hit the scene in the late '80s.

Things done changed.

But have they really?

This is what Michael B. Jordan wants to talk with me about and I with him.

And there he stands, inside a cave-like old warehouse in sun-kissed Los Angeles, one moment costumed as a hybrid of Martin Luther King Jr. and Malcolm X, the next seen in a black beret, like Newton and Seale when "Black Is Beautiful" was in vogue, long before we began using words like "woke" to describe social awareness. Woke he is, Michael B. Jordan, California-born, New Jersey-bred, power on his mind.

Jordan was a child actor who is a man today, marching to a drumbeat tapped out by the freedom shoes of Black artist-activists such as Paul Robeson, Harry Belafonte, and, yes, Nina Simone. Jordan is a bit under six feet tall, both Hollywood and hood handsome with an IMAX smile that could woo ancient bronze church ladies with a single flash. He is polite, humble, and accessible in a way that is highly unusual for a star. Perhaps it is because he was raised by a mother and father—Donna and Michael A.—who taught him early on to appreciate everyone and everything, to take no one and nothing for granted.

KEVIN POWELL: People are calling you one of the most dynamic actors in America. How do you feel about that?

MICHAEL B. JORDAN: Oh, man. It's epic, man. In the beginning, I never really started off acting. I never got into the industry on purpose. My mom was at a doctor's appointment, she has lupus, and I was sitting in the waiting room and the receptionist said, "You know, you should get your son into modeling." She had two boys in the industry so I went and crashed one of their auditions. I booked the first one that I went out on. It was just like a snowball effect. I never really, as a kid, dreamed or watched movies thinking, *I want to be an actor.*

POWELL: What was your first acting job?

JORDAN: It might've been a public service announcement for Big Brothers Big Sisters, something super small. I was on *The Sopranos* as background extra work. All those small little successes added up to this path.

POWELL: When was the first time you actually used the word *actor* to describe yourself?

JORDAN: Probably on *All My Children*. It was after *The Wire*. I got killed off in *The Wire* and then immediately after I went on this audition in New York for *All My Children* and I got it.

POWELL: How old were you?

JORDAN: I was about sixteen. That was the first time I owned up to what I was doing. *The Wire* was the first time I fell in love with acting. Actors like Idris Elba, Dominic West, and Andre Royo, I credit a lot for my drive. That planted that seed in me, but I still had the fear that it was always going to go away.

POWELL: But you were going to regular school, you weren't out of school per se?

JORDAN: No. The first two years of high school I went to Arts High School in Newark, New Jersey. The last two years I got homeschooled because I was just working so much. At that point, I made a decision that I wasn't going to college and I was going to pursue this thing full force. I planned on moving out to Los Angeles when I graduated high school to see this thing through. My parents always really supported me. Family is our support group. We hold each other accountable and we hold each other

up. That was instilled in me as a kid. I celebrated Kwanzaa growing up, the seven principles, those things.

POWELL: Who did you love as an actor when you were a teenager?

JORDAN: The funny thing is, I didn't have that many. I didn't have anyone as a kid growing up. I was more into cartoons and animations: *Dragon Ball Z* and *DuckTales* and any Disney movie. I was the kid watching anime and reading comic books, that type of thing. But I always could appreciate films like *Bad Boys* and *Armageddon* and *Rounders*. Even films that I wasn't supposed to watch [such as] *Scarface* and, you know, *The Godfather* and *Friday*.

POWELL: Did you move to Los Angeles alone?

JORDAN: I came by myself for the first six months. One of my best friends moved out with me a little bit after that. It was tough. I was working but I wasn't working enough. I would doubt and hope and get nervous. Right when I was getting ready to give up, there was something that would keep me there for a little bit longer. Sleeping on my boy's couch, staying with friends, I was blessed to really have a lot of friends in LA. I remember one of my friends, Sterling [MTV host Steelo Brim], and I used to go to Jack in the Box. We were so broke. We tried to fill out job applications to work there after *The Wire*. We were overqualified.

POWELL: What got you past these rough times in Los Angeles?

JORDAN: I was getting ready to call it quits around September 2008.

POWELL: You were about twenty or twenty-one years old.

JORDAN: Twenty-one. I went to Anthony Hemingway's house. I went for Thanksgiving dinner. I knew he was up [to direct] this movie *Red Tails*, with George Lucas producing. He told me he was going to get me an audition. In my head, I was like, *Hopefully it's going to work*. That was the job that gave me enough money to stay in Los Angeles. I remember all of us over his house: me, Nate Parker, David Oyelowo, Elijah Kelley, Tristan Wilds, Leslie Odom Jr. . . .

POWELL: Leslie Odom Jr., the Tony Award winner from *Hamilton*?

JORDAN: Yeah, exactly. We were all in there, and it was one of those things where [Hemingway] was like, "You know, we're going to do something epic." Working with George Lucas, shooting over in Prague, overseas, the whole thing. That movie saved me.

POWELL: *Fruitvale Station* happened and both you and Ryan Coogler, the director, saw your lives change forever. How does it feel when you two are compared to Martin Scorsese and Robert De Niro?

JORDAN: Those guys were making movies longer than I've been alive. It's an incredible honor. Me and Ryan connected on a personal level, on a business level, on a work level, and on a human level. We linked up at a perfect time in my life, in our careers, and we been bopping out ever since.

POWELL: How did you meet?

JORDAN: I met Ryan when I was coming back from shooting *Chronicle* in South Africa, right around the time Trayvon Mar-

tin got shot. I remember feeling sick and wanting to express myself as best I could as an actor, especially a Black actor. Being political and speaking out on issues at that time, I felt a little nervous to really speak my truth. I felt it was really tough. I remember writing stuff on Facebook and deleting it. I reached out to my agent and said, "I want to show I can act. Just give me a gritty independent; let me see if I can do it."

POWELL: This was spurred by Trayvon Martin getting killed?

JORDAN: Yeah. It all happened one after another. It just so happened that [the *Fruitvale Station*] script came through and I read it and I cried. Read it again, cried again. I wanted to sit down and meet [Ryan].

POWELL: That's how it happened?

JORDAN: Yeah. A couple of weeks after that we were talking about *Creed*.

POWELL: That fast?

JORDAN: Yeah.

POWELL: How did Sylvester Stallone get involved in the project?

JORDAN: Ryan did a lot of that work, honestly. He had a vision he pitched to Sly's agent.

POWELL: Ryan came up with the idea of resuscitating the franchise?

JORDAN: Without a doubt. You know, Sly took some massaging to get him on board. Obviously, it's his baby, his franchise

that he created a long time ago. He wanted to do this thing about Apollo Creed's son and Ryan pitched to him a couple times and he still said no. Me and Ryan went and shot *Fruitvale Station*. It won Sundance, premiered in Cannes, got all these accolades, and then Sly slowly started coming around and *Creed* became more real.

POWELL: You're a Black man in the US and a lot of Black men don't get these opportunities. Do you suffer survivor's guilt?

JORDAN: Yeah. I don't know, man. Why me? I'm from Newark, New Jersey. I have friends and peers, other actors that I think are extremely talented. I grew up in an audition room; I see them all the time auditioning for roles. Why am I the only one that gets this? I used to feel animosity from other actors. The way the industry is, it naturally creates this competition between each other and it's not a friendly competition. It becomes more standoffish. We can see each other at a party and no one wants to be the one to come over and say hello—I remember that a couple of times. I never really felt intimidated by anybody, but it got me thinking, wanting to create more, to produce. I want to really change the landscape of the game.

POWELL: You said earlier that you used to be nervous, but now you want to talk about changing things, to talk about race, to talk about diversity. What has shifted for you in these few years of success and stardom?

JORDAN: Becoming more unapologetic, I think. Before, I wasn't that confident in myself. I think the times are changing. I feel the responsibility I have [to] my people, my community—especially through the work that I do and the roles I portray—that I'll be doing them a disservice if I didn't speak up for the people that look to me to set an example. The temperature and the climate

of the world, especially the US, is in a crazy place. People in the older generation have said they've seen it before, but this is the first time I'm seeing it. The Sidney Poitiers, the Harry Belafontes, they've been through this already—a lot worse than it is right now—so it would be disrespectful not to bang down that door, to continue to pick up the baton from where they left off and keep it moving. Obviously, the game's changed a little bit, you're not quite fighting the same, but it's still a fight and I've got to do it my way.

POWELL: Sidney Poitier came from the Bahamas to the US in the 1940s. He was looking for a job and he saw two ads: one said dishwasher and the other said actor. He picked actor. About a decade later Dr. King got his PhD at twenty-six years old and said he just wanted to have a little church with his wife. He landed in Montgomery, Alabama. Then Rosa Parks, the bus boycott—the rest is history. Some people are called to do certain things. Do you feel you have been called to do what you do?

JORDAN: Yes.

POWELL: Why?

JORDAN: I don't know. I feel like doing what I do, it's not just acting; it's what goes into becoming an actor. People see the end results. They see the lights, the premiere, the movie. They don't see the time that you put in by yourself, the lonely journey. They don't see the moments you sleep in your car. They don't see the moment when you have to go into a gas station, swipe your card to pay, then hurry up and go in the convenience store and get chips and frozen pizza before your card gets declined because you don't have that much money in your account. But somehow you still have faith that you are doing what you're supposed to be doing. When you get some success you get ridiculed

and judged by everybody, most of the time by your own people: "You're not this, you're not that, you're not doing as much as possible." It's tough. Being a Black man in America, you have a systemic oppression that's there. A system that's put in place that's always constantly ripping you down, [saying] that you're not good enough. It's tough being a Black man in America. It comes with a lot. So it's why I have chosen to do what I do, because it's a weight I'm willing and able to bear. I'm still trying to figure this shit out.

POWELL: What's the biggest misconception about Michael B. Jordan?

JORDAN: I've been blessed there's not that many things that have been misconstrued, because I stayed out of the way. There's things I've got to do to be the best actor I can be and to be in a position to create my production company, to be able to create more opportunities and more roles for men, women, people of color, all ethnicities, to reverse-engineer this whole prejudiced racist shit.

POWELL: Are you a leader?

JORDAN: Very much so.

POWELL: Why?

JORDAN: Because I have to be.

POWELL: Like Malcolm X or like Martin Luther King Jr.?

JORDAN: I'm a mixture of both. I'm a little bit of Malcolm, a little bit of Martin. You know, you gotta be smart and there's moments where you gotta be a little bit more like Martin and moments you have to be like Malcolm.

POWELL: What does diversity mean to you in Hollywood?

JORDAN: You know, diversity only makes sense in a system where it's lacking. If it's not lacking equal opportunity, there's no need for diversity. Since the beginning of film, it's [been] for White people [who] slowly allowed other ethnicities to contribute and tell stories. As times changed, we got to the point today that you see so many men and women behind the camera. Women are getting more opportunities in all different lanes—politics, scientific, everything. Mankind has been evolving; the technology has changed. I feel like anybody can pick up an iPhone and become a filmmaker.

POWELL: This is the ten-year anniversary of Barack Obama becoming the first Black president of the United States. How far have you come since Obama was elected?

JORDAN: Man, I feel like we've come a long way. Ten years since Obama? That's insane. I remember the day he got elected. I still have the newspapers.

POWELL: That's around the time you were about to quit acting.

JORDAN: Exactly. I feel it's the perfect storm right now.

POWELL: For *Black Panther* or everything?

JORDAN: For everything. Just to get the opportunity to have a conversation about a movie like *Black Panther*, however many millions of dollars the budget is. It had to be a perfect storm. The studio had to feel it was the right time to back a film with a predominantly Black cast, that hasn't been done before with this budget. They felt comfortable enough that it was going to make

an impact, make a statement, and make money, because this is a business and it is about money.

POWELL: How important is *Black Panther*?

JORDAN: I think it's extremely important. I feel like I never had that many actors to look at and inspire me growing up. Black actors that I could identify with, that look like me on-screen. I used to see other films growing up and I would automatically play make-believe, films like *X-Men*. I watched *Blade* and I saw Wesley [Snipes]. I didn't have to try that hard to imagine because I was seeing someone that resembles me. And I'm just thinking about what this movie is going to do to the kids growing up.

POWELL: Which kids?

JORDAN: Black kids, White kids, all kids, because they can imagine just as much as we can, but specifically Black kids who don't have that many positive examples to look at on TV and film. We're giving Black people power, royalty—we don't gotta be crackheads or gangbangers, selling drugs or robbing people. We don't have to be comic relief. We can be *superheroes*. Imagine what that's going to do to the imagination and ambition of kids watching these movies. That's the real impact of this film. When it's a Black cast, everyone wants to act like the project is only for Black audiences. That doesn't make sense to me. Why can't we look at this movie and be inspired and go on that journey? They should be able to do that, and if you can't, that's the problem.

POWELL: You've mentioned women. #MeToo has exploded worldwide. What are your thoughts as a man about what's going on?

JORDAN: I think it's just a cleansing. I think it's a power thing and that's in all industries. I feel like whenever there's power and men in power, there's going to be an abuse of power, that's just human nature. The conversation: how do we hold people accountable and responsible for having that power? The culture of Hollywood is changing now, on all levels, behind the camera [and] in front. And whenever there's a shift in power, it's going to be rough. We're going through that stage right now. I'm glad it's coming out. Because now you have to hold people accountable. People that were scared to say or speak their truth now are feeling comfortable. People are going to be more responsible with the positions that they are in right now and that's taught down. The assistants that are coming up, the producers, the actors coming up—everybody's learning. You have to weed the motherfuckers out so the next crop that come up can learn the right way.

Tupac and Biggie
June 1, 2018

i heard his name first
juiced for freedom
like digital underground
railroads and
the sonic blasts
of brendas having babies
was that a movie or
was that life and soundcloud as art
homies can call
but what do black
boys do when we are
trapped in concrete
boxes forever ever
forever ever
fear is a prison
but so is fame too
but what is fame
is the only bus ticket
you got to make it
from the cradle
to the grave
made me think of
revolutions won
and revolutions lost
of assata's great expectations
of black panthers

dead and gone
while panther cubs
leak tears made of
napalm and the muscular
tails of charcoal-gray hood rats
made me think of
apartheid
winnie and nelson mandela
of run jesse run
of nations of islam
and new africas
blowin' in the wind
say his name
tupac amaru shakur
shining serpent
who is thankful
to be alive in spite of
absent father
imprisoned stepfather
crack cocaine
police raids
and political movements
from one ghetto
to the next
hip-hop
started out in the park
created by black and
brown boys looking
for frederick douglass
the north star
and the perfect
beat
they called him
mc new york in baltimore

a motherless and fatherless
child in the bay area
tupac
who contorted and coiled his voice into
an ebonics symphony
of urban american patois
break-dancing to the malnourished imaginations
of king's and kennedy's poor people's campaigns
tupac
america's most wanted
political rabble-rouser with a drumbeat
beats like the invisible hands of motherlands
come
and motherlands gone
but hip-hop also is the
west indies
and latinx folks too
hip-hop is
christopher wallace
son of jamaican immigrants
jamaica where they toasted
and blew out massive sound systems
jamaica where marcus garvey first
painted it black
the fleshless self-esteem
of ex-slaves asking jah
for a boat ride that drop-kicks them in
an uncolonized and an ungentrified heaven
jamaica that gave us a founding father
of hip-hop kool herc
and half of brooklyn
where brooklyn at
it is right here biggie smalls
cool-posing on an onion-scented street corner

in a tight yoruba prayer circle
they call a cypher
as shorttallfatskinnydamaged bodies
rhyme and shine the shoes of the blues
of palecoconutyellowredbrownjetblack boys
who considered suicide when
rainbows became coalitions
of the haves and the have-nots
biggie
the greatest storyteller
never to win a pulitzer
biggie
who contorted and coiled his voice into
an ebonics symphony
of brooklyn patois
break-dancing to the malnourished imaginations
of king's and kennedy's poor people's campaigns
where brooklyn at
it is right here the notorious b.i.g.
because even gangsters trademark
their names into the history books
of godfathers and macks and superflys
where brooklyn at
right there
where grandmaster flowers
and big daddy kane and stetsasonic
and sawed-off shotguns
and crack vials and crippled
public schools wheelchaired the way
for you
biggie
so that you could
battle royale rhymes
like mario puzo

dry-humping bloody mobsters
and scandalous politicians
and greasy-haired preachers
like don corleone
cupping your chin
the way the devil would cup
death itself
the way bootsy collins would cup and drink
the wet sultry licks of his guitar
just means you tupac you biggie
trade war stories
the way trump trades war stories
with fascist mirrors at the white house
means you all
got soul
like iceberg slim had sold his soul
where brooklyn at
right next to harlem and east harlem
tupac the places you were born and lived
like baltimore and marin city
and the sunny potholed gutters of los angeles
and atlanta
where they birth and bury kings
and call it racial progress
where brooklyn at
in that one time you and biggie
swapped eye sockets and took photos
as friends
together
apart
two black boys about to be their
generation's elvis and buddy holly
their generation's john lennon
and marvin gaye

big yeah like biggie big
peace in the beginning
but then who shot ya
became the soundtrack
for the dirty half dozens
in green camouflaged armor
crooked finger-pointing
contests that turned into
your coast versus my coast
even though ain't nobody own
either coast
but we know they like to
be slave masters and overseers
and loose black boys on each other
like stink-breathed barking dogs
leaping at and gut-bombing marchers
in john coltrane's alabama
except we marching to jail and cemeteries
not toward the moon or the stars or the sun
it is black boys against each other
as poison is poured over
our dream-y american gumbo
hit 'em up
dis you dis your wife dis your life
dis your career
volcano anger stove-boiled by years
of trauma and dear
mamas addicted
to white lines and hypnotic needles
frozen in the medieval times of warriors
as political prisoners
like mutulu like mutulu like mutulu
hypnotized
we eat and swallow ourselves

and each other
the way we eat and swallow watermelon seeds
grow
ride
die
for death
atop death row SUVs
we join elvis in vegas and los angeles
hang lynch-mob ropes around our necks like
they are electric kool-aid acid tests
until we are gunned down
in cars
the way elvis sat on that toilet bowl
waiting for his soul
to flush him into
graceland forever ever
born again six months apart
two dead black boys joined at the lips
of hip-hop's smithsonian institution
gone
because they value you more
dead
than alive
gemini twins that you both are
black boys ain't s'pose to live long
we s'pose to live hard fast short painful
the way they rolled up the torture of jesus
and smoked him on the crucifix
until his humiliation
dripped dripped dripped
an old negro spiritual
into the resurrected earth
of the unbelievable
and our eyes slap-box with the white jesus

as we wait for this or that black jesus
named makaveli or big poppa
eyesfacesskins don't lie
they are permanent graffiti murals
for the brothers who ain't here
these photos of them
permanent graffiti murals
black white
in living color
teardrops
lonely teardrops
jesus-walking
like raindrops
shaped like bullet shells
sculpted by the sawdust hands of the lawd
the fears I we still carry
around all these years later
like prison chains about our tattooed wrists
wondering where all those
bullets came from
wondering why
we they would kill
black boys who only
want to be
free

Friday, June 1, 2018
10:56 a.m.

Aretha Franklin Is America

Originally published in *Vibe*
August 31, 2018

I, too, sing America.
—Langston Hughes

Her words cried, they cried for her, they cried for us. From Dr. King and the Civil Rights Movement, to the presidency of Donald Trump and Black Lives Matter, there has been Aretha Franklin. She was not only the voice of America, but also its heart, its guts, its joy, and, yes, its sorrow songs. I cannot recall when I was introduced to her music, but Aretha, or "Ree Ree" as she is affectionately called by Black folks, has always been there. It was my mother who taught me about her, about her supernatural powers. Aretha, now gone at age seventy-six, is one year older than my mother, and my ma, like far too many women, tragically, has known ugly torrential storms with names like sexism and heartbreak and sickness.

Like Ms. Franklin, my mother has been ill the past few years. Like Ms. Franklin, my mother has had her share of trauma, pain, loneliness. Like Ms. Franklin, my mother has had to fight off no-good men and unequal treatment, professionally, privately, only because she is a woman. Like Ms. Franklin was, my ma is resilient, strong, determined to live and be true to herself, to the final breath.

My mother does not sing. Aretha does, for her, for the masses of people throughout the world. Perhaps that is why my moth-

er's favorite album ever is *Amazing Grace*, the stunningly classic gospel compilation Aretha recorded live in the early 1970s. It is there that we hear Aretha Franklin rip apart every single word she utters, like a guardian angel, and she delivers us reborn, baptized, for a brand-new day.

Alas, how would I describe the voice of Aretha Franklin? It is the mighty work of the God she believed in fiercely, with the Lord's nimble fingers scooping chocolate-brown mud from the earth and shaping it into a hypnotizing human trumpet. That trumpet, like the trumpet of unknown Black Civil War soldiers who helped to create jazz. That trumpet, like the elastic rhythms of Louis Armstrong, Valaida Snow, and Dizzy Gillespie. That trumpet, like the unknown Black women of yesterday, today, tomorrow, in their living rooms, at their places of work, in their bathrooms, on their porches or their stoops, at their sanctified churches, harmonizing the entire history of a people, through dreams and danger, through heaven and hell, through freedom and fried chicken, through love and liberation.

Perhaps this is why, on a very recent road trip to our family roots in the Low Country of South Carolina, my mother requested my wife and I play *Amazing Grace* as we drove. With so much happening in America, including the terrible possibility of our being pulled over by the police along the route, there was Aretha promising us we could make a way out of no way. Because Aretha Franklin, in her essence, is not just a storyteller, but also a healer, one of unparalleled genius. Her inflections, her wails, yes, are the cure-all potion for us, if only we'd listen to the words, and listen, even, to the silent spaces between her words.

This is why Aretha is a goddess to a multicultural and multigenerational march of women when she belts "Respect." That tune made her, instantly, a feminist champion. And she was a champion for Dr. King and civil rights. And she was a champion for legendary activist Angela Davis. And she has been a champion for Elton John and his crusade against AIDS. While

she may have never made very outwardly political or socially conscious music, for the most part, there is no denying that "Respect" was and remains one of the signature anthems for women's empowerment, and easily a one-song soundtrack, in these times, for the #MeToo movement.

This is also why men like me love her, because in her music Aretha has not only taught me to hear and listen to women, but to also understand toxic manhood, and what it does to women, and to us men as well. I do not ever want my wife to feel the depths of anguish that jolts me every single time I hear "I Never Loved a Man (The Way I Love You)." That song is my mother's life, beginning with my father. Because of Aretha, I do not want to be my father, I do not want to be, ever again, any man who would bring a woman, any woman, such great despair.

Moreover, it can never be stated too much the unlimited impact of spirituality, of the Black church, on the earthquake-like tremors in Aretha Franklin's voice. There, additionally, in her royal purse were these ingredients: slave field hollers, the blues, bebop, rock and roll, and the electrifying vocal acrobatics of Black preachers like her daddy, Reverend C.L. Franklin. Artists like Sam Cooke and Otis Redding may be the founding fathers of soul music, but Aretha was not only its founding mother but also its midwife and perennial Olympic champion. She is the gold standard by which any other singer of any era and any genre of music is forever measured. She was, arguably, the best singer ever.

That is because Aretha Franklin forced us to understand the soul of America, the soul of Black America, because of the raw nakedness in her voice's yearning. She comes from a grand tradition, one which includes Bessie Smith, Mahalia Jackson, Clara Ward, Ella Fitzgerald, Sarah Vaughan, and Big Mama Thornton before her. And, quite obviously, there would not have been a Whitney Houston, a Lauryn Hill, an Amy Winehouse, an Adele, an Ariana Grande, a Jennifer Hudson, or a Beyoncé, without the towering influence of Aretha Franklin. Not only was she

universally hailed as the Queen of Soul, but Aretha Franklin is indisputable proof that American music is Black music and vice versa. Then, now, eternally, you simply cannot have one without the other. For as long as things like hate and violence and division and a lack of compassion fester in our America, there will be Aretha Franklin giving color and texture and meaning to what we witness, to what we endure.

And we must not forget that she was a self-taught folk artist, in every sense of the phrase. Aretha is among the countless African Americans who never had formal vocal training but were bestowed, from birth, with the ability to sing. Aretha could not read music either, but she instructed herself, from childhood on, how to play the piano, and became an underrated master at that. We also must not forget that her first recordings happened when she was still a youthful prodigy as a teenager in the 1950s, or that her first major label deal, in the 1960s, did not yield any big hits, but did cement her endless love affair with jazz music, with Broadway numbers, with classical music, nurturing in the process a creative giant who would become, over the span of six decades, a bridge-builder, a unifier, a global ambassador across race and gender and gender identity and class and any other boundaries that segregate the human race. Yes, the Queen of Soul was a direct manifestation of Dr. King's dream, one spoonfed, relentlessly, in the Black experience to the very end, but who belonged to us all.

I only saw Aretha Franklin perform live once in my life, at the *Essence* Music Festival in New Orleans in the early 2000s. As we say, church was all up in her that night. She lifted herself from the piano, she kicked off her shoes, and she danced the way I remember church folks swaying and hopping and chanting and sweating when I was a child: in that moment, Aretha's lifelong balancing act between "God's music" and pop music lay fully exposed, and she did not care; in that moment, put on pause was the fact that Aretha Franklin first became a parent at age twelve,

a second time at age fourteen, and was married by age nineteen to her first husband, a pimp and a businessman, who allegedly beat her savagely for years, sometimes in public; in that moment, put on pause was the fact that her own daddy had fathered a baby, while married to Aretha's mother, with a thirteen-year-old girl in his hugely popular church; in that moment, put on pause was the fact that Aretha's mother took her son from a previous marriage, left Reverend C.L. Franklin and Aretha and her sisters and other brother, left their adopted hometown of Detroit, went to Buffalo, New York, where the Queen of Soul's mother, Barbara Siggers Franklin, would die but a few years later, at the tender age of thirty-four, they say from a heart attack, but just as likely from the sort of massive heartbreak Aretha Franklin would suffer through in her own life; and Aretha, on that New Orleans stage, could have easily been my mother, back home in the kitchen with the radio piped up and the grits bubbling in an old pot, alone, talking to herself, talking with the spirit of her mother, talking in tongues with Jesus, lost in the music, completely, with sadness shoved aside by a ferocious ecstasy that only a Black woman who done seen some things could understand. And *feel*.

Finally, a couple of weeks before we got word that Aretha Franklin was gravely ill, I spent one sleepless night watching an old documentary about her on YouTube. How and why I landed there, I do not know. It was about the first magical year of her enormous success, and there she is, shy, baby-faced, being hailed as a game-changer in the world of American music. And there is Dr. King, friend of her father's and friend of hers, proudly presenting Aretha with a special award. Ain't no way Aretha Franklin could have known what she would become, what her life would become, what it would mean to America, to the entire planet. That a Black girl from Detroit's working-class community, because of her great natural gift, could grow up to be a queen, forever.

Redefining Manhood: A Message to Men, to Boys, to Us All

A speech at the National Bioneers Conference, San Rafael, California
October 20, 2018

NINA SIMONS: America is in a state of turmoil and confusion. There's violence, hatred, and division everywhere, in ways that summon the worst eras in our shared history. The question begs itself: how did we get here? And as Dr. King once wondered, where do we go from here? These are the questions our next speaker dives into with his latest book, an emotionally naked and deeply engaging autobiography of America, by tracing the influence of his remarkable single mother, a woman who shaped his entire life. Threaded with his lived experience, Kevin Powell strips away symbols and pretensions to get to the root of who and what this nation really is, and how it came to be, and why we are struggling so mightily in these times. These notes describe his latest book.

How can we understand gender relations in this country without factoring in how poverty, race relations, politics, hip-hop, and the prison industrial complex affect them? If, as the Kabbalah suggests, healing the world requires reuniting the feminine and masculine aspects of the sacred, how can we address that schism without addressing the whole system? In terms of gender equity, ending sexual abuse, and redefining manhood to address the ways that violence has been baked into our cultural understanding of masculinity, we're still only at the very begin-

ning in the profound transformations we need. A few famous men may have been exposed for their transgressions, but entrenched misogyny is still the norm. And obviously, some of the most brilliant abusers are still in power. And gay marriage may have won widespread acceptance, but homophobia and transphobia are very far from being extinct. In fact, we all know that many of the gains women and LGBTQ folks have made are under threat from the regime currently in power.

In my opinion, we can't ultimately arrive at a more open, loving, and compassionate society by only mobilizing women, youth, and LGBTQ folks, as important as they all are. Unless enough men also come to see that the changes we seek are ultimately liberating, more fulfilling, and better for them, it will be impossible to achieve a fairer society based upon more balanced and equitable relationships. Well, that's what's coming. We hear far too little about the courageous groundbreaking efforts of a few visionary men to challenge the foundations that our current form of toxic masculinity has been built upon. And we need courageous communicators who can make the realities of Black life in America felt and real for all of us . . .

And that's why I'm so thrilled to be able to introduce our next speaker, who in my view is one of the most shining exemplars of a new breed of man. One who has the courage to examine himself and his culture with ruthless honesty, and to do the hard work to rebuild a far healthier identity of manhood. Kevin's story is powerful, which you can learn more about through his thirteen brilliant books, including *My Mother. Barack Obama. Donald Trump. And the Last Stand of the Angry White Man* and *The Education of Kevin Powell*. But let me just say that he was raised in the inner city, steeped in the macho norms of a tough environment. After having to face his demons in young adulthood, he embarked on a remarkable journey to emerge as a great writer and activist, and a leading advocate of a new form of redefined manhood, one anchored in nonviolence, love, and

healthy self-expression. It is with immense admiration that I introduce to you a man who has been unafraid to claim his identity as a feminist and knew he could do so without sacrificing his masculinity. Someone I consider the embodiment of a new form of positive, healing manhood—Kevin Powell. [*Applause*]

KEVIN POWELL: Wow. Good afternoon. Good afternoon. I'm Kevin, from New York City, and I just want to say it's an honor to be here. And I'm especially—it's a lot of people here. How you all doing? Wow. I want to thank—I want to thank God for this opportunity. But I want to respect people who are Christian, who are Muslim, who are Jewish, who are Buddhist, who are agnostic, who are atheistic. I just hope that we all can agree in the times in which we live that we're all part of the human race, part of the human family. Can we agree to that, at least? Yeah? [*Applause*]

And I think we should give another round of applause to Nina, to Kelly, to all the folks who are working with Bioneers. This is a phenomenal gathering. Would you all agree with that? [*Applause*] Yeah. This is my first time here. And when I showed up this morning and I saw all the folks walking around, I was like, *This is serious. This is serious.* And I'm like, *I want a T-shirt and I want a badge. I want one too. And I want my meal ticket. I want my meal ticket.*

I want to also acknowledge all the speakers, presenters. I was looking through the schedule the last couple of days, and it's just an incredible gathering. And I'm certainly excited about the program we're going to do at four thirty, "Sacred Manhood," with other men. We're going to have a conversation. So I hope some of you all can join us for that as well. And I just want to say a few things really quickly. There is so much happening in the country right now, as you all know. And I want to thank Nina for that incredible introduction.

But, you know, last night I was in Oakland, speaking at an

event. And it just hit my heart when a woman spoke. She said, "I want to say something." And she actually said that men are trash. No judgment. Can we say, "No judgment?" And can we say, "Safe space?" But she used the word "trash," but it's no different than what my mother, who turned seventy-five this year, has said my entire life. "Don't be like your father," and, "Men are no good," in the Black vernacular. And so when we look at where we are in this country, with that gentleman—person—in the White House; when we look at Bill Cosby—and I know many of the accusers of Mr. Cosby; we look at Harvey Weinstein. One of my good friends back in New York is the actress Annabella Sciorra, one of the many accusers of Harvey Weinstein.

When we look at all the men, as Nina just said very eloquently, who have been accused, charged with all kinds of deviant behavior, I hope—especially to the men out there, folks who identify, gender-wise, as men out there—that we understand that patriarchy, misogyny, sexism, are not new. Just like this country was quote-unquote founded on racism, the genocide of indigenous people—Native Americans. Some people call them Indians. First Nation people. Just like my ancestors, African people. African people. African people were kidnapped—oh yeah, were kidnapped from Africa and turned into slaves, and built the economic infrastructure of this country. We need to be clear about that. The Founding Fathers—they didn't say Founding Mothers. And we know that those wealthy, heterosexual, White male landowners were engaging in power and privilege, and that was passed to all of us who identify as males in this society. Are you all with me out there?

And so that's the foundation of this country. And so Donald Trump is not some new phenomenon. He's actually a continuum of what we've seen all along. The difference with Donald Trump, he's just raw and completely unfiltered. And that's putting it mildly. But it's patriarchy. Male domination. Male power run amok. You know, I believe—am I right, you all—Dr. Ford is

from this part of the country, am I right? And it took me back to 2011, watching Dr. Ford during the Supreme Court hearings. And 2011, Eve Ensler, who's one of my sheroes and mentors— and if any of you all are from the New York area, Eve and I will be doing a conversation in New York about this very issue on Sunday, November 4. You can look that up. But Eve did a celebration of Anita Hill twenty years after those Supreme Court hearings. And when I was watching and listening to Dr. Ford, she was telling the truth. She was telling the truth. She was telling the truth. [*Applause*]

And as I was listening to Dr. Ford, I kept thinking about Anita Hill telling the truth, telling the truth, telling the truth. [*Applause*] And it hurts my heart as a man, as a cisgendered man, as a heterosexual man, as a so-called straight man who's an ally. Who is an ally. Who had to learn to become an ally. To see so many of us who identify as males in 2018 still saying, "Well, why did she bring it up thirty-five years later?" Well, the same reason why Black folks are saying, one hundred years later, two hundred years later, we still deal with the ills of racism. The same reason why our lesbian, gay, bisexual, transgendered sisters and brothers, people in the LGBTQ community, saying, "We still deal with homophobia and transphobia all these years." Are you all with me out there? [*Applause*] The same reason why poor people of all backgrounds say that poverty is a form of violence. The same reason why disabled human beings are saying, "Hey, able-bodied people, don't forget about us." You know?

And so when I think about where we are with this whole thing called manhood, I want you all to go on a journey with me for a second. Think about who you are, if you identify as a man. And if you identify in other ways, gender-wise, think about the folks who are males in your lives. I was born and raised in Jersey City, New Jersey. As Nina said, I'm the product of a single-parent household, single mother. Shout out to single mothers out there, always. [*Applause*]

My mother, like many African Americans, migrated from the South. From Texas, from Alabama, from Louisiana, from South Carolina, where she's from, to places like Oakland, California, like Richmond, California. Like San Leandro and Hayward, or Brooklyn, or Jersey City, where I was born and raised. She was in her early twenties. She had already survived the racism and the sexism and the classism of the American South, being born in 1943, where her birth certificate said, *Colored*. Not *Black*, not *African American*. *Colored*. She dealt with sexism growing up, because by the time she was eight years old, she and her three sisters—there was four or them. Three sisters—I'm sorry, three sisters and a boy. Only the boy was allowed to graduate from high school. All the girls had to work. My mother started working when she was eight years old, in cotton fields.

She only got to the eighth grade. She was basically groomed not to have a career any other way than being the help for the privileged and powerful in her community. Are you all with me out there? You know, this is where my mother came from. So she got on a Greyhound bus, as many Black women did during those times, and she packed her life into suitcases and they came up north, she and two of her sisters. And they shared one bed in a one-room apartment in Jersey City. And at some point, at some point, at some point, my mother met my father. She was in her early twenties. He was in his thirties. She fell in love with him, and he fell in lust with her. And he manipulated my mother, and he got my mother pregnant. And my mother was forced, when it was time to give birth to me, to call a taxicab because she's a poor Black woman in America. There's no resources, there's no cars, there's no driver's licenses. There's nothing. And she had to go to the hospital in a cab, and that's how I was born.

I only saw my father—my first introduction to manhood—three times in my life between the time I was born and I was eight years old. And my father pretended several times that he was going to marry my mother. He would play games with

her. "Well, let's get married." And then he would pull back. My mother would call him periodically, "Can you help us?" One time, he bought me a watch when I was a little boy. A second time, he bought me a bicycle. A third time, he was a truck driver, so he had money. He actually lived in a house that he owned. But we're living in a rat- and roach-infested tenement. This is where I come from.

My father, the one time I went driving with him in his truck, inside of his truck—I'm six, seven years old—are images of naked women. And when he saw my discomfort at the nudity of these women, he just started laughing and basically said a lot of what I heard from older men throughout my adolescence and youth: "This is what it is to be a man." Are you all with me out there?

When I was eight years old—it was a rainy day. I'll never forget it. My mother—we didn't have a telephone in the house—said we're gonna go to the drugstore down the street. We're gonna go to a pay phone. I know you all are too young to remember pay phones. And she caught my father, and she asked him, again, "Can you help us? Can you help us?" And on this particular day, his toxic manhood said, "You lied to me. He's not my son." And I look like my father. "And I'm not gonna give you another nickel for him ever again." And hung up the phone on my mother. My mother was devastated. And she shared with me what my father had said. And right then and there, this eight-year-old boy, Kevin Powell, had a father hole, a manhood hole, that was as wide as the Grand Canyon. Emotionally, spiritually, and every which way you can imagine.

And whether you have a father or father figure in your life or no father at all, like I did, the reality is, most of us who grew up in this society, whether we're White, Black, Latinx, Asian, Native American, Christian, Jewish, Muslim, atheist, agnostic—most of us who identify as males are still bombarded, just like I was, father figure or no father figure, with the same images. "This is

what boys do. We wear blue. This is what girls do. They wear pink." Are you all with me out there? "These are the kinds of things that boys should be playing with. These are the kinds of things that girls should be playing with." Are you all with me out there? "Boys don't cry. Boys have to be tough."

Boys, from early age—five, six years old, seven years old, eight years old—start to police each other. We start to use sexist or homophobic or transphobic terms to describe boys who might be a little different than the so-called norm. Well, that was me, in this hypermasculine culture. I played sports growing up. I loved football, I loved baseball. I loved every sport. You better believe that I fought every chance I got. Because, "Meet us after school if you want to settle this." "Meet us in the lunchroom if you want to settle this." It's just rites of passage many of us go through in our families, in our communities, all over the country and around the world. And one of the things that's included in that is constantly, from an early age, unless you have a parent or parents or an adult who checks you as a boy and says, "This is unacceptable, to refer to girls in this way. It's unacceptable to dis boys in this way, to police them this way. And it's unacceptable to learn that to be a man is to be violent." [*Applause*]

And so I think about my childhood, and I talk about it in my writings, as Nina said. I mean, we would run around school, fourth or fifth grade, boys grabbing girls' body parts. Not realizing, gentlemen, men out there, we were learning rape culture at eight, nine years old. Not realizing that when we used terms like "gangbang," that's what we were saying. You know? I remember in my neighborhood there was a girl—and I'm embarrassed to admit this. To this day, I don't know her name. But the boys made a decision very early on with this girl, that she was sexually promiscuous—as we say in the Black community, "loose." And so her name became "Whorey Dory." Meanwhile, the boys can do anything we want. But the girls, if it was even thought they had done something, we twisted it around as if there was

something wrong with them, just like what we did with Anita Hill and Dr. Ford. [*Applause*]

But it's not just our families and communities that shape us. It's also the schools that we go to. It doesn't matter, honestly, if you go to public schools or some elite private school. My mother—how far did I say she went to school? Eighth grade. I'm the first generation after the Civil Rights Movement—so I went to the so-called "best" public schools in Jersey City. Integrated schools. I was an A student, K through twelve. My mother did not tolerate bad grades. [*Laughter*] Oh no, she didn't. Momma didn't play. And she still don't play at seventy-five.

But when I think about it, just like I didn't learn anything about Black history or Latinx history or Native American history or Asian history, growing up K through twelve; or queer history, or poor people's history. Guess what, you all? My thirteen years of school, I learned about Betsy Ross sewing the flag. One. I learned about Betsy Ross sewing the flag, one. I learned about Florence Nightingale very vaguely, two. Helen Keller, even more vaguely, three. And then Rosa Parks, because she served double duty—Black history and women's history. [*Laughter*] Now, we're laughing about this. But if you want to understand patriarchy, sexism, misogyny, rape culture—ask the average male in your life, "Name me five to ten women in American and world history," and see how silent most of us go. [*Applause*]

So even though I was raised in a household—single mother, my aunts were around, my grandmother was in the South, there was a matriarchal family—the reality is, when we're talking about the things that we were studying, be it math, science, history, et cetera, everything was through the lens of men. As if women didn't exist. I knew from the time I was eleven, twelve years old that I wanted to be a writer because I discovered this very hypermasculine male writer named Ernest Hemingway. And I loved Hemingway. But in my thirteen years of school, the only woman writer that I remember was Emily Dickinson.

But it's not just there. It's also pop culture. The mass media culture. I mean, I don't know about you all, but it should have broken our hearts when Frances McDormand won her Oscar back in February—remember that, you all? This year. And she asked all the women to stand up in that audience. And you saw all these women. I've worked in the entertainment industry for many, many years. Women are the real leaders in our communities. [*Applause*] However—however, because of sexism, because of our need as men to control everything, we relegate you all to whatever we want you to be. So I grew up loving TV shows like *I Dream of Jeannie*—remember that show? Where she called Major Nelson "Master," and he would put her back in a bottle? And I'm thinking to myself years later, *Wow. Boy was that reinforcing patriarchy and sexism.* Or I'd watch shows that—I mean, it hurts my heart. I loved *Happy Days*. Remember *Happy Days*? The Fonz would snap his fingers and women would just fly out of the ceiling. Now, we're laughing about this. But as a boy taking this in, think about the devastating effect of these images. Just like the devastating effect of Black folks seeing images of us only in certain ways that are stereotypical.

This applies across the board. And so this is how I was socialized. And so fighting was normalized. Violence was normalized. Not respecting women and girls as our equals, as our equals, as our equals, as our equals—which is what women and girls are—was not part of it. So like many boys, I get to college. Rutgers University, New Jersey. First year, first semester—probably the first week—an upper-class male student said to me, "There is so much sex on this campus we don't need electricity to keep the lights on." Now, I'm naive. I'm green, because I was very much a momma's boy. But I get to college, and I realize there's a whole kind of pimp mentality going on. There are student-leader pimps, there's fraternity pimps, there's athlete pimps. There's even faculty and staff pimps. Where the men were running amok with women and girls.

I would hear stories about domestic violence. I would hear stories about rape. You all with me out there? Unfortunately—and I'm not proud to admit this—the boy who grew up where his mother told him, "Do not become like your father," in college is where I began to become like my father. Irresponsible sex. Reducing women to two things again—caretakers or sexual objects. Because I grew up in a violent environment means—I'm being honest with you all—I was violent in my early life. Sometimes toward males, sometimes toward women, in college. It hit a crucible for me after college. I was living in Brooklyn, New York. A girlfriend and I were living together, and we got into an argument. This is in 1991. July 1991. My male rage, my anger, my fragile masculinity, when she challenged me, I pushed her into a bathroom door. Not proud of it. Not proud of it. Years later, I would apologize to her, and she would accept my apology.

But here's what happened in that summer of 1991. And this is why we need to have honest, open conversations with each other. Because when I look at a Bill Cosby, a Woody Allen, a Roman Polanski, a Matt Lauer, a Charlie Rose, a Harvey Weinstein, I'm saying to myself, *No one ever has checked these very damaged human beings as they were doing damage.* There were women—and a few men, but mostly women—who said to me, "Kevin Powell, you're a hypocrite. How can you talk about injustice in the world, and you're participating in the oppression of half the country and the world's population?" That was devastating to me.

Equally devastating is when some women said to me, "You need to read bell hooks." And I said, "Well"—I said, "Well, that's an interesting name. Now, who is that?" We're laughing about it. But not only did I grow up not learning anything about women and girls in our history, my four years at Rutgers University the only woman writer I read in college: Zora Neale Hurston, *Their Eyes Were Watching God.* That was it. And so even in college, when I thought back on it after being challenged around that

bathroom-door incident, here I was thinking I was this brilliant young man, but when women leaders at Rutgers University would challenge us on our sexism, we would say disparaging, disrespectful things to them. Because what men like to do who are engaged in toxic manhood is silence women and girls.

I was told after that incident, "You need to own your mistake, number one." [*Applause*] I was told after that incident, number two, "Men, you need—you need, you must—get help." [*Applause*] What did that look like for me? It meant therapy. It meant therapy. It meant counseling, it meant therapy. All those traumas that I grew up with, I was now passing along and taking out on other people, including women. Are you all with me out there?

What did it mean? Number three: "Kevin Powell, you need to start listening." Men, we need to start listening to the voices of women and girls. [*Applause*] I was in my twenties, taking all of this in. And number four, what was said to me, "You need to become an ally. An ally, a consistent ally to women and girls." [*Applause*] Number five, how do you become an ally? You must read. And I found myself—you must study. I was like, "Well, who is bell hooks? Who is Gloria Steinem? Who is Eve Ensler? Who is Audre Lorde? Who's June Jordan? Who's Sonia Sanchez? Who is Nikki Giovanni?" Because I realized I was completely ignorant about women. Completely ignorant. Like many of us are.

And it was hard to read things where women were saying very powerful things about what they had experienced at the hands of men. But we don't have the kind of transformation that Bioneers represents, if people, if we as a people, no matter how we identify ourselves, are not willing to take hard looks in the mirror. [*Applause*] And the last thing that became a part of it for me is that you have to do the work. And for us, as men, that is—that doesn't mean coming around women all the time. You've got to do that work with men and boys. [*Applause*] It's like when my White sisters and brothers—and I love all people,

I love all people—many White sisters and brothers around the country ask me, "What can I do to fight racism, White supremacy, White privilege?" I always say the same thing: "Work with the White sisters and brothers and challenge them."

So, what can men do, of any background? You've got—we've got to do the work. And so it began in 1991 with a terrible, terrible experience. I never engaged in that kind of behavior again, but I'm gonna be honest with you all. It was a journey to move from toxic manhood, and trying to figure out, *Well, what does healthy manhood look like?* I'd been taught that manhood is violence. I've been taught that manhood is ego. I've been taught that manhood is senseless competition. You know what I mean? I've been taught that men don't cry. They don't express themselves. I was taught that men can't be vulnerable. And I said to myself, *Wait a minute. Here I am trying to figure this thing out, and there's all these wacky definitions out there about manhood in rock and roll. In jazz. In hip-hop. In movies. On TV. In books.* I had to question everything.

That's how you begin to redefine manhood. You've got to question everything. And ask yourself, *What's wrong with love? What's wrong with peace? What's wrong with nonviolence?* In my humble opinion, twenty-seven years later—wow—I've written about it. Essays with titles like, "The Sexist in Me: Confessions of a Recovering Misogynist." I mean, these are the different periods of my life. I wrote a piece in my new book called "Harvey Weinstein and His Toxic Manhood Is Our Toxic Manhood." Because it is. Bill Cosby is us. Woody Allen is us. Roman Polanski is us.

It's not just writing about it. It's speaking about it. Doing workshops. I've worked in prisons. Colleges and universities. Communities, community centers, religious institutions. This is an ongoing conversation. What I'm happy to say to you all is that over the last twenty-seven years, I've seen more men get involved.

To the men out there: if you identify as a male, hold your

hand up for a second. Look at all those hands out there. Let me say this to you all, with all due love and respect. Again, women and girls are our equals, are our equals, are our equals, are our equals, are our equals, in every single way. That's number one.

Number two. Even if you are not the kind of man who would ever call a woman a disrespectful name, touch her inappropriately, touch her without an invitation, rape her, molest her, assault her, God forbid stab her, shoot her, murder her—and all these things happen in our country, on this planet. The *New York Times Magazine* said a few years back that ending violence against women and girls is one of the major human rights issues in the entire planet. Even if you're the kind of man who would never engage in those things, but you have men around you in your family, in your synagogue, in your masjid or mosque, in your church, in your temple, in your fraternity, on your sports team, at work, in your barbershop—wherever you go where men gather and you hear men engaging in toxic manhood, destructive language and behavior toward women and girls, and you say nothing, nothing, nothing about it—you, we, become just as guilty. [*Applause*]

So my hope—my hope, my great hope, because we have to have hope, in spite of all that's happening right now—is that #MeToo, just like the Civil Rights Movement a generation ago, will not only empower women like the Civil Rights Movement empowered Black people, but that movement empowered all of us. My hope, my hope to us as men, is that we understand as women are using their voices, it should be the wind behind us in saying, *I want to be a different, different kind of man and human being.* I love you all. Thank you. [*Applause*]

What Charlie Brown, Snoopy, and *Peanuts* Mean to Me

Originally published in *The Peanuts Papers*
2019

I was born and raised in an American ghetto. I have no direct memory of the Civil Rights Movement, of Dr. King, Dolores Huerta, Fannie Lou Hamer, Bobby Kennedy, Yuri Kochiyama, or Malcolm X. I also have no direct memory of what life was like in America before the 1960s. What I did know was my single mother, my absent father who never married my ma, horrific poverty, violence, abuse, rats, roaches, and much sadness and loneliness as an only child. What I am convinced saved my life was the vision of my mother—in spite of having only an eighth-grade education—to instill in me from the time I could form and comprehend words a love of learning. Even at age three I was already questioning the world, and my place in it: this I do recall.

Apart from reading, which my mother pushed hard and is the reason why I am a writer today, I had a bottomless love for television as a kid, particularly cartoons. I believe, truthfully, that these animated images represented both a feeding of my imagination and an escape, at least temporarily, from our very dire and unpredictable living conditions. We moved much, as poor people often do, but there was always a television, a black-and-white television, with a hanger on top serving as a replacement for the antenna, and a thick line often running through it, distorting the images at times. But I did not care. I loved an-

imation, and I watched them all, *Bugs Bunny*, *Tom and Jerry*, *The Flintstones*, *The Jetsons*. But then there was Charlie Brown, Snoopy, and the entire *Peanuts* gang. I do not remember if I first saw the comic strip in our local Jersey City newspaper, the *Jersey Journal*, or if it was one of the TV specials that hooked me. No matter, hooked I was, and I absorbed *Peanuts* in every imaginable way as a boy.

My earliest memory was of Charlie Brown trying to kick a football and Lucy always removing it just as he was about to do so. That image served as a metaphor for my own tough life. How can we ever *not* be poor? Will we ever be able to leave this ghetto life? Why do I feel so close yet so far from relief, from hope?

There was also a certain kind of melancholy that permeated Charlie Brown that I related to instinctively, a loner mentality in spite of his being a part of a community of other quirky children. I likewise related profoundly to how Charles Schulz rendered the voices of adults, parents, teachers, authority figures, as, well, inaudible. My mother was a mighty yeller, doing the best she knew how to raise me, a man-child, but there was an unfettered pleasure I took in how the youngsters of *Peanuts* had their adult yellers speaking what seemed to be a foreign language. Youth do not want to be yelled at or talked down to; they, we, want to be spoken with, and heard.

I can say now I have battled depression much of my life, and I can say with certainty that *Peanuts*, the comic strip, the television programs, the characters, remain one of the things that still brings me tremendous happiness to this very day. I had a framed image of Snoopy on my wall for many years, and only in storage now because I am married and space is at a premium. This is how deeply connected I am to these characters, even as a grown man.

For sure it has been in my adult years that I have come to love and appreciate *Peanuts* in a very different way. One of the ways I have dealt with the traumas of my past has been years

upon years of therapy. One of the counselors said to me, awhile back, "Find the things that actually made you happy as a child, and keep those things close for the rest of your life." Almost immediately I went out and purchased *A Charlie Brown Christmas*, sat there and watched it alone, and I cried, profusely, as all the memories came flooding back to me.

On another occasion, while I was doing a speech at a historic all-Black private boarding school in Mississippi, it blew my mind to learn that Charles Schulz had donated money to this institution, and there on campus was the Charles M. Schulz "Snoopy Hall." My hosts told me that Schulz, a very shy man, had once been scheduled to come speak at the school, but he called the school's president and said that he would just like to send a check instead. Those funds built Snoopy Hall, the girls' honors dormitory. Mr. Schulz also lent his name to the Charles M. Schulz Scholarship Fund, which still provides tuition for student leaders to this day.

I am someone who has spoken at well over a thousand institutions at this point—me, the poor boy from the American ghetto. But whenever I think of my fondest memories of my speeches and my travels, my mind and soul forever return to that Mississippi dorm named after Snoopy. This, to me, is the essence of *Peanuts*, of the impact it has had and will continue to have on generations of people of all backgrounds. It is the reason why I find myself, even in middle age, posting *Peanuts* quotes and images across social media platforms whenever the mood hits me, whenever I do not have the words myself to express a feeling, any feeling.

I have escaped the worst of what I experienced as a child, this I know. But what I will never escape, what I do not ever want to escape, is the incredible innocence and joy I feel whenever I see or think about Charlie Brown, Snoopy, all the *Peanuts* characters, and the freedom they gave me then, that I still have with me now, to be all of who I am, quirks and all.

Part IV

Between Russell Simmons and the World and Oprah

Originally published in the *Utne Reader*
February 19, 2020

> *'Cause we're alone now*
> *And I'm singing this song to you*
> —Donny Hathaway, "A Song for You"

Take 1

The godfather of hip-hop, Russell Simmons, sits at a table with two elderly White men on either side of him, holding court in the lobby of New York's Mercer Hotel, just days before Christmas. The Mercer is an epicenter of power and wealth, less a lobby than an exclusive living room for Simmons and other visitors. Once you push past the heavy black drapes that separate the outside world from this living room, there are art deco shelves and tables filled with all kinds of books and high-end magazines; there are immaculately scrubbed white walls and comfortably elegant sofas; and there are young, chic, multicultural staffers rocking all-black gear while attending to the godfather of hip-hop and others milling about.

Simmons, with no security detail, is dining on a vegan burger, a salad, and a glass of water, totally at ease, his toothy grin engraved ear to ear, sporting his usual uniform of a New York Yankees fitted cap, a colorful button-up shirt, chiming prayer beads around his neck, blue jeans, and white-on-white Adidas

sneakers. There is a sun-baked glow to Simmons's copper-brown skin, the product of several years of daily yoga and meditation, and every kind of self-care activity at his well-manicured fingertips. Given what is hovering all around Russell Simmons's life this very moment, his Zen-like state is unbelievably jarring in its calmness.

A child of blue-and-white-collar Queens, New York, Simmons and his journey have been a testimony to the surge of hip-hop, the governing culture on the planet since the early 1980s. His vast and layered business interests have grown to include music, film, management, comedy, finance, television, books, fashion, media, technology, the visual arts, yoga, and poetry. There are few in pop culture who can say they have not been affected by Russell Simmons and his monumental reach.

I count myself among the nation of millions. When I was a teenager in the 1980s, I danced to—and worshipped—several of the hip-hop acts Simmons either guided via his firm Rush Management (like his younger brother Joseph's rap group, Run-DMC) or had on his now-historic record label, Def Jam (like LL Cool J, the Beastie Boys, and Public Enemy). In the 1990s, I was a senior writer at *Vibe* magazine, which Quincy Jones owned and Simmons considered joining as a partner. When I was fired from the publication in 1996, it was Russell Simmons, while having a sidewalk lunch with the writer Nelson George at Greenwich Village's Time Cafe, who told me to get over the firing and "go franchise yourself."

In the late 1990s, I wrote cover stories on iconic figures like Lauryn Hill and Chris Rock for Simmons's *One World* magazine, although I never interacted with him directly. A year or two later, when I helped produce the very first exhibit on the history of hip-hop, with the Rock & Roll Hall of Fame and the Brooklyn Museum, it was Russell Simmons who I sat down with, along with the director of the Brooklyn Museum, to get his stamp of approval. And into the 2000s and 2010s I have

become both a vegan and a yogi myself, due in no small part to the health-and-wellness preaching of individuals like Russell Simmons. But the only other time I can ever recall interviewing Russell Simmons was during the 1990s, as he was walking on a treadmill in his home in Manhattan. I have no clue who or what that interview was for, and my only recollection is him telling me I should try yoga.

Russell Simmons and I are not friends and never have been. But there has always been mad respect, and through the years I was certainly in awe of him for curating a soundtrack and a culture that I grew up with, one that provided spaces of expression for me and Black and Brown boys like me from America's ghettos.

Because no Russell Simmons for hip-hop is like no Rosa Parks for the Civil Rights Movement, like no Frida Kahlo or Jean-Michel Basquiat for avant-garde painters, like no Michael Jordan for basketball or Nike, like no Beatles for innovative songwriting and sonic twists and shouts, like no Meryl Streep for method-inspired actors, like no Kardashians or Jenners for reality television and Instagram, and like no Oprah Winfrey for emotion-packed TV talk shows and teary-eyed confessional interviews.

His presence has been revolutionary and deeply transformative for multiple generations of hip-hop heads, a railway bridge between people and possibilities, making Simmons a very potent and very rich tastemaker in the process. As a matter of fact and keepin'-it-a-hundred mythmaking, Russell Simmons is the walking, breathing logo of manifesting something from nothing, of winning on his own terms—the very definitions of hip-hop.

As Simmons sits there with his vegan burger in the lobby of the Mercer, several people, mostly White, stop to pay their respects, to ask how he has been, to say it is good to see him, to shake or touch his hands. You can tell that these admirers have not encountered Simmons in a long while, or are surprised to see

him, by their words, by their body language. That is because the godfather of hip-hop no longer lives in New York, or in America, but has resided, since February of 2018, in Bali, in Indonesia, in Southeast Asia, a nation-state that is a safe and extradition-free haven nine thousand miles away from the allegations of approximately twenty women who have accused Russell Simmons of, among other things, rape.

Take 2

The allegations began in late 2017, just as the #MeToo movement dramatically shifted conversations around sexism, around manhood, across America, across the universe. Hollywood mogul Harvey Weinstein went down first, fast and hard in October 2017, an avalanche of eighty allegations of rape, sexual harassment, and other sexually oppressive conduct. Mere weeks after Weinstein's fall from grace, the first wave of Russell Simmons's accusers came forth, as published in the *New York Times* in December 2017.

Say her name: Drew Dixon, a well-regarded music executive who says that in the mid-1990s, Simmons sexually harassed her during her employment at Def Jam Recordings, exposing his erect penis on several occasions, speaking explicitly to her on work calls, and eventually raping her at his downtown Manhattan apartment. Close friends of Ms. Dixon have corroborated that she immediately told them about these allegations and left Def Jam with a "settlement" of $30,000—only $3,000 of which went to her directly, legal fees swallowing the rest of it.

Say her name: Sherri Hines, also known as pioneering female rapper Sheri Sher of Mercedes Ladies, the first all-women's rap group. In the early 1980s, Hines says, Simmons pinned her down on a couch in his sparsely furnished new offices and "violated" her sexually, after which she left in tears. Sheri Sher told close friends at the time, but never said anything publicly, for fear of being shunned in the music industry, and because she

did not want to bring a Black man down. (Years later, in 2008, Ms. Hines wrote a novel based on the real lives of Mercedes Ladies, which depicts a businessman named "Ronald" who rapes a member of the women's rap group.)

Say her name: Sil Lai Abrams. A former model and currently a longtime domestic violence awareness activist, she says that she dated Simmons off and on for a few years, from the late 1980s through the early 1990s, but one night, while not in a relationship with him of any kind, he took advantage of the fact that she was drunk, and instead of having his driver take her home, she was brought to his residence. There, Abrams has alleged, Simmons raped her, as she laid on her stomach in his bed. It has been reported and confirmed that she was so distraught about the incident that she immediately told close friends; the next day, Abrams says, she downed pills and wine in a suicide attempt.

These three women appear in the soon-to-be-released documentary film, *On the Record,* focusing on the allegations around Simmons, which recently premiered at the Sundance Film Festival to sold-out crowds. All told, there are numerous allegations and complaints against Russell Simmons: everything from rape to sexual harassment, according to various sources. Most of the allegations fall outside the statute of limitations for sex crimes, which is twenty-one years for New York State, where much of this is said to have occurred. While the pattern of allegations ranges from the 1980s to the 2010s, many episodes share a common thread: Simmons's maneuvering women into compromising spaces like an office or an apartment, alone, where they have no escape route.

However, Simmons's supporters—ex-wife Kimora Lee Simmons and about a dozen family members, and some of his past and present friends, colleagues, and business partners I have spoken with—believe that some or all of these women are lying, that Russell Simmons would never be violent toward women. *I*

have known Russell for over twenty-five years, Kimora wrote on Instagram in the aftermath of the allegations. *We were close friends, married, divorced, and have remained friends, co-parents and partners throughout it all. These allegations against him are nothing like the person I have known in all that time. I have known him to be a caring and supportive father and someone who has worked tirelessly to uplift disenfranchised communities.*

I do not know which men are or are not rapists, sexual harassers, abusers, and batterers of women. What I do know is that my friend and fellow activist Tarana Burke coined the term "me too" in the first years of this twenty-first century as she was working with young Black and Latinx girls, and noticed that many of them, barely into their teens, had already been raped by a male figure—a man, a boy, or both. I did not know Tarana was doing this when she and I crossed paths doing relief work in the Deep South in the heartbreaking fog of Hurricane Katrina. By the time actress and singer Alyssa Milano encouraged legions of women to use #MeToo on social media on October 15, 2017, in response to the Weinstein revelations in the *New York Times* and the *New Yorker*, hundreds of thousands of women and girls had posted their own responses.

Yet, when Russell Simmons was accused, he employed a different hashtag: #NotMe. The backlash was swift from women, and men sympathetic to women, on Twitter, condemning Simmons for not taking sexual violence against women and girls seriously. What he does own is his past womanizing. "I'm in this mess because of the amount of whoring I did," he says to me. "I am 1,000 percent comfortable taking responsibility for what I have done, but I absolutely don't want to take responsibility for what I haven't done and that is that I'd never been violent, I've never been forceful, and [it was] never my intention to hurt anyone."

When #MeToo first exploded, there was no way to predict how many women would step forth to speak of being survivors,

to name the men who had assaulted and/or harassed them. Dozens upon dozens of men—executives, elected officials, journalists, names like Charlie Rose and Matt Lauer and Al Franken—have by now been accused of sexual transgression in one form or another. The #MeToo movement has forced a renewed interest in the cases of men like Roman Polanski and Woody Allen, and it landed Bill Cosby in jail. "This is going to go on for years," a famous actress friend told me at the start of the #MeToo movement. "Men being accused and held accountable." Perhaps this is why so many men are frightened, in entertainment, in music, in sports, in politics, in corporate America, everywhere—just like some White Americans were scared, during the Civil Rights Movement, as racism was being tested at every turn. Power forever panics under siege.

If we are to be honest, then we must acknowledge that America was founded not just on racism, but also on sexism. There has scarcely been a time from the beginning of this social experiment in "democracy" that our society has granted any women and girls value equal to men and boys—let alone to Black women and girls. The habitual and continuous rape of Black women by White male slave masters and White male overseers was not merely a passing feature of slavery, but a foundational weapon in its arsenal of dehumanizing tactics. (If you think otherwise, then peep the many colors and complexions of Black folks in this fair land and ask, *How did that happen?* Rape and sexual violence are tools of control, of oppression, of power gone insane.) In her film *NO! The Rape Documentary*, Aishah Shahidah Simmons (no relation to Russell) asserts that Black male slaves consciously and subconsciously absorbed that mindset and began to view Black women and girls as little more than sexual toys, caretakers, or punching bags, just as the White male slave masters and White male overseers did. This was in spite of the fact that Black women and Black men were kidnapped

from Africa together, put at the bottom of those slave ships to-gether, worked in the fields and in the master's house together, celebrated emancipation together, fled white masks and hanging nooses together, and marched and got water-hosed and clubbed in the head together at civil rights protest after civil rights protest.

Evelyn and Daniel Simmons, Russell's parents, civil rights workers themselves, were together as they raised him—the mid-dle child—and his two brothers, Danny Jr. and Joseph. But ac-cording to Russell, "My parents fought all the time." He adds that his mother was fiercely independent, and "was the most nurturing person in my entire life. No one was more supportive of my dreams and my spirit like my mother, no one." Evelyn, a woman small in stature, worked for the Parks Department in Queens while Daniel Sr. was a history teacher, but her true pas-sions were the arts, as she was both a painter and a poet (Danny Jr. would too become a painter and poet). College-educated and a dreamer like her son Russell, Evelyn would divorce her hus-band in the 1970s when Russell was a teenager, on the heels of civil rights, Vietnam, women's rights, and the flowering of major Black women writers like Ntozake Shange.

Russell does not know fully why his parents split, but cou-pled with the sexism and male privilege that all women have endured in this country, and the many movements, from suf-frage to equal rights to #MeToo, that have pushed back on those hateful dynamics—imagine being a Black woman who not only has to deal with racism, but also sexism as well? This is why Gloria Steinem, a pioneer for equal rights for women for over fifty years, has said, loudly, that Black women in America are the original feminists. Because Ms. Steinem, and progressive White women like her, are clear that Black women have had to deal with an extraordinarily disproportionate amount of venom and violence because of their skin color and their gender.

Later, as hip-hop was being birthed by poor African Ameri-cans, poor West Indians, and poor Latinx folks in the Bronx, it

overlapped with the Civil Rights and Black Power movements, neither of which would have happened without Black women front and center, but both of which witnessed men perpetrating sickening sexism and violence against Black women. I can't begin to articulate the number of civil rights–era Black women who have told me of the hate and brutality they endured fighting for a freedom that did not seem to comprise them. Over the past decade or so, I've been working on a biography of Tupac Shakur; Tupac's mother, Afeni Shakur, was one of the few women who fought back—and was vilified for it, her contributions minimized by those men who feared and loathed an outspoken woman.

We know there would be no hip-hop being officially born on a muggy August day in 1973 in the South Bronx if Cindy Campbell had not produced the very first event at which her brother Kool Herc deejayed—thereby predating Russell Simmons's party-promoter hustle by half a decade. But hip-hop would certainly allow and encourage foul behavior toward women and girls, just like rock and roll before it. Giants named David Bowie, John Lennon, Mick Jagger, and members of Led Zeppelin have all been accused of an assortment of things, like sex with underage girls, like domestic violence, like rape. Hip-hop is merely the most recent pop culture phenomenon that is representing what has always been there: unapologetic sexism.

I did not know any of this as a boy who fell in love with hip-hop in the late 1970s. But even if you listen closely to that first major hip-hop hit, "Rapper's Delight," it is riddled with sexism and the objectification of women: "*I can bust you out with my super sperm.*" From childhood on, we learn much of what we know about manhood from music, from television, from movies, from sports, from male-centered spaces. In a call after he had returned to Bali, Russell Simmons speaks directly to these influences, saying, "We grew up watching *The Mack*, I saw so much stuff, and so many people were living in a culture where they devalued women."

As a result, young males, generation to generation and culture to culture, were and are clueless about the male policing we do to each other to "prove our manhood," the sexist or homophobic words we toss at each other like verbal grenades, our brazen grabbing and touching of girls as if their bodies are our playgrounds. We do not know this is assault. We teach each other that there is something wrong with you, sexually, as a boy, as a man, if you do not get sex, if you do not talk or brag about your sexual conquests, whether real or imagined. No, not all of us go on to rape and assault women once we become men, but rape culture lurks all about us, in language and in deed—

Add to this the fact that most of us learned little to nothing about the history and contributions of women and girls in school, in the mass media culture, in our religious or spiritual spaces; it is little surprise that many of us men and boys are entirely clueless about women and girls, about rape culture, about domestic violence, about gender discrimination. It becomes quite easy, with that enthusiastic ignorance, to blame women and girls for everything, to dis them, to never think twice about how they were treated, in my hoods in my hometown of Jersey City, right through my college years at Rutgers University.

For me, it was not until my early twenties in July of 1991, while living with a girlfriend in Brooklyn, that my awakening occurred. How it happened was pitiful and toxic. During an argument, I didn't like a response from her—and pushed her, in a fit of rage, into the bathroom door. I cannot recall what the argument was about, but I do remember feeling a sense of powerlessness as my girlfriend challenged me, so I responded with violence. She bolted from the apartment barefoot, crying, and screaming. I stood trembling, mortified at what I had done. The pathetic thing would have been to say she caused me to do it, or that what she said happened did not actually happen. But I could not lie. My single mother had raised me to always tell the truth, and I thought often of her telling me not to be like my

father. I was never clear what Ma meant until that incident. *Do not become an abuser. Do not hurt women.*

I went for therapy, I consulted both women and men for guidance, I wrote an essay for *Essence* called "The Sexist in Me," apologizing for the incident and taking ownership of it. Years later I would apologize to my ex-girlfriend directly, and I have never put my hands on a woman in any unwelcome manner since that day, but I would be lying if I said I have not said disrespectful and dishonorable things to women since, or that I have not been sexist. Because I have been; I am very clear about that, because all men are either sexist or are easily capable of being sexist instantly.

I struggled mightily, through the 1990s, through the heyday of my years at *Vibe*, as I participated in a culture that I knew was loaded with disgusting examples of manhood, such as Dr. Dre's savage beating of Dee Barnes, or rappers and crews punching hip-hop journalists who had given them negative reviews, or the bottomless survey of songs that called women every kind of name or curse word imaginable, or depicted every kind of sexual aggression, including rape, gang rape, and domestic violence. And just like rock and roll before it, sex, drugs, and liquor were as central to our culture as breathing. While this was happening, women in and around the music industry talked. They talked about rumored assaults and harassment by record executives, including Russell Simmons. They talked about rappers with terrible sexual-assault reputations. I was not aware of much of this back then, but now I know, because several anonymous women have said this to me while writing this piece.

There is not a music industry executive who did not sexually harass me. They used their power, their money, and their resources, and the things that they can offer; they trick us with the glitz and the glamour, and then they use their dicks to try to manipulate the situation.

*They come off as wanting to help you, but when you
do not do what they say, they take everything away.*
—Black woman (name withheld) who has worked in
the entertainment industry for over two decades

This is the culture that spearheaded scenarios of rape and abuse and sexual harassment over and over again, in songs, at concerts, in hotels, in studios, while many of us turned our heads, or enabled it, or acted like it was not happening. Perhaps the most profound thing Tupac Shakur said to me after he was sent to prison for an alleged sexual assault incident with a young woman is that while he maintained his innocence, what he was guilty of was not thinking of her safety as he fell asleep, and as his friends pounced on her.

Take 3

Louis C.K. Brett Ratner. Dustin Hoffman. George H.W. Bush. Morgan Spurlock. Ben Affleck. Casey Affleck. James Franco. Aziz Ansari. Kevin Spacey. Robert De Niro. Antonio Brown. Donald Trump.

These are some more names of famous men accused of one sexual misdeed or another. It is an unofficial but very much alive boys' club that thrives in the corporate and creative worlds, in academia and entertainment, in politics and media, and that has always been the case. There are long days, longer nights; the divisions between work and play are blurred, and if you suffer from an acute case of male privilege, then you believe that everything is yours to take, including women's bodies, without permission.

This is why the #MeToo movement is necessary. This is why I never thought I would ever see anything like it when I confessed those years back to my own toxic manhood, or as I have worked with men and boys to redefine manhood throughout America and globally. Because there has been a staunch resistance to the

truth, an allergic reaction, if you will, to viewing women as our equals. So we go out of our way to deny their voices, to silence them, to say they want money and fame, that they are haters, that they are trying to destroy men. This is what Russell Simmons tells me time and again during our many interviews about the "files" he has on the women accusers.

This is what men do: Men reassert manhood, if you are Harvey Weinstein or Russell Simmons, to highlight the good things you have done for others, for women, while ignoring the fact that doing great things for others does not preclude monstrous acts. Gangsters and drug dealers give away turkeys at Thanksgiving, toys at Christmas, while still damaging the communities they give back to. Because this is about power, and that is what the #MeToo movement is challenging—the unchecked and abusive power of men—just like the Civil Rights Movement and Black Lives Matter came to challenge the unchecked and abusive power of White supremacy.

I wonder about all of this as I am now the one sitting next to Russell Simmons with a vegan burger and fries and a glass of water in front of me. Russell casually reaches across me several times to grab a couple of french fries from my stash. I barely eat my burger, because I want to focus on every word he is saying. I have known him for half my life, but I realize I do not know Simmons, do not know what might have happened with him and women behind closed doors, as he keeps talking: "So anyway, then #MeToo happened, I lost my five charities . . . I mean, I'm happy to live where I live . . . So I have a job and purpose, and I'm thrilled where I am. I don't need to 'come back' as a lot of men do . . ."

I believe the women, Russell Simmons, I believe you raped them, I believe you sexually assaulted them, is what I want to say to him.

Then he says, "I don't want to be an advocate for men. I want to be an advocate for change. And I certainly want to be an

advocate for the shift in consciousness. I think it's more inclusive and has women's energy and in our governance of our planet." I wonder if he realizes he is in fact an advocate for men only, for toxic manhood, every single time he says the women accusers are only doing this for fame and money, every single time he smears their characters, be it publicly or privately. I wonder if he realizes that you just cannot skip from women saying you raped or assaulted them to becoming a spiritual guru on Instagram, using that very spiritual practice as a way not to deal with the reality of damage that has been done to these women's lives.

> FROM: *Russell Simmons Silence Breakers and Survivors*
> *We are more than victims of rape. We are Black women.*
> *We are mothers, daughters, sisters and friends insisting*
> *on our right to live and work free from sexual violence*
> *and abuse. We will not back down, and we will not be si-*
> *lenced. We are not afraid. When we raised our anguished*
> *voices to say, "No! Stop! Don't!" to Russell Simmons,*
> *he ignored us. Now, as we raise our voices in defiance*
> *of a culture that protects abusers and their enablers, he*
> *has tried to discredit us and to deny our truth. Russell*
> *Simmons and his enablers cannot intimidate us, bully us,*
> *or ignore us. Unyielding as a force, united in our resolve,*
> *we are Black women standing with survivors of all col-*
> *ors and we will not be silenced. #silenceisviolence #ustoo*
> *#lifteveryvoice #metoo*

Take 4

When Simmons and I move to a sofa in the Mercer Hotel lobby, I question silently how many men actually know what "consent" means, as discussed in *NO! The Rape Documentary* and on many college campuses I have visited; that having sex with someone who is drunk or high is rape; that having sex with someone who is saying yes but is drunk or high is rape; that hav-

ing sex with someone who is sober or high or drunk who says no or maybe or *I don't know* is rape; that someone who resists at first, then gives in, does not necessarily give consent, which equals rape. While the legal terms may vary state to state, clear consent by a woman is something rarely considered by men of all ages who are later accused of rape.

I ask Russell Simmons what he thinks rape is, and his response is wildly unsettling, naively revealing, and I am both saddened and disgusted that a sixty-two-year-old man with his wealth and power would say these words, referencing the polygraph tests he submitted to regarding the accusations: "I think a lot of people are guilty of a lot of things. What we used to call rape was violent. I took all my tests—one of my tests was: I've never been violent. I thought that was the answer. I said no, no. And then the detective thought—and he had been a detective and he had also worked for the FBI and he was one of the best polygraph people in the country. He explained to me what the definition of rape was."

> *What is required now is a much deeper dive on the part of men. Men have to say, What is sexual abuse? What is harassment? What is domestic violence? What happened in my childhood that made me the kind of man who is capable of degrading a woman, demeaning a woman, beating a woman, hurting a woman, raping a woman? What happened in the culture? What was I taught in the culture? What did I learn? Why? Why am I doing this? What's driving me?*
> —Eve Ensler, author of *The Apology*
> and playwright of *The Vagina Monologues*

The fact that he, like many men, still does not know what rape is speaks volumes about what may have happened to the women who accuse Russell Simmons of that sexually violent

act. My mind is a sagging load of emotions as he continues to talk, nervously, about the many allegations against him, about the "files" he has on his accusers that he insists will prove his innocence. I attempt to tune out some of the things he is saying about the women—about this one having a drug issue, about that one who says she was raped by her father, about her and her and her wanting money and fame—because this is a recurring thing with so many men: to never look inward at themselves, but to instead point fingers outward. This is how power operates inside the music industry, inside any and all spaces where men run things. If men are questioned or prodded, the knee-jerk reaction, time and again, is to say that the woman accusing is wrong, that it cannot possibly be men with the problem, but the women, for even daring to mention ugly and toxic behavior.

Take 5

On another early evening inside the Mercer Hotel, I am with Russell Simmons and two of his longtime associates. Kevin Leong is Russell's close friend and creative director and is helping him to reboot the Phat Farm clothing line. Hasaun Muhammad is a confidant, friend, and associate. Both men have hung for about twenty-five years with Simmons, since the 1990s. We go riding in Simmons's supersized black SUV, to a Uniqlo clothing store, to a cold-pressed juice bar, to a cryotherapy center where he and Leong get a quick treatment, to Simmons's favorite Indian restaurant. We conclude the night at the Roof, a boisterous sky lounge atop Ian Schrager's Public Hotel.

Everywhere we stop, people know Russell Simmons, ask him how he is doing, greet him with reverence. He appreciates the love, is thankful for it, as he sips on a glass of red wine at the Roof. But he is ready to go to bed. The man who has been partying and jet-setting for much of his adult life is more interested, the past several years, in rising early, to meditate, to practice yoga, to teach anyone who will join him about wellness. Mean-

while, I feel as uncomfortable here as I did at the Mercer Hotel, wondering how someone accused of rape and assault and harassment by approximately twenty women can so effortlessly move from place to place, including this lounge, like there are no eyes whatsoever on him. Guilty or not, this is what extraordinary wealth and power, in the hands of a man, look like; no matter the storm, just keep going.

> *I have many prayer beads that I use for meditation.*
> *They all include the image of the holy sound. In the*
> *beginning was vibration and that sound is "ohm."*
> —Russell Simmons, in a text message to me
> about his daily spiritual practice

I watch Simmons's regular Instagram Live chats where he leads dedicated followers in meditation, waxes poetic on the wonders of yoga and his vegan lifestyle, proclaims his love for truth, and seems to relish the chance to be his other self, the higher-consciousness self—"Uncle Rush"—who he says he has evolved into. I wonder how Simmons's soul juggles these two dangerously conflicting realities: the old Russell who is accused by a number of women of rape and sexual harassment; and the new Russell who proclaims he wants to be a part of the women's movement that will change the world, who is proud of the fact his two teenaged daughters with Kimora, Ming Lee Simmons and Aoki Lee Simmons, ages nineteen and seventeen, know what consent is.

I have spoken with Russell many times over the past two months, in person, by cell phone, and I have read and watched and listened to virtually everything attached to these accusations about him. He mentions his daughters regularly, how proud he is that both are in college, what they mean to him. The last time I spoke with Russell was just a couple of weeks ago, one early morning, now that he is back in Bali after spending time both

in New York City and St. Barts during the holiday season. He sounds very much like a man who is afraid and confused, his spirit broken in some ways because of the documentary film that is coming. Once more, he says the words "I am sorry"—this is in relation to being "insensitive" to one of the accusers, Jenny Lumet—but still, he maintains he never raped anyone.

"You know what Ashley Judd told me?" he says. "I was really upset. I called her because I know she's one of the leaders of the movement. I said, 'This is crazy. I would never harm anybody.' She said, 'Revolution is bloody.'

"I'm interested in not having my kids think I'm a rapist," he says. Every time he references his daughters, I think back to something I said a year ago to a group of students at James Madison University in Virginia, where I was a visiting professor: that men need to understand that *all* women and girls are our daughters, mothers, sisters, aunts, grandmothers, nieces. Afterward, a young woman came up to me and corrected me, rightfully. "It should not matter if men have daughters or see any woman as someone close to them," she said. "We should not have to say that all women are this or that. Women and girls should be honored and respected just because we are human beings."

The young woman was correct, is correct: do men value women and girls as human beings, or not? And it is not enough to simply listen to women when they make statements, when they say they have been raped or hurt in some way. Sexism will not end until men are actively engaged in helping to make it end. That is not to say that men cannot grow, change, or at least begin to rethink and redefine manhood. I think of the crisis that unfolded between Beyoncé and Jay-Z when her video album *Lemonade* dropped, an undisguised and public challenge from Bey to Jay to do the right thing, due to his cheating and lack of respect for her. Equally important was Jay's response album, *4:44*. Perhaps with the exception of the evolution of John Lennon from violently abusive boy-band member to grown man

proclaiming his love and reverence for Yoko Ono, we've rarely seen a male public figure with such a massive platform openly apologize the way Jay did. Between Russell Simmons and the world and Oprah, this is what the women I know, including my mother in her seventy-six years of life, have been looking for. A humble, genuine apology, an effort to heal, to grow up—to be, as Lizzo's words are remixed, great, especially when we men need to be great.

This, I believe, is what Oprah Winfrey was trying to say as early as 1991, when she featured the rapper Ice-T on an episode of her talk show. It was a combative segment, when guests and audience members went back and forth, talking over and through each other, dissing each other; you can tell by Oprah's body language and frozen facial expressions that she either hated or strongly disliked hip-hop. I think it no coincidence that through the years hardly any rappers have ever been in her orbit, except for the transcendently wealthy and successful ones, like Jay-Z. In one infamous episode, Oprah welcomed the cast of the film *Crash*, then used it as an opportunity to lambast the rapper Ludacris about his lyrics. And there has been a running beef between her and rapper/actor 50 Cent. All of which is why many in the Black and hip-hop communities called foul when Oprah Winfrey announced that she and Apple TV+ were jumping aboard Amy Ziering and Kirby Dick's *On the Record* documentary featuring at least three of Simmons's accusers. In a society where Black people in general have been historically dissed just for being Black, it is easy to understand why we are hypersensitive to any critiques of, say, Michael Jackson, or Russell Simmons, why we are quick to say, "What about the White men?" As if we Black men should get a pass, just because we are Black, for equally bad behavior.

The way the story goes, Oprah was blown away by a screening of the documentary and instantly jumped on board as ex-

ecutive producer, using her Apple TV+ partnership to lever-
age distribution. The documentary's credibility was already
high—Ziering and Dick are Oscar-nominated filmmakers—but
Oprah's involvement devastated Simmons, who had considered
her a friend. Black people, seemingly spurred from a post by 50
Cent on Instagram, accused the billionaire media mogul of only
going after Black men. A social media pile-on followed, with
commenters on Instagram and elsewhere questioning Oprah's
allegiance to the Black race, calling her an Uncle Tom and even
suggesting she be canceled permanently.

> *Dearest OPRAH, you have been a shining light to my
> family and my community. Contributing so much to my
> life that I couldn't list a fraction of it in this blog. I have
> given you the gift of meditation and the groundbreak-
> ing book "THE POWER OF NOW "we bonded to say
> the least. This is why it's so troubling that you choose
> me to single out in your recent documentary. I have al-
> ready admitted to being a playboy more (appropriately
> titled today "womanizer") sleeping with and putting my-
> self in more compromising situations than almost any
> man I know. Not 8 or 14 thousand like Warren Beatty
> or Wilt Chamberlain, but still an embarrassing number.
> So many that some could reinterpret or reimagine a dif-
> ferent recollection of the same experiences. Please note
> that ur producers said that this upcoming doc was to
> focus ONLY on 3 hand chosen women. I have refused to
> get in the mud with any accusers, but let's acknowledge
> what i have shared. I have taken and passed nine 3-hour
> lie detector tests (taken for my daughters), that these sto-
> ries have been passed on by CNN, NBC, BUZZFEED,
> NY POST, NY MAG, AND OTHERS. Now that you
> have reviewed the facts and you SHOULD have learned
> what I know; that these stories are UNUSABLE and that*

"hurt people hurt people". Today I received a call from an old girlfriend from the early 1980s which means that they are using my words/evidence against me and their COMMITMENT / (all of the claims are 25 to 40 years old) It is impossible to prove what happened 40 years ago, but in my case proof exists of what didn't happen, mostly signed letters from their own parents, siblings, roommates, band members, interns, and in the case of 2 of your 3 accusers, their own words in their books. Shocking how many people have misused this important powerful revolution for relevance and money. Maybe you should name your documentary "FLAVOR OF LOVE"!? In closing, I am guilty of exploiting, supporting, and making the soundtrack for a grossly unequal society, but i have never been violent or forced myself on anyone. Still I am here to help support a necessary shift in power and consciousness. Let us get to work on uplifting humanity and put this moment and old narrative behind us

—Russell Simmons, in an Instagram post

I talked with Simmons practically every single day for a month, and practically every single day he mentioned that he and Oprah had spoken, both before and after this Instagram post to her. She was trying to convince Simmons to do an interview with her, and he was trying to convince Oprah to drop out of the film as executive producer, to stop the film completely. She was doing her due diligence by reaching out to the "witnesses" Russell insisted could prove his innocence, and he was doing his due diligence by sending Oprah his "files" on the women accusers, which he insisted, to her, to me, to any who would listen, poked huge holes in their allegations.

Part of this dance between Simmons and Oprah, I believe, stems from Oprah's controversial interview with Michael Jack-

son's accusers around the time of HBO's *Leaving Neverland*. Many took to social media and suggested Oprah had crossed the line in supporting White people who were badly shredding the legacy of Michael Jackson without sufficient facts. And there has been a perception for many years that Oprah—the most powerful and influential woman on the planet outside of Hillary Clinton and Michelle Obama—goes out of her way to cater to White people, while not extending the same treatment to Black people. The facts make that perception a bit shaky: be it Oprah's generous donations to historically Black colleges, her building of a major educational and art institution for girls in South Africa, her many private donations to help Black folks of all kinds, and her complete and total embrace of the work of Black writers like Toni Morrison and Maya Angelou and Ta-Nehisi Coates, it is simply a lie that Oprah Winfrey does nothing for Black people in America or anywhere else.

> *The woman is an independent entity. She is one of the few that we have, which means that she has not been bowing to White corporate interests for a long time because she owns her own shit. So what Uncle Tom?*
> —Joan Morgan, author of *When Chickenheads Come Home to Roost: My Life as a Hip-Hop Feminist*

But what may be correct is her dislike of hip-hop, the way it has depicted women from the very beginning, and how so few of us in hip-hop culture or the hip-hop industry have been held accountable for our words and deeds, let alone taking responsibility ourselves. We must not forget that Oprah herself was sexually assaulted as a girl, that she herself is a survivor—so part of this work for Oprah, I am sure, is intensely personal. And just because Oprah is a billionaire with power and influence does not mean that she herself does not still carry around the scars, the traumas, of being that young Black girl who was abused, rid-

iculed, shamed, right into her early adult years. Surely, Oprah's story is not that different from many Black women, including my mother's. Oprah, my mother, an endless line of Black women, generation to generation, have not only had to deal with racism, just like Black men, but have also had to suppress, in the past and in the present, over and over, any conversations about sexism or gender oppression, often out of faithfulness to Black men, because of the ever-looming threat of White supremacy, and even if certain Black men are not loyal to them. But at what cost to Black women's bodies, souls, mental health? My grandmother loved my grandfather fiercely to the day he died, but he hit her when he felt like it, cursed her out when he felt like it, and expected her to have babies and raise the children and take care of him, because he, a Black man, had so few places to hold power in this White male–dominated universe, other than over his wife. At home, in sports, in entertainment, in hip-hop, we get to be the kings of the world, while not realizing that our very definitions of manhood are eerily the same as those of White men in power—a bootleg definition of White manhood, yes, that is rooted in a reckless disregard for people.

Because of the marriage of racism and sexism, Black women truly are the mules of the world, as Zora Neale Hurston wrote in her classic and timeless novel *Their Eyes Were Watching God*; and Black women have never been regarded in the same breath as White women, and that would emphatically include this era of #MeToo. If most of Russell Simmons's accusers were White women, some believe, he would have been charged with crimes already, and more than likely on his way to prison, like Bill Cosby.

It was known throughout the music industry for two decades—*two decades*—that R. Kelly was a serial abuser of Black females, particularly young Black girls, but it was dismissed, ignored, joked about, and enabled, because they were Black. Tarana

Burke was only acknowledged as the true creator of the #MeToo movement when Black women took to social media in October of 2017 and pushed back on the notion that Alyssa Milano had coined the phrase. Black women are not, and have never been, valued in the way White women are—in America, or on this planet. Racism has demanded that White women, from slavery forward, represent the standards of beauty, honor, and dignity, that they be the lens through which Black women and other women are viewed. So, yes, Tarana Burke is now widely hailed as the creator of #MeToo, but White women's stories are still elevated in a way that Black women's stories are not. Perhaps this is what brought Oprah Winfrey to this film about Russell Simmons and the Black women who are accusing him: in hearing the stories of women like Drew Dixon and Sheri Sher and Sil Lai Abrams, Oprah was also bearing witness to herself on that screen.

But Black men damaged by both racism and sexism will not grasp this, will instantly become reactionary and defensive, will say that Black women are attacking the Black man, that these Black women are traitors to Black men, to the Black race. This is partially because even in this era of #MeToo, the optics suggest that while Black males like R. Kelly and Bill Cosby are in jail or will wind up in jail, White males accused of comparable crimes and misdeeds will not be. In other words, history and current scenarios paint the picture of Black males as the poster children, time and again, for bad male behavior, even if accused White men have lost careers too. Because we Black males are treated far harsher, condemned far harsher, punished far more severely, in life, and even in death, per Michael Jackson, per Kobe Bryant, while White males who have been accused of similar toxic behavior are either given a pass, or allowed to bounce back, in some form, eventually, in life, in death. That is our perception, what is in our gut, as Black men. Because the image of the Black male as predator, as violent criminal or violent abuser, and so on,

is as old as racism itself, and is a very blatant creation of racism.

Are there Black males who truly are rapists, abusers, batterers, child molesters, serial adulterers, murderers, menaces to society? Without question. But the vicious racism of our world makes it nearly impossible for the average Black male to even grapple with sexism, sadly, tragically, and Black women suffer as a result, because "intersectionality" is as foreign to some Black males, and other men of other cultures, as the word "sexism." Meanwhile, as I write this piece, the Harvey Weinstein trial has been unfolding in New York, with additional charges pending in Los Angeles; yet his insurance company, not he, is paying off a wave of his accusers. Weinstein does his best to solicit sympathy by entering court daily with a walker, appearing to be in feeble health. If Weinstein actually winds up spending a single day in jail, it will come as an astonishment to Black folks of all genders—because even within the era of #MeToo, White male privilege remains alive and well.

> The truth is . . . truth that he's using power? Absolutely, everywhere. All the time. Did he punish people for not agreeing, not doing it? I'm sure. Some people could've got a part if they had done it. And, some people got a part even if they didn't do it. Right? A lot of that. So, did people sleep their way into parts other people should've got? Yeah, probably. Right? And, did people who don't, who couldn't be any good in the movies get the part? Probably not and probably people are mad because they didn't get what they wanted. I don't know, man. I don't want to defend Harvey Weinstein. Fuck him.
> —Russell Simmons

But it is not just about Harvey Weinstein and White male privilege, it is about male privilege period, including, as Russell

Simmons displays above, the privilege of doubting the testimonies of victims, even in the case of someone like a Harvey Weinstein. In other words, either you are a serial rapist and serial abuser, or you are not. Either you stand on the side of women who've come forth, and listen and hear them, or you become an accomplice to the oppression of women. There are no gray areas here. Because Russell Simmons, like Harvey Weinstein, is using the playbook of men who want to duck or dodge truth while holding firmly to toxic manhood. Thus, what men who refuse to be held accountable are guilty of, at the least, is unapologetic sexism in how they respond to accusations, bullying and intimidating women who have accused them, and even going so far as to harass their associates or family members. So in commenting on Weinstein, is Simmons also commenting on himself?

Take 6

People are anxious, nervous, scared. Or so it seems. Over the two months that I have been researching and writing this article, there have been a number of individuals who have refused to talk on the record, or who have completely ignored me, including Oprah Winfrey's office (no reply); the office of the documentary producers Amy Ziering and Kirby Dick (no reply); music industry insiders who know either Russell Simmons or his accusers or both (no one wanted to speak on the record); even the New York Police Department. When I reached out to the person who was the lead detective for the many allegations of rape and sexual violence against Russell Simmons here in New York City, the detective, a White man, responded via a social media platform that he had no comment. I sent another NYPD spokesperson—a Black woman—a LinkedIn message about the allegations, and she replied with an email for me to use, and a number for me to call, to make sure they received my email. When I called the number to see if my email had been received, I was told they had no idea what I was talking about, to call back

later, to talk with the Black woman who had sent me their way in the first place. And, finally, the lead woman accuser in the film, Drew Dixon, via her publicist, opted not to be interviewed by me for this piece either, after agreeing to do so in person, twice, which dejected me. In more than thirty years as a journalist, I have never worked on any article where so many people either ignored my outreach or asked to be off the record, or first said yes to an interview then declined.

Take 7

I have decided that I will no longer be executive producer on The Untitled Kirby Dick and Amy Ziering Documentary, and it will not air on Apple TV+. First and foremost, I want it to be known that I unequivocally believe and support the women. Their stories deserve to be told and heard. In my opinion, there is more work to be done on the film to illuminate the full scope of what the victims endured, and it has become clear that the filmmakers and I are not aligned in that creative vision.
—Oprah Winfrey, in a statement

I was told, privately and by a very reliable source close to the situation, that the Black women in the then-untitled documentary, as well as other Black women who had accused Simmons of various sexual transgressions, felt hurt, confused, scared, and abandoned by Oprah's decision to pull out of the film. This source said it struck them as bizarre that the Oprah Winfrey who raved about the documentary and signed on instantly is the same Oprah Winfrey who now says she and the producers "are not aligned in that creative vision." In the meantime, the producers went on record in the *Los Angeles Times* after Oprah's statement, saying they'd had no indication whatsoever that she

had any issues with the documentary. Then there is the matter of some women, in the film, not being fully told the nature of the film:

> *It's news to me that this is a film about Russell Simmons. It was certainly not presented that way to me when I interviewed for it. The producers, what Amy and Kirby said, was that they really wanted to do an exploration of hip-hop culture in this moment of #MeToo, that they were very honest that they are examining the accusations that were brought about by Drew Dixon. I know Drew. So I didn't have any problem. But the fact that this is now like the Russell Simmons film is news to me. I'll be really honest about that, because that's not the way it was presented.*
> —Joan Morgan

Again, Russell Simmons was hoping, in his almost daily calls or texts with Oprah Winfrey, that she would look at his files, call his witnesses, and rethink her participation in the film. "America trusts her, she's very important," he tells me. "A misstep on her part could really hurt the women's movement. And they need her, we need her for that. We need her to lead the women's movement and add some compassion and some understanding to it. We can't afford for her to be seen as just another finger-pointer, a man-basher."

But in reality, it is not the place of Russell Simmons or any man to say what a woman should or should not do with her voice, her work, her platform. Nor is it our place as men to say how women should respond to allegations of sexual violence against women by men. Nor do we know if the very personal taunts from 50 Cent and others across social media got to Oprah about her race loyalties. What we do know, per her statement, is that she had creative differences with the producers, but still

believes the women. While it is true Russell Simmons took nine lie detector tests, and passed them all, we also know that the way questions are asked during a lie detector test can affect the results, and that has been scientifically proven.

And what I do know is that if several women have said the same man has raped or abused or sexually harassed them, over the course of years, then there is truth somewhere in those many women's stories, because I do not believe that multiple women would be lying about the same man. What I do know for sure is that one out of three women and girls on the planet will be the survivors of some form of sexual violence in their lifetimes—over one billion women and girls. What I do know is that whenever any powerful man, before and during the #MeToo era, has been accused of raping or otherwise injuring a woman or girl, the pattern is always the same: deny, question, and denigrate the character of the accuser; claim, as a man, to be the victim. What I do know is that countless women routinely endure unwanted touching, unwanted comments, unequal pay for equal work, belittlement of their contributions and ideas, attacks on their self-worth, vicious stereotypes, low expectations, ridiculously high standards for certain positions that are not required of men, and a general disregard for their welfare and their safety.

> *We actually don't rape ourselves. This has been an issue about men, and I think we can call out men for eternity, but unless men actually change, we're going to be here for as long as the climate crisis allows us to be.*
> —Eve Ensler

The justifiable rage of many women in this era of #MeToo is understandable, just as my mother's lifelong rage toward my now-dead father has been. But is it enough to simply cancel men who engage in any form of sexual violence or harassment, to exile them so they simply disappear? Is "cancel culture" an

answer to ending sexism? I do not think so: people are gone, but the system of sexism remains in place for the next rapist, the next abuser, the next harasser, to come along. Imagine if the Civil Rights Movement, led by figures like Ella Baker, Fannie Lou Hamer, and Dr. King, among many others, simply canceled White Americans for their physically and emotionally violent racism toward Black people from 1619 onward. Imagine if there had been no love, no nonviolent protest, no forgiveness, no attempts whatsoever to heal the very wicked disease of racism.

Black people and other people of color, then and now, have every right to be angry at White America, from the horrors of slavery, to lynching during segregation, to hideous racial murders like that of Sandra Bland and Trayvon Martin in this century. We have done nothing to deserve this sort of treatment, nonstop, simply because we are Black, just like women have done nothing to deserve rape and harassment and groping and name-calling and more, nonstop, simply because they are women.

Yet I also think about a conference I attended a few months ago in San Francisco, a Women's Funding Network event that featured four hundred participants from across the world. I was invited as a male ally, a male accomplice, to speak about what should be next, for men and boys, during this era of #MeToo. Less important than what I said is what was said to me by many of the women who were trying to figure out what to do in relation to husbands, fathers, grandfathers, brothers, and perhaps, most critically, their sons. Just like we must stop expecting Black people and other people of color in America to do the heavy lifting of ending racism, we as men cannot expect women alone to do the heavy lifting of ending sexism and sexist violence.

Very few women I have ever met and talked with and listened to, who have been hurt in some way by men, have ever said to me very directly, "I want revenge," let alone, "I want money," or, "I want to be famous," or anything else that pow-

erful men so love to attribute to them. Why would any woman willingly subject herself to public scorn and ridicule, as has happened time and again—from Anita Hill to Desiree Washington to the accusers of Harvey Weinstein—for saying, publicly, that a man has raped or abused or harassed them? What they want, I have heard over and over, is justice.

Are there false accusations? Without question. Do I know men who have been accused of foul things that they have not done? Without question. Are men and boys I encounter in my work as an activist and public speaker frightened about what they can and cannot do, what they can and cannot say? Yes, I have heard this, over and over, always in confidence, because of social media's power to destroy people with one click, because these men and boys are afraid that they will be accused of something just because they are men and boys. I have had grown men say to me they now go out of their way to not even look women in the eyes, at work, on elevators, anywhere, for fear of one allegation or another; that they will no longer argue or debate with a woman for fear of being accused of being disrespectful, abusive, or a typically sexist man. I have also found myself staring down at the floor when it is just a woman and me on an elevator, or some other tight space, knowing I am not that kind of man to harass anyone, but terrified that someone will say it anyway. Yet we know fear and avoidance are not a solution.

My hope is that men and boys can get to a space of redemption and reconciliation and love and antisexist actions as ways to combat and end sexism—as Dr. King and Nelson Mandela both once said about racism—where men and boys can be trained and retrained on what is possible with a healthy kind of manhood that uplifts, not hurts, and where men and boys can have honest and vulnerable conversations about who we are, how we got here, and where we can go now that #MeToo has shifted everything, forever.

Take 8

So, no one feels like they owe anybody silence anymore. And for the Black community in particular who have constantly trafficked in that, making women make the choice between the advancement of the race . . . or the battle against racism over the battle against patriarchy, as if that is secondary. If Black men win, then they take care of the community. We've never seen that happen. Between that never happening and this cultural zeitgeist of accountability, it's a real moment for people who have never had to question or think that their behavior was ever going to be called into question or that there would be ramifications about it.
—Joan Morgan

I do not know what is going to happen to Russell Simmons: if there will be more accusations, if he will ever be charged, if he will ever spend a day in jail. Men like Russell Simmons and Bikram Choudhury and Roman Polanski have left the scenes of their alleged crimes, and live elsewhere, away from America where the accusations occurred. To be seen as fleeing is not a good look for men, for women, for humanity; meanwhile, these men continue to do their work, they continue to make money in some way, as Simmons is doing with new business ventures in Asia; and they continue to deny they ever did anything wrong, and people around them and people who admire or worship them, continue to never ask the tough questions of them, of ourselves: Why do so many of us ignore or silence the voices of women when they say they have been hurt in some way? Why do we have such a reckless disregard for the lives and sanity of women and girls, for half the world's population?

You do not have to be a rapist or a batterer or a harasser to be part of the problem. Saying nothing, or acting like the prob-

lem does not exist, or blindly blaming the women, makes you just as guilty. I also do not know if a Russell Simmons can be one of the leaders of a hypothetical men's movement, to help change manhood once and for all, given the huge gaps between what the women accusers are saying and what he is willing to take ownership for. But I do know that Oprah Winfrey was right in a text she sent to him, and that Simmons read to me slowly: that it would be "monumental" if someone with his global platform were to speak freely and honestly about everything—

But is that remotely possible, given how revealing and convincing the women are in the film *On the Record*, and given how damaging that documentary is for Simmons and his claims of total innocence? It is an excellent case study: it is poetically made, handcrafted like the patched-up quilts ancient Black grandmothers fingered together with their souls—inside those patches, stories like those of Drew Dixon, Sil Lai Abrams, and Sheri Sher overlapping, women who refuse to allow men to damage them ever again, just like my mother and countless other mothers will not, ever again. HBO has purchased *On the Record* post-Sundance, and you will have to decide for yourself what all this is, was, and could be. But if you watch this film the way I watched it, you will wonder how and why Oprah Winfrey would walk away, searching for the real reason, and how and why she could separate herself from these Black women and this film, which is like separating herself from herself. Only Oprah knows the whole truth, and perhaps Russell Simmons, godfather of hip-hop, does too—

And, honestly, this has been the most difficult piece I have ever written in my life. My emotions are bleeding, I have had painfully sleepless nights, as this story has dragged on, and on, and on. As a Black man, I do not ever want to see another Black man go down in a world already seemingly designed for us to fall. But by the same token, I do not want to see Black women—or any women of any background—sacrificed just to

spare a Black man—or any man of any background—accused of wrongdoing. This hurts me from all sides, every part of it. I have been a combination of angry and sad, because of the very real and very vivid stories of the many women who've come forth, and because Russell Simmons had been a hero of mine, a hero for many of us boys in the hood. When he made it, we made it. When he dreamed big, we dreamed big. He was us and we were him. I could not have imagined these kinds of allegations against him when I first saw him in person at some New York City event in the early 1990s, when I just stared, because there he was, and I was too timid to greet him. I just stared, hoping whatever magic he had would rub off on me, a poor boy from the ghetto. Nor could I have imagined, all these years later, that he would be a fallen hero, desperately trying to prove his innocence, thanking me just for listening to him, me, the writer who had found his voice, long ago, because of the culture—our culture—Russell Simmons helped to bring to the entire world.

But I believe the women, Russell Simmons, I believe you raped them, I believe you sexually assaulted them . . .

So, yes, it would be "monumental" if Russell Simmons were to come forth in the fearless way he came forth with hip-hop. Yes, if he were to encourage other men and boys to do the same. Russell Simmons is still a hero and a godfather of hip-hop to many, but even heroes and godfathers can be very fragile and very afraid and very much in need of healing too. Russell said many times in our conversations that "hurt people hurt other people," and I now wonder if he meant every single one of us, including himself, particularly because of one phone call from Bali where he struggled mightily to talk about his mother, about his father, about their relationship, and he could not recall which of them died first. This man, with all he has done professionally and all he is dealing with now personally, in that instance, was

reduced to the young boy he once was. Hurt people hurt other people So, alas, what I do know is that real change must occur, and occur very soon, with Russell Simmons, with all of us men, with all of humanity, because women of every race and culture and creed have spoken, are speaking, and they will never be silent again.

Dear Kobe
February 24, 2020

Dear Kobe,
Their eyes were watching
for you the way
they watch for Jesus Shuttlesworth
and Malcolm X and Nipsey Hussle
over on Slauson and Crenshaw
They came in cars
on planes by bus by grit
They got there by foot
They were in wheelchairs
Their sandpaper palms gripped canes and walkers
They were slouching baby boomers
salt-and-pepper-haired Gen Xers
tattoo-faced millennials
They be Beyoncé
and Jimmy Kimmel
and seven-foot ballers who crush the ground
like jolly green giants
They marched from all over
with purple and yellow gold
steamed to their chests
they marched through
the musty scents of downtown Los Angeles
the way twentieth-century Europeans
marched from freedom ships to Ellis Island
the way twenty-first-century immigrants march

from Mexico into the barbed-wire borders
of the promised land
the way chocolate-legged country dwellers
marched from Mississippi
to the salty beaches and sleepy hoods of California
a massive army of humanity hemmed up
block after block
looking for the Staples Center
looking for that angel in America
who got a city of billions
'round the world saying
your name, Kobe
The lines of flesh speed text
as police and arena workers
shoo people to move like
you moved on that basketball court
a Black Mamba
yes
but also an African ballet dancer
who broke a-loose the chains
of plantations and copied and pasted Beethoven and basketball
with Biggie and Beverly Hills
as your body leaped and lunged
into the open mouths of nameless ancestors
who done seen some things
and them ancestors blew Michael Jordan
and Dr. J
and your daddy and your momma
and Philadelphia and Japan and Italy
and the holy ghost of Dizzy
and Coltrane into your veins
just means
the people marching to be like you, Kobe
and they be

White Black Latinx Asian Native American Pacific Islander
Christian Jewish Muslim Atheist Agnostic
This gender That gender No gender
They be Kendrick's cool hip-hop they be Sinatra's cool jazz
They be lakers matching jelly beans
with Amy Winehouse and Marilyn Monroe
as you Kobe and you Gianna wax poetic
with John Lennon and Marvin Gaye about love love love
They be a rainbow coalition
of thousands
marching over
your midrange jumpers and 360-degree dunks
as they scrape field hollers and spirituals and your blues
from their veins, Kobe
Wearing number 8
Wearing number 24
Wearing Gianna's number 2
Street hustlers selling t-shirts posters
clipped and chipped memories of you
putting an entire nation on your shoulders
winning five championships
teaching us the magic of the mamba mentality
telling us to keep shooting
even when the odds are slanted
like that cloudy hillside in heaven
you be heaven to us, Kobe
'cuz you never gave up
That's why they come to you
like you are a saint a king
royalty
yeah
a political leader
yeah
a self-help guru

yeah
a storyteller
yeah
They come to you
because
you could
chest-pass a basketball
through the smashed windows
of centuries of dreams denied
They come to you because
you crumbled in front of us
and got back up
and confessed
and apologized
and sculpted yourself
into a husband
a lover
a father
a girls' dad
Vanessa Bryant's multilingual soul mate
her tears her words
the biblical permission
we need to release
your joyful angel's wings
into the healing arms of the Pacific
Kobe
forever
forever
forever

Monday, February 24, 2020
9:53 p.m.
Los Angeles, California

In Close Quarters, a Mother of Six Battles Coronavirus

Originally published in the *New York Times*
April 17, 2020

On a typical morning during the first bursts of spring, Tanya Denise Fields, a South Bronx mother, is up by six a.m. to prepare her six children, ages four to seventeen, for school: getting the smallest ones dressed, passing out breakfast food or money to grab a snack, and later calling the older ones on their cell phones to confirm they made it safely to class.

Next is a quick HIIT workout to keep off the more than one hundred pounds she proudly lost in a year, then she spends the day administering a nonprofit from her tiny home office. Finally, welcoming her kids back by six p.m., she prepares dinner and helps with homework.

But on this particular April day, everything was different.

Fields, or "Mama Tanya" as many refer to her, a tall woman with flowing dreadlocks and a gigantic smile that makes the hoop dangling from her nose flip up and down, was housebound with the coronavirus. And her children wouldn't be attending school for months to come.

Mama Tanya, thirty-nine, kept her distance from a reporter and photographer so she wouldn't infect them, but agreed to share what life is like for her and her family. She waved frantically at visitors from a small window of the tenement building where she lives with her children and her boyfriend, Mustaphai,

who is not the father of any of her kids but helps to take care of them.

The signs of poverty are obvious up and down her sepia-toned block: bloated and ignored garbage bags lining the streets, folks milling about on street corners doing nothing at all, people begging for change or food, no grocery store in sight but a fully stocked liquor store directly below Mama Tanya's window where residents casually come and go, some wearing protective masks and gloves, some not.

This is Mama Tanya's world where she is raising her family as a single mother. Despite the built-in hardships, she is a dynamic leader—an urban farmer who manages a nearby city-owned plot of land where she grows fruits and vegetables for the community; an outspoken crusader for women whose organization, the Black Feminist Project, works for food justice and reproductive rights; and a gifted public speaker and organizer whose brutally naked musings on social media bring to mind the bottomless courage of Fannie Lou Hamer, the storytelling genius of Toni Morrison, and the self-empowerment ethos of Cardi B.

But most importantly, Mama Tanya is a parent who was terrified when she realized in mid-March that she may have contracted the coronavirus during a recent trip to New Orleans for a conference. Knowing that she could also spread it to her children and her partner was even more frightening.

"I called my doctor immediately," she said. "They called me back in a couple of hours and I gave him all of my symptoms— the chills, the body aches, a headache like I've never had in my life before. My eyeballs hurt."

She lay in bed and kept her eyes closed because they were sensitive to even the dimmest of light. A sore throat and stomach troubles plagued her. "I just could not eat anything. Everything made me nauseous," she said.

There are no nannies or caretakers for women like Mama Tanya, no extended family to help. She is the parent, disciplinar-

ian, educator, nurse, cook, house cleaner, therapist—even when there is no global pandemic. So when her symptoms kicked in with a ferocious intensity, Mama Tanya was emotionally devastated, and she had to wait two weeks to get a test.

"I didn't go to the hospital because I was scared," she said. "I was like, *If they find fluid in my lungs, then I'm gonna die. I'm gonna need to be on a ventilator and we don't have enough ventilators and I'm gonna die.*"

Her fears were rooted in a grim reality: the pandemic has disproportionately affected Black people in New York City, as well as nationwide, in places like Detroit, Chicago, and New Orleans. It does not help that many Black people, like Mama Tanya, harbor a deep distrust of the medical establishment because of past experiences.

"I can tell you horror stories about having my children in hospitals," she said. "Just having a baby, which should be like the happiest part of your life—the microaggressions and the medical racism." She attributes birthing injuries she incurred to the thinly veiled bias of medical professionals she encountered, which drove her to deliver some of her children at home.

Indeed, the Centers for Disease Control and Prevention has found that Black women are 3.3 times more likely to die from pregnancy-related causes than White women are, a fact widely attributed in part to racial inequalities in health care. So what kind of support can a Black mother expect in a pandemic?

Mama Tanya eventually found her way to a makeshift emergency room, where she was given a chest X-ray. She was initially denied a coronavirus test, for fifteen days, but finally tested "presumptive positive" for the virus in the first week of April. Her partner and each of her children, except her four-year-old, have had symptoms of high fever and debilitating nausea, but no one else in the three-bedroom apartment has been tested.

For a working-class family living in one of America's poorest communities, there is no space to social distance, no spare room,

attic, or basement in which to self-quarantine. If one person in the household gets the coronavirus, as Mama Tanya did, it is likely others living there will too.

Mama Tanya was feeling lightheaded on the day the reporter and photographer arrived, but she mustered up the energy to take pictures alone, then with her six children and their dog, Pebbles. The oldest child, her daughter Taylor, is heading to college upstate in the fall to be a filmmaker, if the semester is not postponed. "She's totally stressed about that," Mama Tanya said, "and trying to cope with those feelings."

Trist'ann, fifteen, suffers from severe asthma, and aside from her mother had the most frightening reactions after falling ill, at times unable to breathe.

"I felt very guilty," Mama Tanya said, her voice haunted by sadness. "I gave her this. I was sick and then I made her sick." She'd tried her best to shield the family from the virus, wearing gloves, frequently washing her hands, and disinfecting surfaces regularly. But she's convinced her children and partner caught it despite her precautions.

The family's current location isn't ideal for any child with asthma to recover from a respiratory illness. Inside their apartment building last week the scent of marijuana wafted through the air, accompanied by the loud talk and music of Mama Tanya's neighbors. It is these elements she longs to escape, but cannot, because of her financial situation. She has survived domestic violence and debilitating low self-esteem, and understands the dehumanizing effects of poverty on mothers like her better than any scholar or politician.

"There are people who are living on very fixed incomes who have to decide between, *Do I want to be in debt after all of this is over?* and have to navigate a housing system that is not kind to poor people," she said. "The single mamas have to figure out whether they're gonna use their limited amount of income to pay their portion of the rent, or to buy diapers and formula."

On a different and quieter day, via telephone, Mama Tanya said her health was improving: "I feel much better, but I am concerned how long I'll be contagious." She paused with a sigh, the weight of her thoughts like that heavy load Langston Hughes once described in a poem. "I am tempted to get tested again to see if I'm negative, but don't wanna be bothered with all that is involved with getting tested."

Mama Tanya said people like her are "a miracle"—those from poor backgrounds who, in spite of limited resources, make a way out of no way. So she pushes herself and her children, through her days battling to get well without any treatment other than her homemade remedies and drugstore products like Tylenol. Her partner, Mustaphai, co-parents however he can, but the children have had to, at times, homeschool themselves, clean up when she cannot, and even prepare their own meals. Yet in the midst of that, Mama Tanya is still finding hope, and joy.

"I do feel such a deep happiness right now to be alive," she said. "Because those of us who did get through it have the obligation to create a world that is better able to sustain for all of us. I hope that that is what comes up out of this pandemic."

 The Power of Stacey Abrams

Originally published in the *Washington Post Magazine*
May 14, 2020

There is a big buzz at the Loudermilk Conference Center in downtown Atlanta as a gathering called "Paradigm Shift 2.0: Black Women Confronting HIV, Health and Social Justice" gets underway. Three hundred registered participants have journeyed from across the country to discuss the many challenges and possibilities facing Black women and girls. The second day's morning keynote was delivered by radical activist and professor Angela Davis. The hype has been building exponentially for lunchtime guest speaker Stacey Abrams.

When she is finally introduced, the women shout and leap to their feet. Young women stand on chairs, camera phones flash. Abrams, who appears both amused and slightly disturbed by the fuss over her, takes control of the chaotic scene. I've witnessed this level of affection for very few political leaders in the Democratic circles I've been in since the 1980s. They have the last names Clinton (both Hillary and Bill), Sanders, Warren, Jackson, and Obama (both Michelle and Barack).

"I'm going to make sure there is peace in this room," Abrams says. "Y'all are about to annoy each other with these cameras, so I'm going to stand up and I'm going to stand in front of each group of you. Take pictures so you can put your camera down."

Pandemonium ensues as she walks to the far left of the stage, like a runway supermodel, stops on a dime, poses, tilts her head slightly, and smiles. Camera flashes explode. She next pivots and

walks slowly to the center of the stage, freezes there, and repeats the pose. Again, the flashes explode. Abrams is summoning her inner actress, and she is both enjoying the moment and getting through it to get to the conversation. She then pivots and walks to the far right of the stage, same. You wonder whether she has done this before, because it is not necessarily what one would expect from a forty-six-year-old politician who was nearly elected the first Black female governor in US history. She lost by fewer than two percentage points in the 2018 Georgia race riddled with allegations of voter suppression. Before that, she was a state legislator who had served as a leader in the Georgia General Assembly for a decade. Now her name is on political pundits' short lists of potential running mates for Joe Biden. She also happens to have predicted that she'll be elected president by 2040.

Just as quickly, Abrams leaves the runway and returns to politics. Taking her seat with the moderator, she dives into why she is here and why she believes the leadership of women matters. "We live in a time where we have purported leaders who claim to speak for us but do not know us, and in that ignorance, they make decisions that are designed not for our success but for our demise," she says. "So my deep suspicion is that some people are lying when they say they care about us."

The balloon of silence in the meeting room is punctured, time and again, by "Amen" and "Preach" and "You go, girl."

"When I ran for governor, I did not run simply for me. We went around this state to all 159 counties, and everywhere we went we talked about the power of people to make a choice," Abrams tells the crowd. "On November 6, when malfeasance and incompetence and my opponent who was a cartoon villain stole the voices of Georgians when he purged 1.4 million voters and oversaw the shutdown of 214 precincts that left fifty to sixty thousand people without the ability to vote, when Georgia had the longest lines in the nation and the highest rejection rates

of absentee ballots and provisional ballots," Abrams continues, "it was not just about me. He was doing that to Georgians."

Abrams pauses for a moment, allowing her words to simmer. The audience cheers as she smiles broadly.

"And the thing is, if I had fought back and said, 'I am going to contest this election and make myself governor,' then everyone who loved me and stood with me would have thought, *Well, this is about* her *fight.* My responsibility was instead to focus on the right to vote and not my right to be governor. I had no right to be governor, but I have an obligation to do the work that I said I would do if I were governor."

Voting rights. Responsibility. Possibilities. These are the ideas and values that come up often with Stacey Abrams and her team. I heard them over and over again during the weeks I followed her around earlier this year, in Miami, in New York, in Atlanta, and listened to her give interviews and hold public conversations. She has opened up a nationwide dialogue about voting rights but has also been accused by political pundits of too aggressively pushing herself as Biden's VP choice. What Abrams seems to know is that she must be persuasive and make her own case for her fitness for higher office—and history would suggest that she's right to do so. Commentators have wondered whether Abrams, who has not yet won a statewide election, would be ready to serve as vice president.

Whether or not she's chosen as Biden's running mate, she has moved into a unique space in American politics. DuBose Porter, former chair of the Georgia Democratic Party, told me she is "brilliant," praise that comes in spite of what some view as a relatively thin political résumé. But we live in an era in which an extensive political background hardly matters anymore—Donald Trump had never been elected to office before his 2016 win. Like former South Bend, Indiana, mayor Pete Buttigieg, whose long-shot campaign for the Democratic presidential nomination made him a household name, Abrams doesn't have the baggage

of years of votes on Capitol Hill; she doesn't have a fraught record on criminal justice that comes with having served as an attorney general, nor does she face the accusation of being out of touch because she has spent years in Washington.

At this conference it's easy to be reminded that Black women have long been the most loyal supporters of the Democratic Party. They carried Doug Jones to his senatorial victory in Alabama in 2018 and were key to kick-starting Biden's presidential campaign when it was thought to be dead, helping to lift him to victory in South Carolina's Democratic primary. So perhaps it was only a matter of time before a Black woman, especially a Black woman from the American South, would rise up as a national leader and a power broker for democracy in a way we have not often seen, aside from Fannie Lou Hamer's brief but landmark speech at the 1964 Democratic National Convention and Shirley Chisholm's historic "unbought and unbossed" run for president in 1972.

Abrams's roots and family history have echoes of the Civil Rights Movement, and her Southern heritage is key to her appeal. It helps explain why she has soared to prominence while serving as a standard-bearer for a new kind of multicultural and multigenerational agenda. In the last presidential campaign cycle, the racial breakdown of Democrats outside of the South was roughly 60 percent White, 17 percent African American, and 23 percent Latino, according to a 2016 Blair Center Poll. In the states that form the South, those numbers were 38 percent White, 37 percent African American, and 25 percent Latino. In her runs for the Georgia legislature and governor, Abrams built a coalition that excited this new Georgia. She believes she can do the same on the national stage.

Abrams's special adviser, Chelsey Hall, tells me that in the 2018 gubernatorial race, the campaign had to contend with doubters and "convince her own people that she was viable and electable for that position. Even the people that had been sup-

porting since she became Democratic minority leader [of the General Assembly] or her first race. There were so many times where we would have emotional moments during call time because people that she trusted, that had been supporting her since 2006, 2011 were saying, 'But you are a Black woman. How is this possible?'"

Abrams is the first Black woman in US history to have won the gubernatorial nomination of either major party. She garnered more votes than any Democrat who has run statewide in Georgia. She lost by just over fifty thousand votes to Georgia Secretary of State Brian Kemp.

Kemp was not only her opponent, but his office oversaw everything to do with voting, including how the voter registration rolls were purged. It would be like Tom Brady not only being the quarterback of his team, but the referee and the scorekeeper as well. Kemp's office cut nearly 700,000 names from the rolls in the two years leading to the election, and more than two hundred polling places were closed, primarily in poor and minority neighborhoods.

Abrams chose not to concede to Kemp, because she believes voters were disenfranchised. She has said she went through all the stages of grief for ten days and then got back to work. She has spent the time since leveraging the power she gained and deciding how she wants to use it.

Stacey Abrams lives in a simple blue town house in a diverse middle-class neighborhood on the east side of Atlanta. Her modestly furnished home is filled with a wide range of books, including the four she's currently absorbing: *The City We Became* by N.K. Jemisin, *Huey Long* by T. Harry Williams, *A Problem from Hell* by Samantha Power, and *A Place for Us* by Fatima Farheen Mirza. There is art, some centered on Black America, but also pieces from her travels internationally that are Australian aboriginal, South Korean, French, Chinese. Framed photographs of family and friends are spread throughout as well.

This home is a major expansion of the Gulfport, Mississippi, house she grew up in, where her family of eight had to convert the dining room to a bedroom for her two brothers, Richard and Walter. It feels like a sanctuary to protect Abrams from the many demands on her time. Abrams, who is single with no children, arrived in Atlanta as a fifteen-year-old in 1989 when her parents decided to attend Methodist divinity school. Aside from stints for graduate school at the University of Texas (master's in public affairs) and Yale Law School in Connecticut, Atlanta is where she has mostly lived since departing Mississippi. I ask Abrams about her life in Mississippi.

"I only remember living on South Street in Gulfport, Mississippi," she says. "2020 South Street was a redbrick house with azalea bushes that ran along the front. There was an oak tree in the front yard, and it had such big limbs and so many leaves that grass couldn't grow underneath it. But you could climb that tree, and you could see everything."

Abrams's parents picked that street so that she and her siblings could attend one of the better schools in the area. It was one of many lessons she learned growing up about the division of resources along racial lines and navigating those divisions. "It was less a Black community than we lived on a 'Black street.' There were these two streets that were adjacent to the middle-class, predominantly White part of town to get zoned into the middle-class school . . . We lived on the two streets that were all Black until the Brooks family came . . . All the streets got nicer names as you went farther in, so those were predominantly White. My parents understood that education was the essential ingredient to success for both of them. My mom is the only one of her siblings to finish high school. My dad is the first man in his family to go to college."

Abrams excelled in academics and was always in advanced studies, which meant she was routinely the only Black student in her classes. Because one of the two TV channels that the fam-

ily received was PBS, Abrams watched that network religiously, read the dictionary, and devoured the books and encyclopedias her parents managed to buy for their children.

"I think my mom is the reason I started reading the encyclopedia and the dictionary, because I would ask questions and she was like, 'Go look it up.' Finally, I figured if I wanted to know everything, I just needed to read everything."

Abrams also tells me that she and her sisters like to say their dad—a track star in college who once had pro football tryouts with the Green Bay Packers and the Dallas Cowboys—is the first feminist they ever met. "He will tell you before anyone else will that he thinks my mom is the smartest person he knows . . . It is a true belief that there is no division of capacity that comes along with gender. He raised us with that understanding, and we never questioned it."

Her interests were vast: physics, chemistry, history, psychology, mythologies, biographies, poetry. During our conversation Abrams recalls speeches, debates, and poetry that she studied in her youth, and recites from memory the opening stanza of Paul Laurence Dunbar's poem "We Wear the Mask."

We wear the mask that grins and lies,
It hides our cheeks and shades our eyes,—
This debt we pay to human guile;
With torn and bleeding hearts we smile,
And mouth with myriad subtleties.

Abrams draws no boundaries around most music genres, either: "When I was in tenth grade, I was having a conversation with a friend, and I said, 'I hate country music.' And she said, 'Why?' And I didn't have an answer. So I made myself listen to every station on the radio for two weeks each. But then when I engaged people . . . I could use that complexity of my musical likes to talk. And the same thing was true from what I read. My

mom and dad basically let me read; if I could reach it, I could read it."

When the family moved to Atlanta, Abrams ended up at a performing arts high school, where she became her class's valedictorian. College was next. "I applied to Spelman, Swarthmore, Vassar, Sarah Lawrence. I was leaving the South," she says, recalling that the South was all she knew, and she wanted a different experience. "I only applied to Spelman because my mother tricked me into it."

At Spelman College, a historically Black women's college in Atlanta, she majored in interdisciplinary studies (political science, economics, and sociology), with a minor in theater. It was the first time she would be steeped so broadly in Black life and culture outside of her family home. Johnnetta Cole, who later led the Smithsonian National Museum of African Art and was the school's president at the time, became Abrams's mentor. Cole encouraged young Abrams—who was perpetually raising her voice—to get involved, attend meetings, and bring about change. Abrams did that and then some, on and off campus. When the Rodney King verdict came down in Los Angeles in April 1992, acquitting the four police officers who brutally beat the motorist, Atlanta and many other US cities exploded into protest and violent rebellion. A couple of months later, Abrams was in the back of a protest, watching, when some young Black folks burned the Georgia state flag because it contained the Confederate symbol (she did not personally hold the flag as it burned, but she organized the protest and obtained the permit), a fact that her opponents raised during her run for governor. Soon after that incident, Spelman hosted a town hall with Atlanta mayor Maynard Jackson in which Abrams dissed the work of the first African American elected to lead a major Southern city.

"I berated him for not doing enough for young people," Abrams recalls. "I was very irate and then . . . I gave them my number, and I gave my parents' number. '[Here's] where I'm go-

ing to be, if you have any questions.'" Jackson was very offended and questioned what Abrams knew. It was a bold move for a young woman to challenge a trailblazing Black man who was seen as an important leader throughout the South. She told him that she attended city council meetings and zoning meetings and that she knew he wasn't doing enough. The town hall aired on local television. Despite the confrontation, when Jackson created an Office of Youth Services the next year, 1993, she was the only undergrad college student hired. It was her first taste of life in politics.

After Spelman and graduate and law school, Abrams became a tax lawyer because working in the mayor's office showed her that if she wanted to be a public servant, she needed to learn how the entire system worked. At age twenty-nine, Abrams was appointed deputy city attorney by Mayor Shirley Franklin, another history-making Southern Black politician. Franklin was the first woman to hold the post and the first Black woman to be elected mayor of a major Southern city. Abrams ran for and was elected as a state representative in 2006; she rose quickly in the Georgia legislature and became Democratic Party minority leader in 2011.

She calls herself a "pragmatist," which is a necessary asset for a Democrat in a state long controlled by Republicans. She also embraces the label "progressive"; in the race for governor, she campaigned on expanding Medicaid. Ideologically, she falls somewhere between Bernie Sanders and Joe Biden: as her state's Democratic leader, she worked on behalf of low-income and middle-class residents, defeating sales taxes; she championed reproductive rights, supported military families, and protected public education and Medicaid from budget cuts; and as a mentor, she launched a program to train young people in Democratic Party politics. In my reporting, I have heard grumblings that some Black Democrats in Georgia did not feel Abrams was always with them in political fights, but there's wide agreement

that she is focused on taking action and getting results. To do that, Minority Leader Abrams crossed the aisle, often to work with Republicans. One of her admirers is Nathan Deal, the former two-term Republican governor of Georgia.

"I thought that my working relationship with her, and she with my staff, was very good," Deal says in a phone interview about their partnership to save Georgia's HOPE Scholarship for low-income residents. "We were in the midst of the continuing Great Recession at that period of time, and we had to make some very difficult choices about programs in our state. We did not always agree on all the issues that we were confronted with, but on that one, which was a significant one, I thought she demonstrated the kind of leadership that you hope people would do regardless of party labels."

They made cuts to the program, which upset some liberals, but preserved the scholarship. When asked if Abrams could bring that same tact to national politics, Deal says: "I would think she probably could. Now that's not something that every Republican will say."

Abrams is the author of eight romance novels under a pseudonym, started two small businesses, is a *New York Times* best-selling author under her own name, and is a superfan of *Star Trek* and Southern hip-hop, including one of her favorite rappers, Ludacris. She is scholarly, but she can also wax poetic on football. She is a policy wonk, but she can effortlessly pivot to sending goofy memes to the children of good buddies. She is a pop culture junkie who is also very literate on the sway and potential of technology. She is secure in her identity as a Black woman but also sees herself as appealing broadly to people of all colors and identities. (Exit polls in the Georgia governor's race proved her right about that.) She is effusive about the accomplishments of her sisters and brothers but also talks openly about her brother Walter's long-term battles with mental health

and drug addiction. Politics is a profession that attracts fakers, but it seems to me that Abrams is, for lack of a better phrase, mad real.

In 2018 and immediately after her defeat in 2019, Abrams helped to create three organizations: Fair Fight Action, which advocates against voter suppression (and has a lawsuit in the discovery phase against Brad Raffensperger, in his official capacity as Georgia secretary of state and as chair of the State Election Board); the Southern Economic Advancement Project (SEAP), which aims for equality of opportunity; and Fair Count, which seeks to get communities of color, rural populations, and other marginalized groups counted in the 2020 census. At the Fair Fight office in Atlanta, I meet Abrams's parents in a small conference room. Before the fan frenzy around her, before the passionate support of such A-listers as Will Ferrell, Oprah Winfrey, and Mike Bloomberg, before she found herself the subject of countless media profiles, and before she became an in-demand expert on political talk shows as well as a guest on *The View,* she was their daughter.

Demanding a fair fight is something Stacey Abrams's mother and father have been doing pretty much most of their lives, beginning in Hattiesburg, Mississippi. Both came from generations of churchgoers, cooks, domestic workers, and laborers. They met during the height of the Civil Rights Movement and wound up working together at Hattiesburg's racially segregated swimming pool as lifeguards who became teenage sweethearts.

Says Carolyn Abrams, seventy-one, "I just always believed I can do anything anybody else could do, that there was no limit. And we taught our children the same thing."

"My mom raised me, and we were really, really poor," says Robert Abrams, also seventy-one, "but in our family, anything you do, you do it to benefit others."

These are the people who shaped Stacey Abrams's notions of power and her Southern Black political identity. Robert Abrams

is a tall and nimble man. Carolyn Abrams, his wife and partner of fifty-one years, is short in stature, walks with the help of a cane, and speaks in the perfect diction of an English teacher, or a great debater.

Robert, like other youth of his era in the Deep South, became heavily involved in the Civil Rights Movement, inspired by the founding of the Mississippi Freedom Democratic Party in 1964 and other developments happening in the state. Robert never affiliated himself with any organization but was simply a civil rights "soldier," as many youths were then, and was arrested more times than he can recall. He was, he says, also physically assaulted because he challenged local White authority.

By the time he and Carolyn were both students at historically Black Tougaloo College near Jackson, Mississippi, they had decided to get married; they honeymooned at a local Holiday Inn. A year later, the first of six children came: Andrea in 1970, Stacey in 1973, Leslie in 1974, Richard in 1977, Walter in 1979, and Jeanine in 1982. Stacey and Leslie were born in Madison, Wisconsin, because Robert and the family resided there for a couple of years so that Carolyn could get, with the help of a fellowship, a master's degree in library science from the University of Wisconsin.

After Carolyn Abrams secured her degree, the family returned to Mississippi, this time to Gulfport, a bustling shipping city along the Gulf of Mexico. Carolyn settled into life as a librarian, and because of his dyslexia and difficulties reading, Robert worked at a shipyard. Stacey's mother would come to refer to the family as "the genteel poor" because of their unusual blend of books everywhere and "urban camping" whenever the lights were cut off from a lack of money. They lived by candles or flashlights when that happened. (In my time with Abrams, I noticed that in speeches and interviews she uses the words "poor" and "poverty" in a way most politicians do not, bringing to mind the Reverend Martin Luther King Jr.'s Poor

People's Campaign. But these issues are familiar to her and very personal.)

Carolyn and Robert Abrams would go on, in the years to come, to get master's degrees in divinity from Atlanta's Candler School of Theology and raise their six children to be, among other things, two PhDs, a social worker, a federal judge and a popular politician.

"It was always just a part of what you do," Stacey says. "Your job is to serve."

"My name is Stacey Abrams, and I am not the governor of Georgia. I'm not going to be the senator, ever, but what I am is a proud Southerner, I'm a proud Democrat, and I believe that we will win . . ."

That is how she reintroduces herself at a town hall meeting in Miami in early February hosted by the Florida Democratic Party. This was before Biden overcame early primary defeats to become the Democratic nominee for president, but after Abrams had declined Senate Minority Leader Chuck Schumer's requests for her to run for the US Senate because she'd rather be in the executive branch; and this was before the human and economic devastations of the coronavirus pandemic.

On this muggy eighty-degree day, Abrams paced in front of an interracial crowd in an auditorium at Miami Dade College, North Campus, using a story about her grandmother Wilter "Bill" Abrams to drive home the importance of voting: "My grandmother explained to me that the first time she was truly eligible to vote was after the Voting Rights Act of 1965, but—as with most federal decisions—it didn't really get to Mississippi until '68. So, the first time she was eligible to vote in an election was in the presidential election in 1968, and she remembered that day. My grandfather and his brother were at the house. They had gotten off work, and they were ready to take her to go and vote . . .

"My grandmother said she didn't move. She was sitting back there on that bed and she was frozen," Abrams says, letting the story spool out. "My grandfather became less and less generous with his platitudes and more impatient with her not showing up, and he finally marched back there to get her, and he was like, 'What's wrong? We've got to go and vote!' And she said, 'I don't want to go.' My grandfather was like, 'What do you mean, you don't want to go?' She said, 'I don't want to face the dogs and the billy clubs. I don't want to face the problems.' And he said, 'But we've got the right to vote. We've got the Voting Rights Acts. We can vote!' And she said, 'I'm afraid. I don't want to do this.' And my grandfather looked at her and she said she had never seen my grandfather look so disappointed. He said, 'Your children fought for this . . .'"

Abrams's grandmother summoned the courage to vote that day, and she voted in every election after that until she died. Hearing this, the crowd roars and Abrams rocks back on her heels. She's wearing her now-familiar look of twisted natural hair, short dangling earrings, a solid-colored jacket, and dark blouse and slacks. She speaks without notes, merging front-porch storytelling with a nerdish marshaling of facts and history.

Moments before the town hall, Abrams sat with six students from different Florida colleges to talk about the role of young people in American politics, in protecting the right to vote and building political coalitions—especially in the South. The basic civil right of voting has become a signature issue for Abrams because of her experiences with the 2018 governor's race, because Georgia's racial demographics and voting patterns are shifting quickly, and because of her own family history.

"I started my voting rights activism at Spelman College. I started a voter-registration drive even before I was old enough to vote," she tells the students. "I was probably the only person who turned eighteen in college and got excited to go register and nothing else. But for me, the issue of voter registration is the

beginning of the conversation because it is a conversation about power."

"Power" is a word Abrams uses often in private conversations and in public statements. It's what she wrote about in her political memoir *Lead from the Outside: How to Build Your Future and Make Real Change*: "[T]he questions for those in search of power abound: Who has it? How do we get and wield it? What do we do when we have less than the other guy? What do we do when we lose it? . . . [T]he bald conversation of gaining power—especially for those who rarely hold it—is unusual."

Abrams tells the Florida college students that her political opponents "know how narrow the elections are. Every moment of suppression makes it easier to keep power."

Abrams is not at any of the three offices I visit as I meet and talk with staffers. Each is in a different location: Fair Count in a bland, nondescript house converted to office space next to a gas station; SEAP in a white building that could easily be a school; and Fair Fight in a brownish office building. All are funded by private donations, both large- and small-dollar. Fair Fight Action is a 501(c)(4) and lead plaintiff in the aforementioned lawsuit, and does advocacy work. Fair Fight PAC, with more than 120,000 individual donors and about $24 million in fundraising, works on voter protection with state Democratic parties. Fair Count has raised about $7 million, and SEAP has raised about $1 million. I am told it would be impossible to delineate funds raised by Abrams and funds raised by staff because it's a team effort. Fair Fight Action and its PAC combined have thirty staff members, along with teams at state parties across the country. Fair Count has twenty-six and SEAP four.

On each visit with these organizations, I see that women are in leadership positions, the staffs are a rainbow coalition of identities, and droves of young people, twentysomethings and thirtysomethings, power each group.

Fair Fight Action's chief executive is Lauren Groh-Wargo. Before Abrams began entertaining conversations about the vice presidency, she and Groh-Wargo—a political operative who launched the New Georgia Project in 2014 as a nonpartisan effort to register voters, and who started her career by organizing against slumlords in Brooklyn—would strategize on how to transform their state. They would also discuss why Abrams should run for governor in 2018, with Groh-Wargo as her campaign manager.

Their partnership reflects the bridge-building necessary in the modern Democratic Party—and is a vision, perhaps, of the party's future leaders: Abrams is Southern, Black, straight; Groh-Wargo is Midwestern, White, gay. They share core values: both support abortion rights, the rights of immigrants, marriage equality, economic justice, and environmental protections.

Groh-Wargo says that Abrams also represents a kind of politics that shows "it is possible, and the best option, for Democrats to really aggressively be building this multiracial, multiethnic coalition. We should be leading with that rather than leading with this idea that we have to start with the 'swing voter' concept. We lead with diverse communities of color and really let that drive strategy. What we have learned in Georgia is that no one thought a Black woman would be competitive. We have learned that when you do that work and are also reaching out to White voters of all kinds, you do build a coalition."

This is why, in spite of not being the governor of Georgia, Abrams has become a player in the Democratic Party—in her state and in the country, including her well-reviewed prime-time 2019 response to President Trump's State of the Union address.

In a phone conversation after our in-person interview, Abrams made a point to address the lingering questions raised by pundits about her readiness for national office. "I would say that anyone who believes that they know everything on day one is likely incorrect," she tells me. "Part of any job is being capable

of learning all of the facets but coming with enough knowledge and enough curiosity and enough capacity to adapt quickly either to the challenges you face or to the realities you confront." To that point, Abrams adds that she is a member of the Council on Foreign Relations and has spent the past quarter-century "self-educating" on global affairs with fellowships and other fact-finding missions, including trips to Europe, Asia, and the Middle East.

In that phone conversation, as she was sheltering in place, Abrams was thinking about why the nation was ill-prepared to address the pandemic and how to be better prepared for the next. "What we've watched for the last forty years has been a concentrated assault on public administration and on the public infrastructure that so many Americans take for granted," she says. "And I think because we have not faced an internalized crisis in this country in quite awhile, we have forgotten why we built what we have, and that . . . in times of national emergency we should have an infrastructure that can quickly be scaled up to meet the needs of the moment."

Be it foreign affairs or other topics, Abrams is not a traditional politician—just like Robert Kennedy, who served as attorney general and a US senator, was not your typical politician. Both stepped into massive spotlights in spite of their shyness, both took on the mantle of activist, and both wanted to bring all kinds of people together.

Maybe the signs and troubles of our times are why Abrams has made it no secret that she is very open to a place next to Biden on the Democratic ticket. But the question remains: would a Biden-Abrams ticket work? Word among the political chattering class is that he is looking for a running mate who could step into the Oval Office after one term, and not every pundit is convinced that Abrams has the credentials. Biden is seventy-seven, and Democrats want to be sure they have his successor waiting in the wings. Abrams tells me that she has spoken regularly

with the former vice president over the past year, since they first met to talk about his campaign in March 2019, though Abrams won't divulge the nature of those conversations.

When I press her about the 1990s sexual assault allegation from Biden's former staffer Tara Reade, and how that might affect him or his running mate, Abrams stands firm. "If I am chosen to be his running mate, I will proudly promote his record and his plans to help the women of America," she tells me, noting Biden's leadership of the Violence Against Women Act, his support for equal pay for equal work, and helping to pass the Affordable Care Act.

Even if she's not chosen, it seems that her place in the vice presidential conversation only strengthens her political future. If, for example, she was to challenge Kemp to a rematch in 2022 or run for president in 2024, she'd only have more power.

Before hanging up, we return to that subject, and Abrams again stresses her vision of political power for all people.

"Leadership," she says, "is about answering that question: How can I help?"

we them people

Originally published in *When We Free the World*

June 6, 2020

dream on
dreamer
the way Alvin Ailey
and Maya Angelou
and George Floyd
and Breonna Taylor
dreamed of
southern-baked
pilgrims
dancing and
slow-marching
their sorrows
down the yellow-
brick roads
of
second-line members
humming from
the heels of their dirt-kissed feet:
i wanna be ready / to put on my long white robe . . .
we are survivors
we are survivors
we are survivors
of people
who were free
and became slaves

of people
who were slaves
and became free
we know why the caged bird sings
we know what a redemption song brings
we them people
we the people
we are those people
who shall never forget
our ancestors all up in us as we sleep
our grandmother all up in us as we weep
because we are
native american
black irish welsh french german polish italian
jewish puerto rican mexican greek russian
dominican chinese japanese vietnamese
filipino korean arab middle eastern
we are biracial and we are multicultural
we are bicentennial and we are new millennial
we are essential and we are front line
we are everyday people and we are people every day
we are #metoo we are #metoo we are #metoo
we are muslim christian hebrew too
we are bible torah koran atheist agnostic truer than true
we are rabbis and imams and preachers and yoruba priests
tap-dancing with buddhists and hindus and rastafarians
as the nicholas brothers
jump and jive and split the earth in half
while chloe and maud arnold
them syncopated ladies
twist and shout and stomp and trump
hate
again—
again—

again—
yeah
still we rise still we surprise
like we got judith jamison's crying solo in our eyes
every hello ain't alone every goodbye ain't gone
we are every tongue every nose every skin every color every face
mask
we are mattered lives paint it black
we are mattered lives paint it black
we are mattered lives paint it black
we are every tattoo every piercing every drop of blood
every global flood
we are straight queer trans non–gender conforming
we are she/he/they
we are disabled abled poor rich
big people little people in between people
we are protesters pepper-sprayed with knees on our necks
we are protesters pepper-sprayed with knees on our necks
we are protesters pepper-sprayed with knees on our necks
we them people
we the people
we are those people
who will survive
these times
because we done
survived
those times
where pandemics were
trail of tears and lynchings and holocausts
where pandemics were
no hope and no vote and no freedom spoke
we them people
we the people
we are those people

while our planet gently weeps
we bob and bop
like hip-hop
across the tender bones
of those tear-stained photographs
to hand to
this generation
the next generation
those revelations
yeah
that blues suite
yeah
that peaceful dance
inside a raging tornado
we call
love

Saturday, June 6, 2020
5:37 a.m.

I Was Hugged for the First Time at 18

Originally published in the *Guardian*
July 15, 2020

I had grown up in brutal poverty, and saw touch as a privilege for those with less traumatic backgrounds. Then a friend and mentor changed my life.

It happened one day during my first year of college at Rutgers University, in my home state of New Jersey. The anti-apartheid movement was raging on my college campus, there was still a massive buzz about Jesse Jackson's first run for president, and I had instantly become woke, as we say, because of names such as Winnie and Nelson Mandela, because of the AIDS and crack epidemics, and because of my adopted big sister on campus, an older student named Lisa Williamson, who would later become the famed activist and best-selling author Sister Souljah.

For sure, Lisa was one of the most incredible speakers I had ever heard. She was a fearless leader, and I became so instantly fond of her, I even called her "Ma" just like I did my own mother. And she adored me, taught me, and shared with me everything that she knew and was learning, in real time.

On one of those many occasions we were together, as we were about to part ways, Lisa did something she had not done before: she leaned in to hug me goodbye, and I recoiled with unimaginable terror, my body trembling. Lisa was stunned, asked me what was wrong, and I was profoundly embarrassed by my reaction. I said nothing.

"You have never been hugged before, have you?"

My eighteen-year-old eyes tumbled to the ground, along with my self-esteem. I felt weak, exposed, and shook my head no so slightly that it could barely be seen.

"Well, I am going to keep hugging you until you get used to it. You cannot live like that, Kev, afraid of people hugging or touching you."

And with that Lisa was gone, as I stood there still staring at the asphalt, my sweaty palms shoved deeply into my pockets.

It was the first time I had been confronted about my fear of physical touch. I was raised by a single mother in brutal poverty, no father and no father figure those first eighteen years of my life, and my ma did the best she could with what she had. But there were no hugs, no kisses, no *I love yous*—never. The only touching I ever received from my mother were the severe beatings whenever I was "bad," sometimes when I was awake, sometimes when I was asleep.

This went on from birth until I was about eleven or twelve and finally taller than my mother. But the emotional and verbal assaults never ended. So somewhere in my mind I had come to associate touching with violence, with someone trying to hurt me, and it would take several years of therapy, and mighty and consistent spiritual work, for me to forgive my mother, to understand that she was simply doing to me what had been done to her by her father, by our society.

Touching, hugging was a privilege reserved for those who had lives that were not traumatic like ours. Touching, hugging was for people who were "weird," different, like the Puerto Rican kids I would observe from a distance at my Jersey City grammar school openly offering love and affection to each other. As a youth, I was stunned by their behavior; it was foreign to me, and I could not imagine someone, anyone, touching me.

Yet little did I know that, in time, because of that singular act

by Sister Souljah when I was eighteen, I would fall in love with hugs, with touch.

It would happen slowly, through my twenties and thirties and into my forties, this love of touch, of hugs. It would come as I would get over my dread of holding a girlfriend's hand in public. It would come as I would learn, from a woman, from women, the difference between having sex and making love. It would come as I cried my eyes out in therapy session after therapy session over the course of three decades about the many traumas of my childhood. It would come to me as an activist, as a public speaker, when complete strangers would touch my shoulder, my elbow, my back, grab me, hug me, as a sign of appreciation. It comes when I try to touch my mother, on her shoulder, on her elbow, on her back, when I try to hug her as a sign of forgiveness and she recoils, as I had done long ago, with Sister Souljah; but I keep trying, hoping, praying that my mother, in her late seventies now, will finally allow herself to be touched or hugged, with love.

So here I am, sitting in my Brooklyn apartment, alone, during this pandemic, craving the presence and energy of human beings so intensely that it has left me in a flood of tears pretty much every single week.

Touching is magic for the soul, it is healing. I ache badly now, as I did during the first eighteen years of my life, because I do not have it, because I am just newly divorced from my wife after twelve painful months of separation and loneliness. I will have touch again, this I know, but I wonder, daily, *When?*

To John Lewis, with Love

Originally published in the *Guardian*
July 18, 2020

Dear Mr. Lewis,

I gasped when I learned of your death, after your courageous battle against cancer. I think of your December statement, when you said: "I have been in some kind of fight—for freedom, equality, basic human rights—for nearly my entire life. I have never faced a fight quite like the one I have now."

I shed tears then and I shed tears now, at what your passing represents to America and to the world. You do not know this, but the very first time I heard of you, in 1986, I was a Rutgers University student, asked by the Commission for Racial Justice to be part of a group of young people recreating the Freedom Rides you led during the Civil Rights Movement.

We stopped in Atlanta, where you were running for Congress. You encouraged us, you gave us an on-the-spot civil rights history lesson, you told us not to be afraid. You seemed to know that some of us, including me, were absolutely terrified.

Our bus went on to Alabama, to help African Americans protect their voting rights, just as you had done a generation before. When we heard troubling rumors of White supremacists "coming to get us" for repeating and continuing your work, I held tightly to your words in Atlanta, urging us to never give up—never.

That was thirty-four long years ago. I watched you become a congressman, an elder statesman, the humble and unassuming moral voice of America. I sat on panels with you at the Congres-

sional Black Caucus Annual Legislative Conference. I saw you publicly saddened by attacks on the civil rights for which leaders like you were savagely beaten. That is why you were forever committed to making "good trouble" on behalf of democracy.

I myself have walked across the Edmund Pettus Bridge in Selma, Alabama, many times. But my memories there are of you: of the bloodthirsty hatred of the police cracking your skull, how you could have died there on that ground, in your white trench coat, in 1965, just because you believed that Black people, all people, had the right to vote. I vote, Mr. Lewis, because of you, because of people like you. I exist because of you, because of people like you.

And I have wondered, as you witnessed president after president, one racial murder after another, from your childhood until your death, how you could still possess such a massive capacity to love people, every kind of people, in spite of what you experienced in your eighty years on this planet, in this country. You did not merely preach love, you embodied it, and were clear that love was forever the answer.

Is that who you were, Mr. Lewis, when you were a boy practicing your sermons to your chickens in your hometown of Troy, Alabama?

Is that who you were in 2017, when you led a thousand people through Comic-Con, a march to celebrate the trilogy of comic books you had written, based on your life?

What a life it was, Mr. Lewis. To be able to say you spoke at the same majestic March on Washington in 1963 where Dr. King gave his "I Have a Dream" address, and to be the last living speaker from that sweltering August day. To be able to say you were there in Indianapolis, Indiana, on the day Bobby Kennedy announced to a mostly Black crowd that Martin Luther King Jr. had been killed, Kennedy's words rivaling King's as one of the greatest speeches ever. To also say you were there, just two months later in Los Angeles, when Bobby himself was assassinated.

To be able to say that your cracked skull and many arrests in the 1960s led to Barack Obama becoming our first Black president, and to also be able to say you lived long enough to witness #MeToo and Black Lives Matter and protests unlike anything we have had since you yourself led nonviolent demonstrations those many years ago.

You never stopped protesting, Mr. Lewis. In the final months of your life, there you were in Selma, honoring the fifty-fifth anniversary of that march. There you were in a virtual town hall meeting with Barack Obama. And there you were, in June, a mere month before your death, admiring the Black Lives Matter mural on the street leading to the White House.

You never gave up, Mr. Lewis, and neither will I, and neither will we who believe in freedom, justice, and equality for everyone. You, sir, were a living, breathing history book of America, a living, breathing example of the best of the human race.

The greatest thing you gave us, besides your entire life, was your entire love. The greatest salute to you we can give is to love ourselves and each other as fiercely as you did us, to the very end.

To Be Young, Gifted, and Chadwick Boseman

Originally published on CNN.com
August 29, 2020

We've lost a humble superhero, and his name was Chadwick Boseman. Like everyone, I am shocked at the news of his death on Friday at the age of forty-three. That he suffered with colon cancer for four years, telling hardly anyone except those in his inner circle, shows us the kind of human being he was.

In those last four years of his life, Chadwick appeared in ten films, including his historic and thrilling performance as the title character in *Black Panther*, and underwent treatment. It's difficult to imagine the suffering he must have endured—how taxing the surgeries and chemotherapy sessions must have been on his body and what mind games he must have faced in his quiet moments, knowing his life could be tragically short. It was an incredible act of selflessness that Chadwick continued to work and bring people joy, in spite of the cancer that ravaged his body.

When I heard the sad news, my thoughts flashed back to the 2000s, when I first met Chadwick, who at the time had just graduated from the historically Black Howard University. I had published a collection of autobiographical essays, and a mutual friend who is a theater director suggested I ask this young actor to interpret parts of the book on stage. It was remarkable and humbling to see Chadwick, a native son of South Carolina born to working-class parents, embody me on that stage. And yet he

thanked *me* for the opportunity, and I never forgot him, his dedication to his craft or his humility.

Like many, I followed Chadwick's career as he landed bit parts on television and in film. I surged with pride when the Hollywood doors opened, and he played sports pioneer Jackie Robinson in *42*, civil rights icon Thurgood Marshall in *Marshall*, and music legend James Brown in *Get on Up*.

Chadwick seemed to know that acting was not merely his career but his spiritual calling. Through acting, he depicted cultural giants and brought each role to life as the everyman, in the vein of James Stewart and Sidney Poitier. He also channeled his cultural heritage into films that stirred and fed his soul—much like Robert De Niro and Denzel Washington—which, in turn, nourished so many of us. He channeled the Black Lives Matter movement too, knowing that the roles he played required the same kind of grace and dignity he manifested in every part of his life; that he represented not only himself, but the hopes and aspirations of an entire community of people.

That is why there is so much hurt and sorrow around his death. For Black people worldwide, Chadwick Boseman's performance in *Black Panther* felt like it had single-handedly erased centuries of racist pop culture stereotypes. Chadwick as T'Challa proved to us, to Hollywood and to viewers around the world, that a Black superhero could be celebrated, beloved, and make over a billion dollars at the box office too.

Black Panther was hugely inspiring, and people of all ages and identities took to making the same cross-armed Wakanda greeting that Chadwick Boseman did in the film. As his fame exploded, I thought of how different my life would have been, as a poor and profoundly self-hating Black boy, had I grown up with a movie superhero who was Black like me.

Chadwick's screen portrayals offered a hopeful counter-narrative amid the barrage of video footage showing Black men being shot and killed by police or racist vigilantes. Chad-

wick was the seed planted long ago by ancestors who wanted to be treated as equals. Chadwick was a superstar with cross-generational and crosscultural appeal for our still-new and troubled century.

In 2018, Chadwick was hailed as one of *British GQ*'s international men of the year, and I was lucky enough to write a cover story on him for the magazine. His own modesty was stunning in its plainspokenness. Despite his astounding success, it was as if we were transported back to our first meeting more than a decade earlier, when he was just a college graduate. Once again, he thanked me for the opportunity.

Little did I know, as I interviewed Chadwick over the phone, that that would be the last time I would speak with him. Little did I know, as he shared with me the many projects he was working on, that he knew cancer was destroying his body. And yet he did not hesitate to discuss his future with childlike joy and amazement.

Chadwick Boseman was nothing but a man who wanted to make a difference in the lives of others. And that he has done, forever.

For V
(formerly Eve Ensler)
October 20, 2021

one billion apologies are due
to the women and girls
of the world
who are you
and had to bear
sledgehammer hate
from the violent paws of men
even men we call
our fathers
i am sorry
your introduction to human-hood
was a biological not
bothering
and incapable
of taming his own traumas
but instead
terrorized you
with exploding hand grenades
chained to his teeth
you
a little girl
whose body
was lit a-fire
whose smile
eyes

childhood
were hung and burned away
the way my ancestors
were hung and burned away
by nameless naked cowards—
i am also sorry your
mother
could not protect
you
because she too
lived in a land
littered with
rape and abuse
and revenge
a land held
hostage
by broken little boys
in men's bodies:
why does a monster
call himself a man?
why does a little girl
pray
that mister alligator
will rescue her
from a monster
who calls himself
father?
we wear
the permanently
bandaged scars
of our childhoods
as my mother wears
the rage and sadness
of what she might have

been
had girls like her
been encouraged
to be
not do
what freed you
what will free
women like my ma
was/will be the vagina monologue
scat-singing in tongues
like sister so-and-so
sifting through nature's church pews
for sanctified sounds
in the holiest city of joy
'bukin' cancer
'bukin' cancer
'bukin' cancer
from the body of the world—

Wednesday, October 20, 2021
9:15 a.m.

Melvin Van Peebles
Was My Father Too

Originally published in the *Washington Post*
September 23, 2021

My heart pumped fast when I saw the news alert Wednesday that Melvin Van Peebles—filmmaker, actor, poet, songwriter, author, playwright, painter, options trader on the American Stock Exchange, father of modern Black cinema—had died. Though he was eighty-nine and ill the past few years, I texted one of his three children in disbelief to confirm.

I wept. Not just for Mr. Van Peebles, but for the seemingly endless list of Black male cultural figures we've lost since the Kobe Bryant tragedy: Bill Withers, Little Richard, John Lewis, Chadwick Boseman, Hank Aaron, DMX, Shock G, Biz Markie, Michael K. Williams, Melvin Van Peebles …

It is not that these deaths are more important than others. But as someone who grew up a fatherless and poor Black boy, I did not learn any semblance of Black cultural or political history until financial aid got me to college. Seeing people who look like you, whose stories are your stories, matters. Having a father figure, even from a distance, matters. It is the difference between knowing what is possible and a life stuck in fear and hopelessness.

Melvin Van Peebles gave me courage and hope. The first time I heard his name, it was in the 1990s when I was a twenty-something writer for Quincy Jones's *Vibe* magazine. I was told

I needed to watch *Sweet Sweetback's Baadasssss Song*, Van Peebles's 1971 magnum opus that kick-started the modern Black film movement in America—a movement that continues to this day with Spike Lee, Ava DuVernay, and many others.

I had never seen anything like *Sweetback*. A Black man as the hero, with barely any dialogue, fleeing White police attempting to capture him for a crime he did not commit. Mind-blowing allusions to America's history of slavery and segregation. Wildly provocative sex scenes that upended racial stereotypes. A Black Power middle finger to racism. Directed, written, produced, and scored by Van Peebles (although he couldn't read music), with an original soundtrack by the then-unknown group Earth, Wind & Fire. And for good measure, Van Peebles was also the star, did his own stunts, and spearheaded the marketing campaign.

Largely financed by himself and a few friends, *Sweetback* premiered in just Atlanta and Detroit at first. It received an X rating, but over time would rake in the rough equivalent of $90 million in today's dollars, single-handedly launching the Blaxploitation film era. All because Van Peebles was habitually a self-made man.

I spent a day with him somewhere in the mid-'90s, interviewing him for HBO. There he was, the obligatory hat atop his head, the half-smoked, half-chewed cigar either in his mouth or between his curled fingers, with the ultra-lean physique of a man, in his sixties then, who ran eight miles every single day.

I was mesmerized. By his humble roots in Chicago. By his bachelor's degree from an Ohio college when Jim Crow reigned supreme. By his three years in the US Air Force with that rebellious persona. By his self-proclaimed boring stint working in San Francisco on a cable car where he decided he would become a filmmaker while flipping through a picture book—despite no filmmaking experience.

Nor would Van Peebles allow racism to stop him. He tried to penetrate Hollywood in the late 1950s but was told he could be

an elevator operator or, at best, a dancer. Upset but unfazed, he moved his wife and three children to Europe, not unlike many African Americans who had fled there for the freedom they could not obtain here.

As Van Peebles told me during the time we spent together, freedom for him was landing in France and writing novels and producing films. But he eventually returned to America by the late 1960s to direct his first Hollywood-backed picture, *Watermelon Man*.

Ever the restless spirit, Van Peebles wanted more. He wanted full creative control over his films in his native land. He wanted his voice to be heard in every way, so he created spoken-word albums that foreshadowed the verbal acrobatics of hip-hop. And with the stunning success of *Sweetback,* Van Peebles found himself on Broadway creating plays.

No, he was not a perfect man, none of us are. But he did the best with what he had and was never afraid to seize the time. That, to me, is his greatest legacy. Indeed, there would not be multimedia visionaries like Lena Waithe or Jordan Peele had there been no Van Peebles. Nor would there be the self-empowerment ethos of a Jay-Z or a Cardi B without the director's fearless trailblazing.

When I watched director Mario Van Peebles's breathtaking Instagram tribute to his dad, I cried again. Mario said Melvin was all our fathers. Indeed, he was mine.

From a distance, he gave me a blueprint on how to be an artist, a content creator, a voice for the voiceless.

From a distance, I saw in Melvin Van Peebles myself, telling me as he told countless others of his children to always "keep on keepin' on."

Greg Tate Showed Me What Being a Writer in America Could Mean

Originally published in the *Washington Post*
December 8, 2021

You do not have to be famous or a best-selling or award-winning writer to influence multiple generations of singers, rappers, musicians, filmmakers, journalists, cultural critics, visual artists, public intellectuals, poets, dancers, DJs, novelists, playwrights, politicians, community activists, and multimedia content creators of all colors and identities.

You just have to be Greg Tate, arguably the best American writer and thinker of the past forty years, easily one of the greatest wordsmiths we've ever been blessed to have.

This is why I pushed my phone away in horror when I received a text on Tuesday from my former *Vibe* magazine editor Rob Kenner that read, *Greg Tate R.I.P.* This is why I hyperventilated and cried in disbelief on the phone with Joan Morgan, a fellow writer, when she confirmed it was true: Greg Tate had died, at age sixty-four.

I had seen Greg a month before, at a crowded and very lit New York City art opening for Radcliffe Bailey. He greeted me, as he always did, with a from-the-gut-up shout of "KP!" He was wearing a mask, a trademark hat, and a variety of colorful fabrics wrapped around his plump frame like the sacred garments worn by a priest. And he was there by himself, as he often

was, lurking on the edges of the event, shy in a crowd despite his warmth with those he knew. Sometimes his eyes met yours, sometimes they did not.

We spoke about the new autobiography of his late mother, civil rights pioneer Florence Tate, and the possibility of my interviewing him for my forthcoming biography of Tupac Shakur. Greg is widely considered one of the godfathers of hip-hop journalism, among many other accolades, because of his prolific coverage of the culture from the early 1980s forward, just as rap was becoming a cultural juggernaut. We agreed I would email him to arrange that interview. I never got to send that email.

I cannot recall when I first met Greg Tate or how or where, but I do know as a ridiculously young writer in the late 1980s I found my way to the pages of the *Village Voice*, and to his by-line. The first piece I read by Tate was on the legendary painter Jean-Michel Basquiat, in 1989. It was titled "Nobody Loves a Genius Child," in a nod to a poem by Langston Hughes.

"The ones who keep up the good fight with a scintilla of sanity," Greg wrote, "are the ones who know how to beat the devil out of a dollar while maintaining a Black agenda and to keep an ear out for the next dope house party set to go down in Brooklyn, Sugar Hill, or the Boogie Down Bronx."

His words were hypnotic, and they lit my brain like a fuse. Greg was writing, with unparalleled honesty, about the perils and pitfalls of fame and its toll on the Black mind and the Black body. He was also showing me the possibilities of what a writer could do and be: poet, cultural curator, memory-keeper, visionary, and unapologetic truth-teller for the people.

From then on, I digested everything Greg Tate penned, including his earlier work, and to this day I thumb through his writings for inspiration. When I was a cast member on the very first season of MTV's *The Real World* in 1992, in my hands was Greg Tate's first book and collection of essays, *Flyboy in*

the Buttermilk, during one of the many heated arguments about race and racism.

He wrote powerfully not just about race but also sexism, about homophobia, about anti-Semitism, about hate in all forms. I mean, it was mad bold for Tate to take on Public Enemy and its landmark album *It Takes a Nation of Millions*, regarded by many as the *Sgt. Pepper's* of hip-hop.

"PE wants to reconvene the Black Power movement with hip-hop as the medium," Greg wrote. "From the albums and interviews, the program involves rabble-rousing rage, radical aesthetics, and bootstrap capitalism, as well as a revival of the old movement's less-than-humane tendencies: revolutionary suicide, misogyny, gay-bashing, Jew-baiting, and the castigation of the White man as a genetic miscreant, or per Elijah Muhammad's infamous myth of Yacub, a 'grafted devil.'"

Never have I read a man, other than James Baldwin, who was so unafraid to challenge both White and Black America and the messy madness of race in this country. Other than *The Autobiography of Malcolm X*, never have I read work by a man, any man, who not only made me think new ideas but who made me feel transformed, like my very life had been saved. As someone raised by a single mother, I hungered for new definitions of manhood, and Greg was giving it to me without my even realizing it.

That is why I am mourning the loss of this hugely influential writer who moved from his native Ohio to Washington, DC, in the early 1970s, who grew up on everything from Motown, the Beatles, and Led Zeppelin, to DC go-go, early punk, and hip-hop, and comic books and science fiction too, cementing his stature as a game-changing ink-slinger with his uncanny gift to turn a missive about an album, a film, a scene, about anything, into a master class on the craft of being a writer steeped in the improvisational traditions of Negro spirituals, jazz, and a Black mama singing alone in her bedroom.

Because Greg Tate was brave, free, and unapologetically

Black. Because Greg was hip, hip-hop, *and* a hippie; and Greg was American-made in every sense of the phrase, like his artistic heroes Miles Davis and Amiri Baraka, like all Black music, which is undoubtedly American music.

For sure, his words could reach the bourgeoisie and rock the boulevard, because Greg blurred and burned class lines every chance he got. For sure, he was one of the many Black men sitting on sagging milk crates on a street corner in Anywhere America, woke to the daily news and woke to the ways of his hood, and able to flip that wisdom into observations and wordplay as genius as Joan Didion, Norman Mailer, Joni Mitchell, Smokey Robinson, Nikki Giovanni, or Bob Dylan.

This is why he mattered even in his final years, be it his work as a musician with his funk fusion band Burnt Sugar, his nearly forty years with the Black Rock Coalition, of which he was a cofounder, or his insights into Kendrick Lamar.

Because Greg Tate never stopped creating and fighting, because he never stopped dreaming, in the form of words strung together like a Pablo Neruda poem, of love, of his vision for a future he will not get to see himself.

A Love Sonnet
December 29, 2021

I've waited a life for a love like yours
It appeared as a red moon from the south
I feel warm fingers orbiting my pores
I taste joy at the corners of your mouth

I did not know that I was mad hungry
That I was this starved for a simple touch
My love, I must enjoy this reverie
From bone to skin I adore you so much

Our legs interlaced like rope when we rest
Hearts race each other like African drums
I've laid burdens upon the sun's bare chest
I've blown the tops off mountains with your lungs

Together we jump the broom's tulip floor
And when we die, I'll love you even more

Wednesday, December 29, 2021
9:12 a.m.

A Praise Song
for Sidney Poitier

January 7, 2022

what kind of man
was he
money-poor Bahamas boy
airlifted from the womb
a few months too soon
during Evelyn and Reginald's
mad dash to Miami
to hustle tomatoes
to survive
hardly weighed any pounds
teeny enough
to rest inside
the mud-soiled
palm of Reginald the father
what kind of man
was he
likely to be dead
in two or three days so his father
readied a shoebox
for the infant funeral
but the ears of
Evelyn the mother
clanged
of colonizers and overseers
in break-dance battles with

Maroons and Lucayan people
and her ears clanged too of a runaway ghost
slouching toward Bethlehem
while sheltering in Griffin Bat Cave
on Cat Island
the same Cat Island
her child will smell and
eat with his Caribbean eyes
the first ten years of his life
if she can resurrect him like Jesus
what kind of man
was he
Mother Evelyn's miracle
born yet again as she laid hands
on the congested pathways of Miami
her own private ghetto
knocking over the bowls
of Negro folks until a sister prophetess
struck a match with her mouth and foretold
the boy will live
and he will walk with kings
and it does not matter
that the boy's hair
is wooly like a seaman's cap
that the boy's feet
are bronze like tobacco-bleached grass
that the boy's face
is pitch-dark like a West Indian nightfall
that the boy's lips
are full like the stomach of a pirate's ship
that the boy's spoken-word poetry
unloads with thick African-English creole
because the boy
Sidney

is beautiful
like Black is beautiful
like the world before Columbus
and the transatlantic slave trade
and its toxic residue
might have been
beautiful
because the boy
Sidney
was begat from coinless dirt farmers
on an island with one thousand Black souls
and two White souls
and race was not yet a savage
interruption of his imagination
thus he registered all souls as all souls
he was merely
Sidney with flour sacks as clothing
who barely ever saw
reflections of himself
because the Poitier family of two parents
and seven children
had no mirror
had no nothing
what kind of man
was he
the first movies he witnessed
were wavy and jagged renderings
of himself in a pond
the first movies he witnessed
were wavy and jagged renderings
of himself in the shattered glass of a rum bottle
the first movies he witnessed
were wavy and jagged renderings
of Bahamian insects and birds and fish

breathing in the earth with their heartbeats
what kind of man
was he
the first sound that squared his
shoulders and yanked his head to attention
was the booming noise of nature's silence
the first sound that squared
his shoulders and yanked his head to attention
was the distressed plea
from his father
that fifteen-year-old Sidney go back to Miami
so that he the rebellious youngest child
would not dagger himself on that island
take care of yourself son
his father said to him
as Sidney was put on a boat
with three dollars and two years of formal schooling
the measure of a man
dripping with tears in the
mangled goodbye wave
of a parent who had done
what they could to prepare
a child for yesterday
what kind of man
was he
a teenage boy
with elastic troubles
in an outer space called Overtown
Miami's version of the barbed wire of racism
coloreds only signs
as poisonous nooses hung tightly around the possibilities
of a people
they did not know you were
an undereducated man-child

who had never been told
what was impossible
they did not know you were
an undereducated man-child
unwilling to gash and stab
your own flesh with that barbed wire
that is why you fled Miami
for Harlem New York City
the land of Southern
and West Indian fugitives
the land of Marcus Garvey
and I-too-sing-America
blues and bebop revolutions
what kind of man
was he
if there was any life for you
your hands would have to make
that life happen
hands that washed dishes
became the hands banging
on the door of the American
Negro Theatre
became the trembling hands wrestling
with the words of a script
be an actor or be a dishwasher
a newspaper ad had
dry-cemented a seed that became
the rose that busted through concrete
those hands washed more dishes
but those hands were also held by an aging Jewish
coworker who decided to help
you conquer reading
night after night after work
those hands touched and grabbed

syllables
those hands funneled and fed
sentences
those hands retrieved and embraced
new meanings
those hands raised the banner on a lifelong
unity with Harry Belafonte
and those hands spun the knob
of a radio so that you could
learn how to speak
as a Shakespearean actor might speak
as Paul Robeson or Spencer Tracy might speak
as kings and presidents might speak
as Frederick Douglass might speak
after learning how to read as a slave
your freedom was in reading
your freedom was in speaking
your freedom was in acting
the urgency like sticks of lit dynamite
inside your membrane
I have to learn to read
to articulate me as a human being
what kind of man
was he
transporter of a nation
of millions on his watch
no eyes bugging out like a broken-back minstrel
no lips quivering like a terrified sambo
he the defiant one
with a patch of blue to garbage-can his rage
the Martin Luther King Jr. of American movies
who I am is my father's son
I will scrub my knees with Porgy's shame
I will be a purple lily in the field of daisies

but I will also be a raisin
in the sun trolling like an endless road
I will sledgehammer my Paris blues
I will shape-shift my skin like sand
and slap a White man back
with such force it will echo through galaxies
from Chicago to Nigeria
to Brixton
a slap so dope and layered by trauma ropes
that when I die
they will say
this is evidence of things not seen
that I was not your Negro
nor your Uncle Tom
they call me Mister Tibbs
I Sir Sidney Poitier
what kind of man
was he
I am the me
I choose to be

Friday, January 7, 2022
12:38 p.m.

The Emancipation of Kendrick Lamar

Originally published in *Complex*
May 14, 2022

To be, or not to be, that is the question . . .
—William Shakespeare

I want you—the right way . . .
—Marvin Gaye

My mother used to say to me, when I was a youth, that she did not know if I would make it, if I would have a long life. Because I was Black. Because I was male. Because I questioned and talked and did too much. Because my emotions were unpredictably wild: sometimes unbelievable joy, sometimes unbearable depression, both rooted, to be blunt, in childhood traumas and generations of abuse and neglect.

Plus, my ma knew, stored deep in the guts of her own history, that I—we—lived in a land that did not seem to want us or want us the right way, except to entertain, except for sport, play, jokes, except for our culture. Because I could get killed, crucified, crushed, for real, by the ugly and oppressive racism of White people, and by the ugly and internalized racism of Black people. Many of us feel this way, whether we say it loud, as Kendrick Lamar has done brilliantly and unapologetically on albums like the Pulitzer Prize–winning *DAMN.*, or largely keep it to ourselves for years, as Kendrick has similarly done since he

was a shy and socially awkward ghetto boy just like me. Because to be Black in America—especially the urban poor Kendrick focuses much of his art on—is to be a trapped and pimped-out butterfly with battered and bloodied wings as you struggle to soar inside a concrete box.

This is why Kendrick Lamar matters. His very spirit gives voice to what it is to be who we are, particularly the Black male experience, the way fellow Black male writers named Langston Hughes, Richard Wright, James Baldwin, Amiri Baraka, Curtis Mayfield, Stevie Wonder, August Wilson, and Kanye West did before him. But, likewise, his art squeezes and pulls nearer to thee all people, all identities, because who has not felt the brutal loneliness of simply existing that Kendrick rhymes about? Or the belly-churning hunger for freedom that his verbal gifts evoke? Or those close cousins, mentioned above, we call joy and depression that he relentlessly excavates in his art, sometimes in the very same line or song?

But I would be lying if I did not say that legions of Black men and Black boys, specifically, desperately seek, consciously, subconsciously, something, someone, who can speak for us, who is unafraid to be us when we are wholly afraid to be ourselves. Hip-hop has lacked a dope and self-aware and self-critical superhero since, well, Kendrick's last solo album five years ago. To cut and paste some old-school sayings, hip-hop has saved a nation of millions, my life included, but we must also honor the truth that hip-hop has been as dumbed down and socially ignorant as reality television and the worst aspects of social media for, say, at least the first two decades of this century. That said, Kendrick ain't perfect, never claimed to be, which is what makes him so refreshing, his unbandaged scars there for everyone to download: he got into this game mad young, a Charles Dickens–like character with a Forrest Gump lucky streak, and has had to grow up fast in a blinding spotlight of celebrity and great expectations; Kendrick has been accused of sexism because of joints

like "Be Humble"; and for sure he has used language that has made me cringe mightily, including his overwhelming fondness for the n-word and the b-word.

But then I recall the toxic things I have said, written, done when I was so much younger than today, not really considering every part of humanity either. My hope, as he continues to grow as both a man and an artist, including with and beyond this new album, *Mr. Morale & the Big Steppers*, is that Kendrick Lamar understands, or will, that saving half the race (if we are speaking of the binary), Black or human, means we are not saving the entire race, Black or human, and that we need far more than the limited Black boys club thinking; we need a steady and heavy dose of the equal legacies of Zora Neale Hurston, Gwendolyn Brooks, Lorraine Hansberry, Nina Simone, Maya Angelou, Toni Morrison, Angela Davis, Alice Walker, bell hooks, Audre Lorde, jessica Care moore, Lynn Nottage, and the mother of his two small children, Whitney Alford. Or, recall, there would not be one of Kendrick's major idols, Tupac Shakur, without the giant of a woman and human and thinker and doer that was his mother, Afeni Shakur, she of the Civil Rights Movement, she of the Black Panther Party, she the mama in Tupac's "Dear Mama." Her life matters too.

Or, moreover, while Kendrick has been away these five years, we've seen the meteoric rise of Lizzo, Cardi B, and Megan Thee Stallion. But I dream a world, this very minute, where a Black woman rap or pop star can be as celebrated as a Kendrick Lamar no matter what she has on, or not, where we talk about her genius, and the content of her lyrics, whatever they might be, as much as we cite the genius and content of a Kendrick Lamar. And where a woman rap artist—Megan—is shot and it is not savagely skipped over like it did not happen, yet we make waves, or mourn, or memorialize, or muralize Black male artist after Black male artist when something violent happens to them. Say their names loud and consistently please, Kendrick—Megan

Thee Stallion, Breonna Taylor—not just the dudes. Their lives matter too.

But I digress, because this I do know as an avid listener of his music from his liftoff in the 2000s: Kendrick Lamar is the chanting revolutionary drums of the Last Poets. Kendrick Lamar is the mystical liberation theology of Bob Marley. Kendrick Lamar is the holy water blues of Donny Hathaway. Kendrick Lamar is the shirtless political manifestos of Fela Kuti. Kendrick Lamar is the bombed-out hood journalism of hip-hop forebears Ice-T, KRS-One, Chuck D, Ice Cube, Snoop Dogg, and Jay-Z. And Kendrick Lamar is the Basquiat portrait of the artist as ever-shifting rabbit hole in the persons of Charlie Parker, Little Richard, Sun Ra, Miles Davis, Thelonious Monk, George Clinton, Prince, Slick Rick, André 3000, and Robert Glasper. That just means that Kendrick Lamar, Gemini card-carrying member like Lauryn Hill, like Prince, like Tupac, like the Notorious B.I.G., like Kanye, is in a league of his own.

But Kendrick Lamar is not Frederick Douglass, nor W.E.B. Du Bois, nor Marcus Garvey, nor Malcolm X, nor the Reverend Dr. Martin Luther King Jr., nor Nelson Mandela, and he may never be a leader on that level the way some think he is already. Nor is he even a full-time activist like me. Kendrick Lamar is a truthful and critically thinking artist, one with a conscience, one with a soul plugged into the sorrow songs of the wretched and ignored of this earth.

This is why Kendrick Lamar can be famously out of sight for five years, save a few guest appearances here and there; have two children on the relative-low with Whitney, his high school sweetheart and rumored fiancée; start new brands and business ventures with his from-way-back artistic collaborator, Dave Free; and drop this message on his website in months past:

Love, loss, and grief have disturbed my comfort zone, but the glimmers of God speak through my music and family.

While the world around me evolves, I reflect on what matters the most. The life in which my words will land next.

Because we have been waiting for Kendrick Lamar the way die-hard Black believers like my mother have been waiting for Jesus—

Thus, and seriously, how does any human being, let alone an artist as sensitive and emotionally naked as a Kendrick Lamar, digest and interpret Donald Trump, a global pandemic, endless mass shootings and murders and violence, the explosion of #MeToo and Black Lives Matter, Russia's war on Ukraine, tragic deaths like that of Kobe Bryant and Nipsey Hussle, and the gruesome videotaped murdering of a breath in the form of George Floyd?

What must you feel when one of your tracks, "Alright," becomes a universal anthem for protest and change as omnipresent as John Lennon's "Imagine" has been for half a century?

Or what do you do when the multitudes are begging for a hero, a savior, and they choose you? A chosen one because Kendrick Lamar, like Marvin Gaye and Tupac Shakur, is unafraid to machete his mind in half and let the blood flow where it may.

Take his teaser latest single not on the new album, "The Heart Part 5." It is a pulsating five-plus minutes of a sermon to himself, to Black America, low-riding atop an interpolation of Gaye's underappreciated romance opus "I Want You."

What Marvin is crooning about is the flesh, but so is Kendrick, kinda. The difference is, Gaye wants a sensual love here while Kendrick wants to be mentally and spiritually hugged by Black communities, and for us to put arms around ourselves, around each other, to stop destroying ourselves, each other. The mind-jarring part of the cut is when Kendrick slides into the persona of Nipsey Hussle philosophizing from the heavens to his family, to his fans, even to his alleged killer.

There are few songs in pop music history that so boldly probe who and what we are. Think Billie Holiday's "Strange Fruit." Think Bob Dylan's "Blowin' in the Wind." Think Nina Simone's "Mississippi Goddam." Think Lauryn Hill's "Doo Woop (That Thing)." Think Marvin Gaye's "What's Going On." And think Tupac's "Keep Ya Head Up."

That the accompanying promotional would be a starkly minimalist Kendrick on-screen with white T-shirt, black bandanna around his neck, a maroon-ish background, and semi-twisted locks framing his weary eyes like a lion's mane, was surprising, given his penchant for music videos as cinema verité short films. Until we see him deepfake into the faces of O.J. Simpson, Kanye West, Will Smith, Jussie Smollett, Kobe Bryant, and Nipsey Hussle. Some of these Black men are dead. Some of these Black men are alive. Each of them controversial for one reason or another, and some of them totally problematic. But Black men, nonetheless. And the questions they have in common with Kendrick, with me, with pretty much every Black man who has had to battle racism and the contradictions within ourselves, are these: When can my life stop being the amusement park and punching bag for y'all? When can I stop being the envy of the world, and its number one enemy too?

This brings me to *Mr. Morale & the Big Steppers*. My mind is on fire and my mind is blown. It is Kendrick Lamar's masterpiece, the way *Tapestry* is that for Carole King, the way *What's Going On* is that for Marvin Gaye. Meaning it is a remarkably personal record of a life and a time, and times past, and times yet to be. And yeah, Gaye is an immediate inspiration, with Kendrick sonically vomiting his heart across eighteen songs, nine each on the two-part album. It is a forehead-gripping therapy session that seemingly admits that there is an epidemic crisis of manhood in America, and like everywhere, through the lens and multiple lives of this thirty-four-year-old Black male born Kendrick Lamar Duckworth.

It is Nelson Mandela in that South African prison cell for twenty-seven long years shadowboxing with his mortality. It is Shakespeare's Hamlet rassling, in excruciating ways in the mud with himself, with the meaning of life; it is James Stewart's George Bailey in the film *It's a Wonderful Life* pleading to God for answers on why he should live, and how. It is a cry for understanding, and for help, I feel, from an artist literally praying and meditating not to go the path of Elvis Presley. Or Marilyn Monroe. Or Jimi Hendrix. Or Janis Joplin. Or Marvin Gaye. Or Tupac Shakur. Or Michael Jackson. Or Amy Winehouse. Or Whitney Houston. Or Naomi Judd. It is what I have been waiting for from a musical artist, particularly a male musical artist, since the golden era of hip-hop in the late 1980s and 1990s, since the heyday of Kurt Cobain and Nirvana, the Red Hot Chili Peppers, and R.E.M., when Bill and Hillary were in the White House. It is the counterpart to Lauryn Hill's *The Miseducation of Lauryn Hill* a generation later; but it is also what I fantasize Beyoncé's *Lemonade* and Jay-Z's *4:44* would have been had they done a public conversation as an album, together, during that tumultuous part of their marriage. It is free jazz, loose funk, imperfect harmonies, jagged edges, screaming splinters everywhere; it is spoken-word masquerading as hip-hop, often, Kendrick on an intimate platform at Los Angeles's World Stage or New York's Nuyorican Poets Cafe; and it is as hood as one can get at the barbershop, at the beauty salon, at the fried chicken spot, at the dusty storefront church, at the California swap meet, on the street corner in slippers sucking on a cig. *Mr. Morale & the Big Steppers* is blowout combs and curling iron burns, it is baby mommas and baby daddies, and it is a very necessary venting for Whitney and Kendrick of their love for each other, Kendrick's blatant and disturbing adultery notwithstanding. Like what man admits to these things so publicly without the pressure of his wife, as Jay-Z was forced to do because of Beyoncé's bold *Lemonade* checkmate in the same 2017 as Kendrick's *DAMN.*?

And *Mr. Morale* ascends to heights of soulful musings with Eckhart Tolle, the self-help guru, interspersed throughout the record. Yet it also lags, pitifully, when you realize Kendrick's opposition to cancel culture is so severe that Kodak Black, a hugely problematic brother with countless sexual and criminal accusations on his résumé, also populates *Mr. Morale*. Not sure what point Kendrick is making; perhaps he is genuinely mentoring K.B., or thinking he is, but the entire album would have been better served leaving someone like Kodak Black completely off. Same with Kendrick Lamar's excessive use of the n-word and b-word I noted previously. He is too dope of a poetic prophet to be sandbagged with those dangerous words forever.

That notwithstanding, what makes *Mr. Morale* a masterpiece, to me, is its spare but impactful music, which feels, frankly, like a movie score that a Terence Blanchard or a John Williams might have concocted. Because what matters most are the words, the bars and beats that have clearly been tugging at Kendrick's brain cells for a long minute. There is the supremely progressive lyric that challenges homophobia and transphobia ("Auntie Diaries"); there is the scathing but sympathetic assessment of his father and fathering ("Father Time"); and there is the holistic breakdown of Black America's posttraumatic stress disorder that unfolds his mother's sexual and physical abuse and scratches furiously at the mental health challenges, and abuses, Kendrick himself warded off as a child, challenges and abuses that dog him into adulthood, that have fed his reckless disregard for women, including Whitney.

To say *Mr. Morale & the Big Steppers* is dense would be wrong. It is a purging, a baptism, it is the self-surgery of a Black man trying not to fall into that gutter permanently like Ralph Ellison's invisible man; but also, a Black man who does not want to be Richard Wright's Bigger Thomas from *Native Son*, either. As I listened to the voice of his partner, Whitney Alford, narrate parts of *Mr. Morale*, I could not help but think of the power-

ful cover image featuring Kendrick and Whitney and their two children, as beautifully photographed by Renell Medrano. The man has hundreds of millions of YouTube views. The man has sold tens of millions of records. The man has won every kind of award imaginable. The man has traveled to places some of us will never see, doing sold-out concerts. But there he is, in this scrunched-up box of a space, standing, holding their daughter, a gun peeking ominously from his waistband, while Whitney sits on the bed holding their son. I don't own a gun, never have, never will, but as a Black man I get why Kendrick, symbolically at least, has the gun in the photo. Who will protect him if he does not protect himself? His family is what he has, what he needs, the cover art is stating emphatically. And the way Nipsey Hussle was blown away, in broad daylight, will leave any Black man super paranoid, be it me or Kendrick Lamar. Especially if you were also badly violated as a child, as he was, as I was.

Better yet, what is manhood if it is just a cycle of chaos and violence and damaging all around you? Or how can you ever love another if you never knew how to love yourself? That is the beautiful struggle, the spiritual tug-of-war of *Mr. Morale & the Big Steppers*. I ain't saying Kendrick Lamar has the answers, because he does not. But he is trying, and that, no doubt, is half the battle.

The above said, if you can survive what many of us have been forced to survive, only because we are Black and male, then you just want a peaceful life, a peaceful home, and it does not matter that the bed is unmade, that there is a lonesome radiator in the corner, that paint is peeling from several parts of the wall. That is the hand-me-down life I came from, that Kendrick Lamar came from, that many of us know, from Brooklyn to Compton to Kingston to Brixton to Soweto. It is a universe you never really escape no matter how much money or fame you might achieve, no matter how much career success you might obtain. Because there is lurking always, like a masked mugger in the al-

ley, that survivor's guilt: *Why me, God, when others are dead, or in prison, or otherwise broken?* There is the sense of doom that your life still might end prematurely, as it did for Marvin Gaye. For Tupac Shakur. For Nipsey Hussle. For Trayvon Martin. For George Floyd.

Therefore, we need Kendrick Lamar, and Kendrick Lamar needs us. *Mr. Morale & the Big Steppers* is not only his emancipation proclamation, but also a love letter to us, the way Dr. King's "Mountaintop" speech was a love letter to us.

That gun is on Kendrick's hip because he is not willing for *Mr. Morale & the Big Steppers* to be his eulogy. The crown of thorns decking Kendrick's head on that album cover says he does not want to be betrayed, and crucified, like Jesus. He is not done yet; he is not done with us yet.

Last, I cried, as Kendrick says on the album men should, when I listened to the song about his mother, "Mother I Sober," because just like Kendrick is me and I am him, that is my mother he is rapping about as well. And all the Black mothers who have been treated like trash, kicked to the side, and discarded; and all the Black mothers with Black sons who fear for the safety of their boys, whether those boys are five or fifty. Kendrick has a right to live a long life, and so do I, so do we all.

Merely the fact that to be Black and male means we are forced to think of death frequently, of not living long lives, is also the reason why we need a Kendrick Lamar. Because there is no better spokesperson for our hopes and anguish and confusions right now than he, not in hip-hop, not in pop music period, not even in politics. Because with *Mr. Morale & the Big Steppers*, Kendrick Lamar has decided to be free—by any means necessary.

Acknowledgments

This book of some of my many writings and conversations is an incredible blessing, and I do not take that for granted. Thank you so very much, Johnny Temple, cofounder and publisher of Akashic Books, for even suggesting *The Kevin Powell Reader* to me as a project, as the title. I am humbled and grateful. I similarly thank the Akashic team, everyone associated, including Johanna Ingalls, Aaron Petrovich, and Sohrab Habibion. I also thank and love madly my own circle that worked hard to pull this book together in a short period of time: Regan Richardson, Michael Cohen, Wendy Morrill, Liv Jordan, Veronica Cooper-Tucker, Evangeline Lawson, Hilary VanWright, Rob Kenner, Joanna Parson/ Letter Perfect Transcription, and the many magazines, newspapers, websites, individuals, and libraries that helped find pieces of mine from way back to the present.

Previous Books by Kevin Powell

2022. *Grocery Shopping with My Mother* (poetry); Soft Skull Press

2020. *When We Free the World* (essays); Amazon and Apple Books

2018. *My Mother. Barack Obama. Donald Trump. And the Last Stand of the Angry White Man.* (essays); Atria Books/Simon & Schuster

2015. *The Education of Kevin Powell: A Boy's Journey into Manhood* (autobiography); Atria Books/Simon & Schuster

2012. *Barack Obama, Ronald Reagan, and the Ghost of Dr. King: Blogs and Essays*; lulu.com

2009. *Open Letters to America* (essays); Soft Skull Press

2008. *The Black Male Handbook: A Blueprint for Life* (edited by Kevin Powell, foreword by Hill Harper); Atria Books/Simon & Schuster

2008. *No Sleep Till Brooklyn: New and Selected Poems*; Soft Skull Press

2006. *Someday We'll All Be Free* (essays); Soft Skull Press

2003. *Who's Gonna Take the Weight? Manhood, Race, and Power in America* (essays); Three Rivers Press/Random House

2002. *Who Shot Ya? Three Decades of Hiphop Photography* (photographs by Ernie Paniccioli, edited by Kevin Powell); HarperCollins

2000. *step into a world: A Global Anthology of the New Black Literature* (edited by Kevin Powell); Wiley

1997. *Keepin' It Real: Post-MTV Reflections on Race, Sex, and Politics* (essays); Ballantine/Random House

1995. *recognize* (poetry); Harlem River Press

1992. *In the Tradition: An Anthology of Young Black Writers* (coedited by Kevin Powell and Ras Baraka); Harlem River Press

Permissions

Grateful acknowledgment is made for permission to reprint the following essays in this volume. "The Sexist in Me" was originally published in *Essence*, September 1992; "Native Sons" was originally published in *Vibe*, September 1992; "A Dialogue with Audre Lorde" was originally published in *Emerge, November* 1992; "Hero Today" was originally published in *Vibe*, October 1994; "Ready to Live" was originally published in *Vibe*, April 1995; "Uncut Funk" was originally published in *Vibe*, May 1995; "Right On" was originally published in *Vibe*, August 1995; "Colin Powell: Generally Speaking" was originally published in *Vibe*, November 1995; "Live from Death Row" was originally published in *Vibe*, February 1996; "Ready for the World" was originally published in *Vibe*, August 1996; "The Breakdown" was originally published in *Code*, December 1999; "Hip-Hop Is the Most Important Youth Culture on the Planet" was originally published in *Time*, September 22, 2000; "Looking for America" was originally published in *SPIN*, November 10, 2004; "Heaven, Hell, Dave Chappelle" was originally published in *Esquire*, May 1, 2006; "September 11" (essay excerpt) was originally published in *Someday We'll All Be Free* by Kevin Powell, Soft Skull Press, 2006, reprinted with the permission of the Permissions Company, LLC, on behalf of Soft Skull Press, an imprint of Counterpoint Press, softskull.com; "A Psalm for New Orleans, Verse 5" was originally published in *Someday We'll All Be Free* by Kevin Powell, Soft Skull Press, 2006, reprinted with the permission of the Permissions Company, LLC, on behalf of Soft Skull Press, an imprint of Counterpoint Press, softskull. com; "Kerry Washington: Woman on Top" was originally published in *Ebony*, May 9, 2013; "Why Is Baltimore Burning?" was